Edmund's

UNITED STATES

COIN

PRICES

COMPREHENSIVE CURRENT MARKET PRICES
FOR ALL U.S. COINS

**COMPLETE WITH
OVER 350 ILLUSTRATIONS
AND
VALUABLE COLLECTING INFORMATION
AT YOUR FINGERTIPS**

"THE ORIGINAL CONSUMER PRICE AUTHORITY"

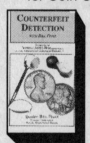

UNITED STATES **COIN PRICES**

Vol. 15 No. 1 / April 1994

Publisher: Peter Steinlauf

Published by: Edmund Publications Corp.
300 N Sepulveda Boulevard, Suite 2050
El Segundo, CA 90245

Editorial Director: Robert I. Belloch

Contributing Editors: Daniel J. Goevert
Robert S. Riemer

Photographs by : Robert I. Belloch

Coins for Photography Courtesy of
The American Numismatic Society, NY

Pages 199-209:
Official United States Mint Photographs

Photography (pages 192-206) Courtesy of
The Museum of the
American Numismatic Association

Art Direction/Design: Julie Finger

Production Coordination: Margalit Ward

Production: Kevin McMillan, John Ward

Advertising Manager: Barbara Abramson

Special Thanks to: Dr. Richard Doty
for his assistance in preparing this book.

United States Coin Prices
is published quarterly.

Library of Congress
Catalog Card Number: 80-65937

SBN: 87759-434-1

On The Cover:
The 1804 Silver Dollar
"The King of American Coins"

Printed in the United States

TABLE OF CONTENTS

Preface

This book is intended to be a useful guide for collectors of United States coins as well as the investor who wishes to include rare U.S. coins in his investment portfolio. At the time that this book is being written, the entire United States coin series is experiencing a dramatic upswing in prices. Although this series of increases has been unusually large, the continuous increase in the price of U.S. coins is by no means unusual.

To the serious numismatist, the investment potential of coins is secondary to their historical and educational value. However, he cannot ignore the increasing value of his collection over the years. This is one hobby in which one cannot lose, either financially or educationally.

The prices listed in this book have been carefully compiled by studying the current trends in the coin market. This includes auction results, dealer prices, and various references as to the relative values of various coins within a series.

In some instances, due to the increased bullion values of coins in some modern series, a minimum numismatic value has been set. In these series it would be unwise numismatic practice to purchase coins in lesser grades than the lowest priced grade because their price would be the same due to the bullion content of the coin.

On the Cover

The **1804 DOLLAR - "THE KING OF AMERICAN COINS"** pictured here is one of the most sought after American rarities. It is a prime example of scarcity and demand. There are fifteen known specimens of the 1804 Dollar. There are several specimens of this rarity permanently impounded in the collections of museums, leaving very few specimens available to the private collector. Due to this extreme rarity and considerable demand for the coin, the price of this coin increases considerably each time a specimen is put on the market.

There are, however, several other coins in the United States series that are even rarer than the 1804 Dollar. Some of these coins can be purchased for considerably less than the 1804 Dollar because they are not as popular for one reason or another. An example of this is the 1829 Large Planchet Half Eagle. There are only six known specimens of this coin, making it more than twice as rare as the 1804 Dollar. However, the 1804 Dollar, renowned as the "King of American Coins," brings considerably more money when sold because of the greater demand.

Introduction

It is a well demonstrated fact that investing in United States coins can be one of the most profitable ventures an individual can undertake. A few years ago, the Salomon Brothers of New York, a well known investment firm, conducted a survey on various investment vehicles and discovered that United States coins enjoyed a compounded annual return of 21.4 percent over the previous ten years. In the early 1990's, the same company reported a 14.6 percent return on a selected group of coins over a twelve month period. Even though the percentages are down in recent months, these returns still out-distanced more notable performers such as real estate and stocks by a considerable margin. This is not to imply that a person can simply walk into the nearest coin shop, purchase the first coin he sees, and expect that coin to appreciate at a compounded rate of 21.4 percent. Having some basic knowledge of the mechanics propelling the coin industry forward is a very important factor in wisely purchasing American coins as investment mediums. The following is intended to provide the reader with some essential background information.

The coin industry has witnessed significant changes over the last decade. Inconsistent grading practices had become a highly vocalized issue by the mid 1980's. While one dealer might assign a coin a certain grade, another dealer might give the same coin a slightly higher or lower grade. In the numismatic profession, subtle grade differences can mean literally thousands of dollars in trading value. In 1986, several companies began offering third party grading services. Coins submitted to these organizations were evaluated by a panel of expert opinions. Each coin was then encapsulated in a tamper evident container and returned to the owner. The coins submitted were mostly high grade uncirculated and proof specimens, or otherwise "expensive" material. By the late 1980's, the large grading services captured the trust of the coin industry, at last providing the much desired consistency in coin grading.

The impact of the grading services was enormous. Encapsulated coins (known as "slabs" by insiders) became highly liquid commodities, being traded readily by confident buyers and sellers, often sight unseen. Computer networks connected bidders to further facilitate coin transactions more quickly. Suddenly, coins were being merchandised much in the same way as stocks, resulting in extremely volatile price movements, generally upward. This activity won the attention of millions of first-time coin investors and several large Wall Street brokerage firms, pushing the slabbed market to dizzying heights by the spring of 1989.

Eventually, many slabbed coin prices plunged back towards reality as grading services began releasing their population reports. These reports indicated how many of what types and grades of coins passed through their systems, thus revealing a more likely approximation of each coin's true scarcity. Especially hard hit were the "generic" coins (i.e. common date coins), which even in very high mint state conditions were much more abundant than realized just a few years earlier. In the early 1990's, the great run-up of the 1980's crash landed to become nothing more than a memory.

In the aftermath of the slabbed market's collapse, numerous bargains exist today, and for those able to react in an informed manner, great purchases can be made. A good rule of thumb to obey is to focus on acquiring slabbed coins in the $250 to $10,000 price range. Naturally, there are exceptions, but contained in this range are true collectibles within the reach of most serious would-be buyers. Because this segment of numismatics is so active, a prudent investor should establish a relationship with a professional engrossed daily with the slabbed coin business.

While the higher end investment side of the coin industry has changed radically, collectors are still actively purchasing their favorite interest. Public awareness of the coin hobby has grown, as evidenced by the record turnouts at coins shows across the nation. In truth, collector purchases have increased over the last several years, a fact overshadowed by the monumental transformations mentioned above. The demand for key and semi-key dates in lesser grades than top quality is generally getting stronger. Although not nearly as volatile as slabbed items, some of these coins have been known to experience downward price corrections as well, and go up again in value as interest expanded. On the other hand, certain key and semi-key dates have risen consistently over time, with virtually no record of abrupt reversals. The collector pressure presents investment opportunities as well. By studying retail price trends, an informed investor may have a clue about future performance. He can learn how to recognize which coins have temporarily reached their maximum value levels and which ones are due for several more years of healthy appreciation. In addition, he can spot those "blue chips," which have solid, long term investment potential, and identify "dogs"...those coins with poor investment potential. Armed with this knowledge, these investors maximize their chances to realize profit in the numismatic marketplace.

Much of today's numismatic investment literature deals only with the slabbed material, practically ignoring the less expensive market currently occupied by collectors and a relative few investors. The scope of this book explores not only the terrific potential of purchasing certain slabbed coins, but also those "collector" coins as investment possibilities. Hopefully, along the way, the reader will be encouraged to study and learn about coins as a hobbyist might. Not only will it be a help in reaching financial objectives, it will open avenues of adventure not found in other income producing vehicles.

A Brief History of the American Coinage System

Understanding the historical aspect of coins is an important factor in adopting a successful investment program. From the earliest colonial times to the birth of our nation, through the great gold and silver debates dominating American politics for much of the 19th century, and during generations of war and peace, American coins have always been indicative of the times. Coins are visible links to the past, placing us face-to-face with history itself. If only that 1839 half dollar in your collection could speak, what stories it could tell!

The story of American money goes back more than three centuries ago. The early settlers of New England relied heavily upon foreign coins for conducting their day to day business affairs. At any given time, coins from England, France, Germany, Holland, Spain, and many other countries could be found in circulation. Also in use, and of special importance, were the coins that migrated to the colonies from Spanish possessions in the New World. Included in these were the Spanish milled dollar and the doubloons (worth about $16). The Spanish milled dollar, also called the "piece of eight" or the Upillar dollar" was the equivalent of eight Spanish reales. One real equaled 12½ cents and was known as a "bit." Thus a quarter came to be known as "two bits," an expression still used today. The Spanish milled dollar and its fractional parts were the principal coins of the American colonists, and served as the model for our silver dollar and its sub-divisions in later years. For the most part, however, much larger quantities of coins were needed. Because of the scarcity of coins, especially in the more remote areas, the colonists sometimes used other mediums of exchange, such as bullets, mussel shells (called wampum) and animal skins.

Unfortunately, for the early American settlers, our mother country, England, failed to seriously consider the coinage problems mounting in her colonies across the Atlantic. Since the English Parliament evidently was not going to provide more coins for the hard-pressed colonists, some of the more industrious Americans opted to take the matter into their own hands. Whether or not it had the authority to do so, the General Court of the Massachusetts Bay Colony granted John Hull permission to begin minting coins. Hull set up a mint in Boston and began producing the well-known "N.E. pine tree" coins in 1652, the denominations being threepence, sixpence, and one shilling. These were the first coins ever minted in the New World, outside of Mexico. As time went on, other coins and tokens of various types were introduced and used by the colonists regularly.

After the Revolutionary War broke out, there was little change in the pattern of coins circulating in America. To be sure, there were new pieces always entering from abroad, as usual, which were quickly accepted in the coin starved colonies. It was during this time that the first unified currency system was established. This consisted of notes issued by the Continental Congress to finance the Revolution.

Although these notes were originally declared to be redeemable after the war in gold and silver coins, such redemption was found impossible because of the excess of printed notes over metal reserves. Consequently, the notes depreciated rapidly and became worthless. Following the Revolution, the governing document of the infant nation, called the Articles of Confederation, adopted March 1, 1781, maintained that Congress had the authority to regulate coinage, but specifically reserved the right of coinage to each individual state. And so, during the 1780's we find a healthy variety of these state issues, minted mostly in copper, circulating throughout the country. These post-Revolution, pre-Constitution coins represent a truly unique era of American history, and are admired by all true numismatists today.

By the mid 1780's, many Americans began to conceive of the advantages of having a national mint and a standardized coinage system. The money situation at the time was still woefully inadequate and confusing. To further promote this cause, Thomas Jefferson recommended the use of the decimal system with the dollar as the basic unit of trade, in 1784. On July 6, 1785, the United States Congress voted in favor of Jefferson's plan, but took no action on account of more important issues confronting the young nation. Not until after the Constitution was implemented and George Washington sworn in as our first president did the Congress again investigate plans for solving the "money mess," also known as the United States coinage system.

On April 2,1792, Congress approved a law allowing coins to be minted bearing the words "United States of America." This was the first major step in establishing our national coinage system. President Washington appointed a famous scientist and philosopher named David Rittenhouse to be the first Director of the Mint. Construction of the new minting facility, located in Philadelphia, began in the summer of 1792. The coin denominations specified in the 1792 law were as follows:

	VALUE OF
Gold Eagle	$10.00
Gold Half-Eagle	5.00
Gold Quarter-Eagle	2.50
Silver Dollar	1.00
Silver Half-Dollar	.50
Silver Quarter-Dollar	.25
Silver Dime (originally spelled disme)	.10
Silver Half-Dime (same as above)	.05
Copper Cent	.01
Copper Half-Cent	.005

The first coin struck by the United States was the half-dime in July 1792, several months before the mint facility was fully completed. Fifteen hundred of these pieces were minted, but only as pattern coins, and were not intended for circulation. The first coins to reach the general population were the copper half cent and one cent coins of 1793. The following year, the first silver issues were released: the five cent silver piece (the half-dime), the half-dollar, and the silver dollar. Dimes and quarters were first issued in 1796. Gold coins arrived on the scene in 1795, in the form of the ten dollar gold eagle and the five dollar gold half eagle. Quarter eagles, valued at two and one-half dollars, were introduced in 1796. Because the minting process was primitive by today's standards, some of the early United States coins bear file marks, a result of weight adjustment by the mint's original employees.

For many years after the Philadelphia Mint began operating, coins failed to appear in sufficient numbers throughout the United States. This problem did not arise because of the mint's inability to produce money in adequate volumes. The expected movement of new coinage into the channels of trade was greatly impaired by metals speculators, who exported overseas as many gold and silver coins as they could obtain. The basic reason for this one-way flow was the existing weight ratios between the American money and foreign currency. On the European market, the bullion value of the American coins caused them to find their way to the melting pot.

It wasn't until 1834 that Congress reduced the weight standard of gold, a move which helped to alleviate the exportation of American coins. The passage of another act in 1837 to further revise and standardize the mint and coinage laws proved to be beneficial to the American nation as a whole. More Congressional legislation in 1853 reduced the weight of silver coins by about 7%, to make their metal value less than face value, causing more smaller coins to be retained in circulation.

As the number of United States coins in circulation increased, the necessity for the use of foreign and private coins decreased. Congress enacted a law in 1857 to prohibit the continued use of foreign and private coins in circulation. When the Philadelphia Mint began regular production in 1793, it was thought at the time that this facility would fulfill the coinage demands of our new nation. Within forty years, however, pioneers had extended the boundaries of the American frontier so distant from Philadelphia that the mint could no longer viably serve the entire nation. In order to meet the needs of the growing country, several branch mints were opened, the first ones in 1838. To distinguish the place of origin, small letters, or "mint marks," were added to the coins' surface, differentiating one mint from another. A quick rundown of all United States mints that ever saw active duty follows:

Charlotte, North Carolina—Mint Mark "C"-in operation from 1838-1861. One of America's earliest productive gold mining districts, situated in the southern Appalachian region, was concentrated sixty miles west of Charlotte. The mint here created a boom for the mining industry nearby. The Charlotte mint struck only gold dollars, quarter eagles and half-eagles.

The Confederate States of America seized the mint in 1861 and operations stopped after the remaining gold bullion had been coined into half-eagles of the federal design. Although reopened as an assay office in 1868, this facility never produced coins again. The original building was relocated and reconstructed and today is known as the Mint Museum of Art.

Dahlonega, Georgia—Mint Mark "D"-in operation 1838-1861. The story of the Dahlonega Mint is similar to that of the Charlotte Mint. In addition to the gold dollars, quarter-eagles and half-eagles, this mint produced a few three dollar gold pieces.

Soon after the Civil War began the mint closed its doors. In 1871, the state of Georgia became the rightful owner of the property, and converted the building into an agricultural college. That same year, a fire destroyed the former mint. Today the administration building of North Georgia College sits atop the foundation of the original building.

New Orleans, Louisiana—Mint Mark "O"- in operation 1838-1909. The New Orleans Mint was the third mint opened in 1838. This facility was much larger than its sister branches and eventually produced all gold and silver coins with the exception of the twenty cent piece.

In 1861 operations ceased when the government of Louisiana took control of the mint, which later relinquished control to the Confederacy. It was here that coins began bearing the identity of the Confederate States of America. Also struck by the Confederates were some 1861 half dollars of federal design, which are impossible to distinguish from the halves issued by the United States government in early 1861.

Following the demise of the South, the New Orleans Mint was closed, but was reactivated in 1879 with the production of silver dollars, gold eagles and double eagles. After the mint permanently shut down as a coinage facility in 1909, it continued to serve as an assay office until 1942. Parts of the old mint building have been restored within the last few years, and are now open to tourists.

San Francisco, California—Mint Mark "S"-in operation 1854 to present. The discovery of gold at Sutter's Mill in 1848 started a westward stampede and brought both statehood and a mint to California. During the early days of the gold rush, coins were badly required to fill the needs of the growing population. Several private mints popped up in the San Francisco area prior to the establishment of the government mint. The San Francisco Mint has been housed in three separate buildings, the last move taking place in 1937.

The Old Mint Museum, housed in San Francisco's second mint building at Fifth and Mission streets, is open to the public free of charge. The spectacle was expanded in 1993.

Carson City, Nevada—Mint Mark "CC"-in operation 1870-1893. The discovery of silver at Nevada's famous Comstock Lode brought another westward migration of fortune seekers. Although established perhaps because of political pressure from the powerful mining industry, the Carson City Mint produced some of the coins most highly prized by today's collectors, because of scarcity and the allure of owning an artifact from the "Wild West." The Carson City Mint passed into oblivion for several reasons: the glitter of silver eventually dimmed, there was an overabundance of coins available to the local economy, and because the Mint was unable to cleanse its reputation following a government scandal resulting in the suspension of the mint from 1886 to 1888.

From 1893 to 1933, the Carson City facility operated as an assay office. In time, the old mint became occupied as the Nevada State Museum, where visitors will find an exhibit dedicated to the building's original purpose.

Denver, Colorado—Mint Mark "D"-in operation 1906 to present. The establishment of this mint was provided for in a law passed in 1862, but operations did not begin until 1906. The mint mark ("D") cannot be confused with that of the Dahlonega Mint (also "D") because the Dahlonega Mint last issued coins in 1861. The Denver Mint is still housed in its original building, completed in 1904, and of course has been upgraded and modernized several times since then.

In recent years, the Denver Mint has been one of the world's most prolific producers of coins, with billions of coins turned out annually.

West Point, New York—Mint Mark "W"-the newest facility, granted mint status in 1988. Actually, coinage has taken place at this location since 1974, to help the Philadelphia Mint meet the demand for one cent coins. The 1984 Olympic commemorative coins were struck at West Point, and carry the mint mark "W," the first coins to bear a distinguishing mark from West Point. Today it is used primarily to produce coins for collector programs and bullion coins, although it has struck coins for circulation in recent years. The coins released into general circulation are identical to those struck in Philadelphia.

Philadelphia, Pennsylvania—No Mint Mark, except "P" on 1942-1945 nickels, 1979 Susan B. Anthony dollars, and all coins 1980 or newer, except cents - in operation 1792 to present. Today the largest and most modern mint in the world, this facility creates all dies for United States coins and sends them to the branch mints (dies are pieces of metal, with designs imposed upon them and are used in pairs to strike a blank disc to make a coin). The present mint was dedicated in 1969, just a short walk from the original 1792 building.

Since the inception of the United States coinage system in 1792, mint officials have attempted to monitor the number of coins struck each year. Collectors should be advised that these mint reports were probably not always accurate, and should not be the sole factor in estimating rarity of coins. To confuse the matter even more, large quantities of gold and silver coins were never released for actual circulation, but were stored in United States Treasury vaults as backing for paper money. Many of these were eventually melted and re-minted into new coins. The reports from the Mint Directors do have some merit, however, as they provide a starting point for a numismatist to estimate scarcity of certain coins; but there are many many other factors that must be considered before arriving at an accurate estimation.

Why Coins Are Desirable Investments

In recent decades, the price appreciation of many United States coins has been spectacular, capturing the imagination of countless investors. Many collectors have joyfully discovered that one of the world's most productive investment vehicles also happens to be their favorite hobby! For example, the collections of R.H. Gore Jr. and Dennis I. Long were auctioned off together in 1990 for a combined total of nearly $5 million; the collections were assembled at only a small fraction of that total!

What makes a coin valuable? Ultimately, coin values are based on essentially the same set of rules as any other investment medium. If everyone wants to buy, prices go up, but if everyone wants to sell, prices drop. For coins, however, the supply/demand factor is closely associated with a number of other factors specific to the coin industry. Each of these must be carefully considered to arrive at a general evaluation of any single coin, and it is smart to analyze which particular factor has the greatest influence on the price movements of that coin. All collectors and investors should learn to recognize how these diverse factors determine the market value of a coin.

First of all, let's take a look at the supply/demand theory and how it relates to coin values. What exactly is the supply? Simply stated, the supply can be defined as the number of coins available for sale at a specific point in time. Mintage is the first indicator to be studied when guessing the available supply of a given coin. The mintage figure for a given date and mint mark tells you that the existing total today can be no larger than this number. Survivorship is the key modifier to the original mintage figure. As mentioned earlier, many coins were never released by the Mint, or were melted down. For instance, the Pittman Act authorized the melting down of over 270 million silver dollars in 1918! In 1979 and 1980, bullion prices set record highs, causing more coins to be withdrawn and converted to their metal form and resold at a profit. Moreover, millions of coins have been lost or destroyed by methods other than melting, further reducing the supply. To state the situation more concisely, the volume of coins issued in the past is finite, can never increase, and in all likelihood will shrink even more over time due to attrition. These facts provide the basic upward momentum behind the coin market.

Collectors and investors comprise the demand position of the equation. If there is no demand, there is no market. Over the past thirty years, a higher and higher percentage of our population have become coin buyers. The number of collectors and investors has increased from about half a million in the 1950's to perhaps as many as 20 million today, depending upon one's definition of a collector. In all likelihood, that number will continue to increase. With more buyers competing for, at best, a fixed supply of collectible coins points to only one thing: higher prices in the future.

Besides the supply/demand factor, there are several other considerations determining the value of a coin. The most critical of these is condition, or state of preservation, of a coin. Coins are very durable, but seldom can collectible coins be found in the pristine condition they had when first minted. From the moment a coin is removed from the dies, it is scratched, scraped, mishandled, and worn from everyday use. The degree of deterioration is measured by the "grade" or "condition" assigned to a coin. There are several typical grades widely recognized by numismatists, and just as with diamonds or antiques, these grades can significantly affect a coin's value. For instance, take a look at the 1892-S Morgan silver dollar. In Almost Uncirculated grade, the coin retails for around $1750. In the next grade up, MS-60 Uncirculated, it sells for around $10,500! Such an incredible jump in price from one grade to the next is not uncommon, so you see how critical the coin's condition is in determining its value.

A common misconception held by the general public is that age is an important factor in setting coin values. Actually, it is one of the least important considerations. Many of the coins of the 20th century are far more expensive than some of the coins of the ancient Greeks or Romans, which can be purchased for as little as $5. To be sure, age does have some indirect impact on the rarity of a coin, in that the older the coin, the longer the time for more of the original total to perish.

The design of a coin can have a bearing on its value. Many collectors enjoy acquiring every date and mint mark of an individual series of United States coins. Such a collector who focuses on, let's say Buffalo nickels, would want a specimen from each mint for every year the Buffalo nickel was issued. After the Buffalo nickel collection is completed, the collector may move on to some other series. While some collectors practice their hobby this way, others like to acquire a specimen of each design change in the entire United States series. They are called "type set collectors," and this method of collecting puts pressure on certain designs minted for only a short period of time. The 2½ dollar quarter-eagle design of 1808 lasted for that year only. Although not much rarer than other quarter-eagles of its time, demand from type set collectors has pushed the value of the 1808 quarter eagle to at least three times that of its contemporaries!

Coin collecting is a profitable hobby. That's why millions of investors sink their financial reserves into coins. While the appreciation rate in many instances is nothing short of spectacular, a word of warning to those hoping to use coins to turn a fast buck: forget it! Coins usually are a long term blue chip investment, not a short term 'get rich quick' scheme. The people who have earned the most outstanding profits on their coin investments held them for the long term. In other words, be prepared to hold your coins for a minimum of two to five years before selling.

In summation, few investments opportunities offer as many advantages coupled with impressive performance and outstanding potential as numismatic investments do. The governing precept is this: In order to maximize your chances of value appreciation, obtain quality, scarce coins at competitive prices, and hold them for a reasonable length of time. Several negative aspects exist too, but they can be minimized through studying the subject and using good old-fashioned common sense. It's no wonder why coins receive so much attention from so many investors, large and small.

Speculators, Investors, and Collectors

There are basically three categories of coin buyers: speculators, investors, and collectors. A combination of these groups comprises the demand side of the numismatic industry. However, the make-up of the buyers may vary from one small segment of the market to the next, not necessarily in concert with any other part of the market. Should you have the ability to identify what group exerts the greatest pressure on any one segment of the market at any particular time, you have in your hands a valuable clue as to what direction prices will take in the very near future. Each group possesses distinct personality traits, and you need to learn how to recognize them.

A speculator is someone who follows promotional advertising and hops aboard bandwagons when they appear. Speculation is based or the concept that another buyer will pay a still higher price for an item than what the seller paid for it. Speculators operate with mass psychology. When the word gets around about a certain 'good' investment, everyone wants to get in on the act and make money. It doesn't take much arm twisting to convince a speculator to jump into a bull market.

In the coin world, an influx of speculators is evident when a coin series (or even a single coin) experiences sudden sharp price increases. The pandemonium continues until interest shifts to some new areas, which could be in a few days, a few months, or a few years, depending on how much promotion was involved. Because of their nature, speculators don't stay with anything for a long period of time. When they lose interest in an item and move on to greener pastures, prices fall.

Typically, very few speculators familiarize themselves with the machinations of any investment vehicle, and for some reason, numismatics seem to always be at the top of this list. They simply migrate to wherever they believe most of the money is going.

A perfect example of the speculator phenomenon has already been touched upon in this book. For a period of several years it became very popular to invest in high grade generic certified coins (i.e. common-dated slabbed Morgan silver dollars, Walking Liberty half dollars, etc., grading MS-65 or better). Interest in these issues heightened to unbelievable levels, causing prices to escalate accordingly, even though supplies were plentiful. In March 1990, interest waned markedly, triggering a sharp fall in prices.

Today the money is in the stock market and other high-yield securities. Mass psychology indicates real estate, gold and silver, and collectibles are "dead." When the economy eventually changes gears, it will be almost incomprehensible how fast the forgotten "dead" will be resurrected to life!

A coin investor is a person who strategically spends money on coins regularly, with the hope that someday he will be able to resell at a substantial profit. A notable difference between an investor and a speculator is that an investor doesn't jump in and out of the market when he sees someone else doing it. He's consistently active in the marketplace year after year. The true investor understands the basic reasons underlying the value of a coin, the cyclical nature of the coin market, and other related facts. He observes, compares, and rationalizes before each coin purchase is made, and leaves hysteria to the masses of speculators. Most investors initiate their numismatic careers as speculators or collectors, and cross over into the investor class later on. For instance, during the 1979-1980 bull market, countless thousands of speculators became collectors and investors upon discovering the rewards of owning historic United States coins. At the same time, some collectors realized how they could benefit financially from their numismatic skills, and they too became investors.

Collectors of coins have been around for many centuries. One definition of a coin collector is a person who assembles coins principally for the enjoyment received during the search. For them, coins are a hobby. Collectors come in all sizes and shapes, young and old, rich and poor. These days, a collector can't find too many worthy coins out of general circulation, and so is willing to pay a price to a dealer to acquire a desired specimen. The chief determinants for a collector to buy a coin is whether or not it's needed to fill an empty slot in a coin album, and of course, it must be affordable. When certain coins rise quickly in value, collectors typically redirect their enthusiasm to another segment of the market and return when prices have fallen.

Even though the slabbed market has been declining for several years, collectors still remain consistent buyers of specific coins needed for their collections. Unquestionably, collectors serve as the price foundation of the coin market as a whole. Any coin of numismatic interest will have some value as far as collectors are concerned. Collectors are the reason why prices will never fall beyond a certain point.

If you're an investor, watch closely the activities of the collectors and speculators. When the collector gets pushed out of a market because of escalating prices, and the buyers are made up almost entirely of speculators, that segment of the market is probably headed for a fall. Conversely, when collectors have shaped the basis for demand and prices have been stable for some time, the market is at basement levels and can only go up.

More Advice About Coin Investing

Simply stated, as an investor, your objective with numismatic coins is to assemble a collection of coins (or portfolio if you wish to call it that) that will appreciate handsomely over the years. There are numerous options available for achieving this goal, but you should adopt a strategy beforehand structured by your desires and circumstances. You must determine, for instance, whether you want long term growth or short term growth coins (or both), and how much investment capital you can safely afford to tie up in each. Also, since there are many good investment prospects on the market at any given time, you have to decide which coins and in what condition will be the most profitable to add to your numismatic portfolio. You should take all angles into consideration before you spend any of your hard earned money. It's alright to be skeptical. Remember, it's better to be safe than sorry, and for every "good" opportunity that slips through your fingers, there is always another to take its place.

Even though the basic motive for an investor in buying a coin is to resell someday at a profit, strategies change depending on your future goals. You may want to accumulate wealth for a down payment on a new home in five years or so, or perhaps you're starting a nest egg for retirement thirty years down the road. Persons wanting to register shorter term profits should get into what industry analysts call "short term" coins. Begin by looking at the track record for different coins in various grades. There are literally thousands to choose from with no particular preferred beginning point; the main thing is to start investing. Short term coins are those that rise fast in a relatively short time and drop quickly later on. Not coincidentally, short term coins historically have been linked with speculative involvement, ala slabbed coins. When short term investment coins are clearly undervalued in the present market, and are therefore due for a price increase, that is the time to buy. You should expect to hold these coins an absolute minimum of two years, possibly as long as five years, and maybe even a little bit longer. After the short term coins have recorded their anticipated increases, be disciplined enough to sell them. Many investors have the misconception that the coins will continue to perform fantastically every year, but they won't. Sell them and funnel you profits into other coins which are underpriced.

"Long term" coins are coins which cannot be expected to increase substantially within the next few years. These coins, when graphed, display a steady upward movement, with a few minor dips here and there. Typically, a long term coin is one which has wide appeal among collectors, which explains its relatively smooth performance over the years. An investor should be prepared to hold these coins for at least ten years. Visualize long term coins as the "blue chip stocks" of the numismatic world because you can count on good, steady growth. If you're a fairly young person especially, you ought to seriously consider obtaining a fair number of long term investment coins for your future.

What percentage of income should an investor spend on coins? Obviously the answer varies from person to person. Since you know your financial situation more intimately than anyone, including your income, obligations, plans, spending habits and lifestyles, you alone are the one who can best make that decision. Be careful: buying coins is enjoyable for many investors, and some find they cannot resist the temptation to convert all their cash into numismatic holdings. Always leave yourself an emergency cash cushion, or you may be forced to liquidate some of your investment coins before they have reached their full potential.

The price of a coin gives little indication of whether or not it is a good investment. What is needed to determine the investment potential of a coin is an analysis of the demand for it, and its directional trend, not simply what it is priced at today. A coin currently selling for $3000 sounds impressive, but in reality, a coin selling for less than $100 may be a far better investment. When ready to buy, always keep in mind that good investment coins do not necessarily have big price tags.

After studying this book, the investor should develop a pattern for adding good potential coins to his portfolio. As with so many other financial areas, it is best to diversify. By diversifying, when some of your coins don't perform quite as you had anticipated, others will do well in the meantime. Should you ever be faced with having to sell some of your coins, a diversified portfolio will enable you to liquidate coins which have more closely reached their maximum potential. Prominent coin expert David Hall, along with a number of other numismatic advisors, recommends this diversification program:

25% Type Coins   20% Modern Singles   10% Commemoratives
25% Gold   20% Silver Dollars

In each investment area, there are short and long term prospects available at any given time. Plan your purchases according to your objectives, but concentrate on maintaining desired percentages for maximum satisfaction. Type coins are coins in all denominations minted in this country between 1793-1916. "Type coin" got it's name from collectors trying to obtain an example of each type of coin minted during this period, because complete sets were too costly to assemble. Gold coins are generally the most expensive coins a collector can buy. In fact, the price of choice gold coins has put them out of reach for smaller investors. For marginal investors, you're best advised to buy the less expensive dates without compromising on quality or condition.

Modern singles are the coins of the 20th century. They include:

Lincoln Cents	1909-Present
Buffalo Nickels	1913-1938
Jefferson Nickels	1938-Present
Mercury Dimes	1916-1945
Roosevelt Dimes	1946-Present
Standing Liberty Quarter	1916-1930
Washington Quarters	1932-Present
Walking Liberty Half Dollars	1916-1947
Franklin Half Dollars	1948-1963
Kennedy Half Dollars	1964-Present
Eisenhower Dollars	1971 -1978

These coins in particular offer an array of tremendous long term investment opportunities. The prices of many of these coins can fit nearly anyone's budget, while even MS-65 coins can be had for only a few dollars more than MS-60. Great potential exists in the modern singles. Although gaining in value, the best is yet to come for modern singles. The top grade coins from this area will no doubt become extremely valuable in twenty or thirty years, in comparison to what they cost presently.

Silver dollars are the most commonly bought investment coin today. Dollars minted from 1794 to 1873 are not as widely traded as the more common Morgan and Peace dollars of 1878-1935. Probably in no other series has there been more price manipulation and speculation than here. Extreme caution is advised because of this unnatural pressure, but therein lies fantastic possibilities. See the section on silver dollars for more information.

Commemoratives are coins specially minted to commemorate an event or honor some person from the past. Commemoratives are sanctioned by Congress. Speculation influence has been heavy here also.

Don't be uneasy if you can't adjust your coin portfolio immediately to reflect the guidelines listed above. Naturally, if you purchase only one coin at a time, it will take a while to diversify your collection accordingly.

One very important decision an investor must make is what condition of coins to buy. Dealers usually tell customers to buy coins in the very best conditions...Uncirculated and Proof. From an investment viewpoint, this is generally good advice. However, all grades can do well from time to time and from coin to coin. For instance, scarce coins and many early American coins have done extremely well in Good and Very Good condition at various intervals in the past. To no one's surprise, countless issues in Uncirculated and Proof have performed super spectacularly too. There is no absolute rule of thumb when it comes to grade selection. Each coin in every condition must be judged on its history, potential, and current price.

Certain circulated coins merit a home in your investment portfolio. They have fantastic potential and represent solid buys when compared to lots of high priced Uncirculated and Proof coins. Very early American coins grading Good and Very Good have performed superbly in the past, and should do so in the future. In fact, pieces minted in the late 18th century and early 19th century are so highly valued today in upper grades, that as a practical matter, Good and Very Good coins may be the best you can afford. That's all right, because the potential is still there. For coins a little over a century old, the Fine to Extremely Fine grade ranges especially offer many good affordable prospects too. Of course, certain Extremely Fine and Almost Uncirculated of any century are good investment material too.

Always avoid coins that have been bent, holed, gouged, or damaged in any way. They almost never possess good investment potential.

If you're seriously contemplating spending Investment dollars on coins, it is highly recommended to first spend a little money on building a small numismatic library. It's a purchase that can literally pay for itself many times over. "Buy the book before the coin" was a quote attributed to Aaron Feldman, a well-known dealer for many years. See the recommended reading list on page 212 before beginning your reference library.

Buying and Selling Coins

More often than not, when you buy or sell a coin, you will be doing business with a coin dealer. It is worth the effort to check out the background of any dealer you're considering working with, because there is a small minority of dealers out there waiting to sell overgraded and overpriced coins, among other things, to unsuspecting customers in order to pad their profit margins unfairly. By carefully choosing a dealer whose expertise is great and reputation unchallenged, you will take yet another step toward becoming a successful numismatic investor.

If you are considering doing business with a dealer, first ask a lot of questions. A legitimate dealer expects to receive many questions, and he'll be happy to answer them for you. Questions to bring up are: What return privilege, if any, does the dealer offer? Does he guarantee his coins to be genuine? Does he belong to any of the trade organizations, such as the American Numismatic Association or the Professional Numismatic Guild? Professional affiliations are clues that the dealer is willing to obey certain industry guidelines and accept responsibility, at least superficially. Also, the memberships are indicators that the dealer has an established network of contacts within the industry.

Be sure to inquire outright if the dealer uses the A.N.A. grading standards, and if not, how does he determine the grade of a coin. Will he allow his coins to be submitted to an unbiased grading service? What price guides, if any, does he base coin values on? Does he both buy and sell coins based on that guide? Will he buy back coins that he originally sold to you? Examine his policies in depth. If an individual or company can't answer all of your questions to your complete satisfaction, or if the firm simply won't take the time to field your inquiries, take your business elsewhere. There are numerous other honest companies in the coin business which will work hard to serve your needs, whether you are a small collector or a wealthy investor.

The best place to start in your search for a good dealer is the community where you live. Most cities of 10,000 or more usually have a least one coin dealer. Get answers to questions similar to those above. In addition, contact a coin club in your area, if any, and listen to what they have to say about the dealer. Try to obtain references from the banks, the chamber of commerce, credit bureaus, or anywhere the dealer has done business in the past. Bad reputations are hard to shake, and chances are good that if the dealer has been incompetent or dishonest, you'll discover it, but only if you investigate. On the other hand, a good reputation is difficult to build, and is usually well deserved.

There are hundreds of very fine coin dealers scattered across the nation who do a large volume of business through the mail. Unfortunately, there are a few con artists using the postal system to their advantage also. Before you send off any money in the mail, you should adopt investigative tactics for out of town dealers as you would for any other dealer. One good aspect of mail order firms is that they usually maintain a much larger inventory to choose from than your local dealer. A quick check with the publisher who prints their advertising can also yield useful information.

One area that has given the numismatic industry a black-eye is telemarketing fraud. Not every company using this approach has sinister motives, but a good rule to abide by is this: if you receive an unsolicited phone call from someone in an attempt to sell you coins, be on guard. What occasionally happens is that a slick talking sales man disguising himself as a knowledgeable numismatist tries to impress you with his fantastic stock of coins, part of which he is willing to "sacrifice" for you, his prized customer. In reality, what he has is a group of overpriced coins, worth only a fraction of its cost to you. If you feel a necessity to do business with a telemarketer, at least follow the guidelines mentioned above. Also, ask them if you could stop by their place of business the next time you're in their area. Most con artists don't want you to see their operation in person. Even if a telemarketer has "good" answers to your questions, never abandon caution. Some of these professionals are so clever at handling objections that even a well-versed customer can be fooled. (If only these crooks would just focus their talents in honest endeavors, they could probably make a good living legitimately.) At the risk of offending sincere telemarketers, the safest and best advise is to avoid numismatic telemarketers altogether.

Once you select a dealer you feel comfortable with, it is still wise to proceed with caution. Buy only a few coins at first, resisting the temptation to start out big. Examine your new purchases carefully. Don't be embarrassed to request another opinion from an informed, but impartial source. If you conclude that the coins are properly graded and accurately priced, feel free to order more next time. Always be sure to inspect your coins immediately after you receive them. Some unscrupulous dealers will bait you by filling your orders correctly at first, but after they gain your trust, they'll supply you with overgraded, overpriced items.

If you believe that you have been cheated by a coin dealer, there are several options available for you to achieve satisfaction. If the dealer's stated policy includes a money back guarantee, use it. Be sure to retain copies of all receipts and written correspondence between both parties. If you're still not satisfied, complain to the A.N.A. or P.N.G. if the offending dealer is a member. These organizations carefully monitor their members under a strict code of ethics. If you purchased your problem coin through an ad in one of the hobby publications, file a grievance with the publisher against the dealer. Publishers don't want unhappy readers spreading bad news about their magazines, so they may exert pressure upon the dealer, threatening to refuse him advertising space, unless the problem is rectified promptly. Another recourse is to notify federal and state authorities who enforce mail fraud laws. They can assist you if you've been the victim of blatantly deceitful advertising.

Assuming that you have chosen to buy coins of sound investment quality, and you have maintained them in as good a condition as when they were bought, you should have little difficulty in finding a buyer. However, there are a few facts you should be mindful of before you approach a dealer to ask him for an offer on your coin.

Coin dealers are in business to make a profit. Numismatics is their chosen profession and so they are certainly entitled to one. Like any other businessman, a coin dealer has numerous overhead expenses, including salaries to his employees, rent, taxes, advertising, insurance, travel, and many other miscellaneous items. About 70% to 90% of the retail value of a coin is the best a dealer can offer to buy for, sometimes even less.

When a dealer is solicited to buy a coin that he thinks will sell quickly, he'll probably be willing to pay closer to the 90% figure. If there is a chance of a slower sale, the dealer will discount his offer accordingly. Slow selling coins are the dread of coin dealers. It means having capital tied up while the coin lies idle. He cannot buy other coins or pay expenses with the money he spent for the idle coin.

Other factors make it worth your while to shop around when selling your coins. Understand that not all dealers are in identical economic positions, and while one dealer may want your coin to replenish his inventory, another may be well stocked with the same coin. These and other unmentioned factors can have a bearing on how much a dealer will offer for your merchandise.

An alternate method of liquidating your investment coins is to sell them to other investors. Should you opt for this method, be prepared to allot more time and out-of-pocket expenses than if you sold them directly to a dealer. A classified ad in the local newspaper or hobby circular usually brings respondents willing to buy your coins at or near their fair retail price. Try to avoid letting strangers know much about yourself and your investment. Take precautions not to publish your phone number and home address, and if at all possible, meet with interested buyers on neutral ground. A good option would be the bank where you keep the coins.

Putting your coins on the auction block is a choice you may decide to exercise. Many of the larger, better known coin auction companies are always seeking collectible coins from the general public as a way to round out their sales, and would welcome your contributions. The average auctioneer commission ranges from 12% to 20%, usually paid by the seller, but increasingly today the commission charge is split evenly between the buyer and seller. Frequently, an auction sale for an especially "hot" coin is likely to draw a higher price than if you sold it otherwise, because auctions are emotional platforms where bidders often react beyond reason to acquire a popular item. Be certain to make all the usual inquiries about the auction company before you go this route.

Yet another method of selling your coins is to consign them to a dealer. Since the dealer does not incur any expenses in a consignment agreement, he can afford to charge a smaller percentage for his services, normally around 10%. Your coin will remain on his store shelves until the time it is sold, (unless the consignment period expires first), at which time you and he will divvy the sales figure according to your prearranged agreement. The major drawback about consignment sales is that you may have to wait a considerable length of time before one of his customers buys your coin. Also, when you enter into a consignment arrangement, make sure everything is in writing, right down to the final detail.

Most dealers are honest, forthright professionals committed to helping their customers find the right coin in the right grade at the right price. Because there are a few bad apples in every barrel, a coin investor should never abandon caution when dealing with an unknown company. You may never be as familiar with grading and numismatics in general as professional coin people are, but if you arm yourself with some knowledge about the hobby and always be inquisitive, the rip-off artists will have to look beyond you to carry out their scams.

An Introduction to Grading

As stated earlier, grade (the condition or state of wear of a coin) is one of the main determining factors of a coin's value. Until relatively recent decades, grading was by "instinct." Based on his own knowledge and personal observations, one seller would have his own system, and another seller with another set of observations, experiences, and opinions, would have a different one. There was little standardization.

In recent times coin values have increased sharply. In many instances coins that were worth $10 twenty years ago are worth $200 or more now. A very small difference in grade can mean a very large difference in price. The exact grade of a coin is more important now than ever before.

Recently, the continued escalation of coin values has brought about finer grading distinctions than ever before. For example, the Mint State or Uncirculated grade is often divided into three classifications: Uncirculated (typical) or, in the numerical scale MS-60; Choice Uncirculated or MS-65, and Perfect Uncirculated or MS-70. The official ANA Grading System defines these and many other distinctions. It also gives important information concerning surface characteristics, methods of striking, different gradations of wear, and much other information which enables the user to accurately grade any United States coin from 1793 to the present.

In the pages immediately following, you will find basic information from the official ANA Grading System. This information is far from complete because of the size limitations of this book. The complete official ANA Grading System is a sizable reference book of 352 pages and is highly recommended by the editor as a very useful adjunct to this book.

Basic Grading Information for United States Coins

OFFICIAL ANA GRADING SYSTEM

The grading information on the following pages is intended to inform the reader about the basics of grading United States Coins. This information is being reproduced from *The Official American Numismatic Association Grading Standards For United States Coins* with the courtesy of the American Numismatic Association.

For more detailed grading information, the above reference is highly recommended.

PROOF COINS

The term "Proof" refers to a manufacturing process which results in a special surface or finish on coins made for collectors. Most familiar are modern brilliant proofs. These coins are struck at the mint by a special process. Carefully prepared dies, sharp in all features, are made. Then the flat surfaces of the dies are given a high mirror-like polish. Specially prepared planchets are fed into low-speed coining presses. Each Proof coin is slowly and carefully struck more than once to accentuate details. When striking is completed, the coin is taken from the dies with care and not allowed to come into contact with other pieces. The result is a coin with mirror-like surface. The piece is then grouped together with other denominations in a set and offered for sale to collectors.

From 1817 through 1857 inclusive, Proof coins were made only on special occasions and not for general sale to collectors. They were made available to visiting foreign dignitaries, government officials, and those with connections at the mint. Earlier (pre-1817) United States coins may have proof-like surfaces and many proof characteristics (1796 Silver Coins are a good example), but they were not specifically or intentionally struck as proofs. There are sometimes designated as "specimen strikings."

Beginning in 1858, Proofs were sold to collectors openly. In that year 80 Silver Proof sets (containing silver coins from the three-cent piece through the Silver Dollar), plus additional pieces of the Silver Dollar denomination, were produced as well as perhaps 200 (the exact number is not known) Copper-Nickel cents and limited number of Proof Gold coins.

The traditional or "brilliant" type of proof finish was used on all American proof coins of the nineteenth century. During the twentieth century, cents through the 1909 Indian, nickels through the 1912 Liberty, regular issued silver coins through 1915, and gold coins through 1907 were of the brilliant type. When modern proof coinage was resumed in 1936 and continued through 1942, then 1950-1964, and 1968 to date, the brilliant finish was used. While these types of proofs are referred to as "brilliant proofs," actual specimens may have toned over the years. The mirror-like surface is still evident, however.

From 1908 through 1915, matte proofs and sandblast proofs (the latter made by directing fine sand particles at high pressure toward the coin's surface) were made of certain gold coins (exceptions are 1909-1910 proofs with Roman finish). While characteristics vary from issue to issue, generally all of these pieces have extreme sharpness of design detail and sharp, squared-off rims. The surfaces are without luster and have a dullish matte surface. Sandblast proofs were made of certain commemoratives also, such as the 1928 Hawaiian issue.

Roman finish proof gold coins were made in 1909 and 1910. These pieces are sharply struck, have squared-off edges, and have a satin-like surface finish, not too much different from an Uncirculated coin (which causes confusion among collectors today, and which at the time of issue was quite unpopular as collectors resented having to pay a premium for a coin without a distinctly different appearance).

Matte proofs were made of Lincoln cents 1909-1917 and Buffalo Nickels 1913-1917. Such coins have extremely sharp design detail, squared-off rims, "brilliant" (mirror-like) edges, but a matte or satin-like (or even satin surface, not with flashy mint luster) surface. In some instances matte proof dies may have been used to make regular circulation strikes once the requisite number of matte proofs were made for collectors. So, it is important that a matte proof, to be considered authentic, have squared-off rims and mirror-like perfect edges in addition to the proper surface characteristics.

Additional Points Concerning Proofs: Certain regular issues or business strike coins have nearly full prooflike surfaces. These were produced in several ways. Usually regular issue dies (intended to make coins for circulation) were polished to remove surface marks or defects to extend use. Coins struck from these dies were produced at high speed, and the full proof surface is not always evident. Also, the pieces are struck on ordinary planchets. Usually such pieces, sometimes called "First Strikes" or "Prooflike Uncirculated" have patches of Uncirculated mint frost. A characteristic in this regard is the shield on the reverse (on coins with this design feature). The stripes within the shield on proofs are fully brilliant, but on proof-like no-proofs the stripes usually are not mirror-like. Also, the striking may be weak in areas and the rims might not be sharp.

The mirror-like surface of a brilliant proof coin is much more susceptible to damage than surfaces of an Uncirculated coin. For this reason, proof coins which have been cleaned often show a series of fine hairlines or minute striations. Also, careless handling has resulted in certain proofs acquiring marks, nicks, and scratches.

Some proofs, particularly nineteenth century issues, have "lint marks." When a proof die was wiped with an oily rag, sometimes threads, bits of hair, lint, and so on would remain. When a coin was struck from such a die, an incuse or recessed impression of the debris would appear on the piece. Lintmarks visible to the unaided eye should be specifically mentioned in a description.

Proof-70 (Perfect Proof). A Proof-70 or Perfect Proof is a coin with no hairlines, handling marks, or other defects; in other words, a flawless coin. Such a coin may be brilliant or may have natural toning.

Proof-65 (Choice Proof). Proof 65 or Choice Proof refers to a proof which may show some very fine hairlines, usually from friction type cleaning or friction type drying or rubbing after dipping. To the unaided eye, a Proof-65 or Choice Proof will appear to be virtually perfect. However, 5x magnification will reveal some minute lines. Such hairlines are best seen under strong incandescent light.

Proof-60 (Proof). Proof-60 refers to a proof with some scattered handling marks and hairlines which may be visible to the unaided eye.

Impaired Proofs; Other Comments. If a proof has been excessively cleaned, has many marks, scratches, dents or other defects, it is described as an impaired proof. If the coin has seen extensive wear then it will be graded one of the lesser grades--Proof-55, Proof-45, or whatever. It is not logical to describe a slightly worn proof as "AU" (Almost

Uncirculated) for it never was "Uncirculated" to begin with--in the sense that Uncirculated describes a top grade of normal production strike. So, the term "Impaired Proof" is appropriate. It is best to describe fully such a coin, examples being: "Proof with extensive hairlines and scuffing," or "Proof with numerous nicks and scratches in the field," or "Proof-55, with light wear on the higher surfaces."

UNCIRCULATED COINS

The term "Uncirculated," interchangeable with "Mint State," refers to a coin which has never seen circulation. Such a piece has no wear of any kind. A coin as bright as the time it was minted or with very light natural toning can be described as "Brilliant Uncirculated." Except in the instance of copper coins, the presence or absence of light toning does not affect an Uncirculated coin's grade. Indeed, among silver coins, attractive natural toning often results in the coin bringing a premium.

The quality of luster or "mint bloom" on an Uncirculated coin is an essential element in correctly grading the piece, and has a bearing on its value. Luster may in time become dull, frosty, spotted or discolored. Unattractive luster will normally lower the grade.

With the exception of certain Special Mint Sets made in recent years for collectors, Uncirculated or normal production strike coins were produced on high speed presses, stored in bags together with other coins, run through counting machines, and in other ways handled without regard for numismatic prosterity. As a result, it is the rule and not the exception for an Uncirculated coin to have bag marks and evidence of coin-to-coin contact, although the piece might not have seen actual commercial circulation. The amount of such marks will depend on the coin's size. Differences in criteria in this regard are given in the detailed individual grading sections of the *Official ANA Grading Guide.*

Uncirculated coins can be divided into three major categories:

MS-70 (Perfect Uncirculated). MS-70 or Perfect Uncirculated is the finest quality available. Such a coin under 4x magnification will show no bag marks, lines, or other evidence of handling or contact with other coins.

A brilliant coin may be described as "MS-70 Brilliant" or "Perfect Brilliant Uncirculated." A lightly toned silver or nickel coin may be described as "MS-70 Toned" or "Perfect Toned Uncirculated." Or in the case of particularly attractive or unusual toning, additional adjectives may be in order such as "Perfect Uncirculated with attractive iridescent toning around the borders."

Copper and Bronze coins: To qualify as MS-70 or Perfect Uncirculated, a copper or bronze coin must have its full luster and natural surface color, and may not be toned brown, olive, or any other color; (coins with toned surfaces which are otherwise perfect should be described as MS-65 as the following text indicates).

MS-65 (Choice Uncirculated). This refers to an above average Uncirculated coin which may be Brilliant or Toned (and described accordingly) and which has fewer bag marks than usual; scattered occasional bag marks on the surface or perhaps one or two very light rim marks.

MS-60 (Uncirculated). MS-60 or Uncirculated (typical Uncirculated without any other adjectives) refers to a coin which has a moderate number of bag marks on it's surface. Also present may be a few minor edge nicks and marks although not of serious nature.

Usually deep bag marks, nicks, and the like must be described separately. A coin may be either brilliant or toned.

Striking and Minting Peculiarities on Uncirculated Coins

Certain early United States gold and silver coins have mint-caused planchet or adjustment marks, a series of parallel striations. If these are visible to the naked eye, they should be described adjectivally in addition to the numerical or regular descriptive grade. For example: "MS-60 with adjustment marks," or "MS-65 with adjustment marks," or "Perfect Uncirculated with very light adjustment marks," or something similar.

If an Uncirculated coin exhibits weakness due to striking or die wear, or unusual (for the variety) die wear, this must be adjectivally mentioned in addition to the grade. Examples are:"MS-60, lightly struck", or "Choice Uncirculated, lightly struck," and "MS-70, lightly struck."

CIRCULATED COINS

Once a coin enters circulation it begins to show signs of wear. As time goes on the coin becomes more and more worn until, after a period of many decades, only a few features may be left.

Dr. William H. Sheldon devised a numerical scale to indicate degrees of wear. According to the scale, a coin touched by even the slightest trace of wear (below MS-60) cannot be called Uncirculated.

While numbers from 1 through 59 are continuous, it has been found practical to designate specific intermediate numbers to define grades. Hence, this text uses the following descriptions and their numerical equivalents:

Choice About Uncirculated-55. Abbreviation: AU-55. Only a small trace of wear is visible on the highest points of the coin. As in the case with the other grades here, specific information is listed in the Official ANA Grading Guide under the various types, for wear often occurs in different spots on different designs.

About Uncirculated-50. Abbreviation: AU-50. With traces of wear on nearly all of the highest areas. At least half of the original mint luster is present.

Choice Extremely Fine-45. Abbreviation: EF-45. With light overall wear on the coins highest points. All design details are very sharp. Mint luster is usually seen only in protected areas of the coin's surface such as between the star points and in the letter spaces.

Extremely Fine-40. Abbreviation: EF-40. With only slight wear but more extensive than the preceding, still with excellent overall sharpness. Traces of mint luster may still show.

Choice Very Fine-30. Abbreviation: VF-30. With light even wear on the surfaces; design details on the highest points lightly worn, but with all lettering and major features sharp.

Very Fine-20. Abbreviation: VF-12. As preceding but with moderate wear on highest parts.

Fine-12. Abbreviation: F-12 Moderate to considerable even wear. Entire design is bold. All lettering, including the word LIBERTY (on 28 coins with this feature on the shield or headband), visible, but with some weaknesses.

Very Good-8. Abbreviation: VG-8. Well worn. Most fine details such as hair strands, leaf details, and so on are worn nearly smooth. The word LIBERTY if on a shield or headband is only partially visible.

Good-4. Abbreviation: G-4. Heavily worn. Major designs visible, but with faintness in areas. Head of liberty, wreath, and other major features visible in outline form without center detail.

About Good-3. Abbreviation AG-3. Very heavily worn with portions of the lettering, date, and legends being worn smooth, the date barely readable.

Editor's Note: The exact descriptions of circulated grades vary widely from issue to issue, so the preceding commentary is only of a very general nature. It is once again highly recommended the Official ANA Grading Guide be referred to for specific information about grading the various types.

SPLIT AND INTERMEDIATE GRADES

It is often the case that because of peculiarities of striking or a coin's design, one side of the coin will grade differently from the other. When this is the case, a diagonal mark is used to separate the two. For example, a coin with an AU-50 obverse and a Choice Extremely Fine-45 reverse can be described as: AU/EF or, alternately 50/45.

The ANA standard numerical scale is divided into the following steps: 3, 4, 8, 12, 20, 30, 40, 50, 55, 60, 65, and 70. Most advanced collectors and dealers find that the gradations from AG-3 through choice AU-55 are sufficient to describe nearly every coin showing wear. The use of intermediate grade labels such as EF-42, EF-43, and so on is not encouraged. Grading is not that precise, and using such finely split intermediate grades implies a degree of accuracy which probably will not be verified by other numismatists. As such, it is discouraged.

A split or an intermediate grade, such as that between VF-30 and EF-40 should be called choice VF-35 rather than VF-EF or about EF.

An exception to intermediate grades can be found among Mint State coins—coins grading from MS-60 through MS-70. Among Mint State Coins there are fewer variables. Wear is not a factor; the considerations are the amount of bag marks and surface blemishes. While it is good numismatic practice to adhere to the numerical classifications of 60, 65, and 70, it is permissible to use intermediate grades.

In all instances, the adjectival description must be of the next lower grade. For example, a standard grade for a coin is MS-60 or Uncirculated Typical. The next major category is MS-65 or Uncirculated Choice. A coin which is felt to grade, for example MS-64, must be described as "MS-64, Uncirculated Typical." It may not be described a Choice Uncirculated for the minimum definition of Choice Uncirculated is MS-65. Likewise, an MS-69 coin must be described as: MS-69, Uncirculated Choice. It is not permissible to use Uncirculated Perfect for any coin which is any degree less than MS-70.

The ANA Grading System considers it to be good numismatic practice to adhere to the standard 60, 65 and 70 numerical designations. Experienced numismatics can generally agree on whether a given coin is MS-60 or MS-65. However, not even the most advanced numismatists can necessarily agree on whether a coin is MS-62 or MS-63; the distinction is simply too minute to permit accuracy. In all instances it is recommended that intermediate grades be avoided, and if there is any doubt, the lowest standard grade would be used. The use of plus or minus signs is also not accepted practice.

GRADING ABBREVIATIONS

Corresponding numbers may be used with any of these descriptions.

MS-70	Perfect Uncirculated	Perf. Unc.	UNC.-70
MS-65	Choice Uncirculated	Ch. Unc.	UNC.-65
MS-60	Uncirculated	Unc.	UNC.-60
AU-55	Ch. Abt. Unc.	Ch. Abt. Unc.	CH. AU.
AU-50	About Uncirculated	Abt. Unc.	AU
EF-45	Choice Extremely Fine	Ch. Ex. Fine	CH. EF
EF-40	Extremely Fine	Ex. Fine	EF
VF-30	Choice Very Fine	Ch. V. Fine	CH. VF
VF-20	Very Fine	V. Fine	VF
F-12	Fine	Fine	F
VG-8	Very Good	V. Good	VG
G-4	Good	Good	G
AG-3	About Good	Abt. Good	AG

CLEANING COINS

Experienced numismatists will usually say that a coin is best left alone and not cleaned. However, most beginning collectors have the idea that "Brilliant is best" and somehow feel that cleaning a coin will "improve" it. As the penchant for cleaning seems to be universal, and also because there are some instances in which cleaning can actually be beneficial, some important aspects are presented here.

All types of cleaning, "good" and "bad," result in the coin's surface being changed, even if only slightly. Even the most careful "dipping" of a coin will, if repeated time and time again, result in the coin acquiring a dullish and microscopically etched surface. It is probably true to state that no matter what one's intentions are, for every single coin actually improved in some way by cleaning, a dozen or more have been decreased in value. Generally, experienced numismatists agree that a coin *should not be cleaned* unless there are spots of oxidation, pitting which might worsen in time, or unsightly streaking or discoloration.

PROCESSING, POLISHING, AND OTHER MISTREATMENT OF COINS

There have been many attempts to give a coin the appearance of being in a higher grade than it actually is. Numismatists refer to such treatment as "processing." Being different from cleaning (which can be "good" or "bad"), processing is never beneficial.

Types of processing include polishing and abrasion which removes metal from a coin's surface, etching and acid treatment, and "whizzing," the latter usually referring to abrading the surface of a coin with a stiff wire brush, often in a circular motion, to produce a series of minute tiny parallel scratches which to the unaided eye or under low magnification often appear to be like mint luster. Under high magnification (in this instance a very strong magnifying glass should be used) the surface of a whizzed coin will show countless tiny scratches. Also, the artificial "mint luster" will usually be in a uniform pattern throughout the coin's surfaces, whereas on an Uncirculated coin with true mint luster the sheen of the luster will be different on the higher parts than on the field. Some whizzed coins can be extremely deceptive. Comparing a whizzed coin to an untreated coin is the best way to gain experience in this regard.

The reader is advised that the American Numismatic Association's bylaws make a member subject to disciplinary action if he advertises or offers for sale or trade any coin that has been whizzed and is represented to be of a better condition than it was previously.

Often one or more methods of treating a coin are combined. Sometimes a coin will be cleaned or polished and then by means of heat, fumes, or other treatment artificial toning will be applied. There are many variations.

When a coin has been polished, whizzed, artificially retoned, or in any other way changed from its original natural appearance and surface, it must be so stated in description. For example, a coin which is Extremely Fine but whizzed to give it the artificial appearance of Uncirculated should be described as "Extremely Fine, Whizzed." An AU coin which has been recolored should be described as "AU, Recolored." The simple "dipping" (without abrasion) of an already Uncirculated or Proof coin to brighten the surface does not have to be mentioned unless such dipping alters the appearance from when the coin was first struck (for example, in the instance of a copper or bronze coin in which dipping always produces an unnatural color completely unlike the coin when it was first struck).

NATURAL COLORATION OF COINS

Knowledge of the natural color which coinage metals acquire over a period of years is useful to the collector. To an extent, a coin's value is determined by the attractiveness of its coloration. Also, certain types of unnatural color might indicate that a coin has been cleaned or otherwise treated.

The basic coinage metals used in the United States are alloys of copper, nickel, silver, and gold. Copper tends to tone the most rapidly. Gold is the least chemically active and will tone only slightly and then over a long period of years.

Copper. Copper is among the most chemically active of all coinage metals. Half cents and large cents of 1793-1857 were made of nearly pure copper. Later "copper" coins are actually bronze.

When a copper coin is first struck it emerges from the dies with a brilliant pale-orange surface, the color of a newly minted Lincoln set. There were some exceptions in the early years among half cents and large cents. Copper was obtained from many different sources, traces of impurities varied from shipment to shipment, and some newly minted coins had a subdued brilliance, sometimes with a brownish or grayish cast.

Once a freshly minted coin enters the atmosphere it immediately begins to oxidize. Over a period of years, especially if exposed to actively circulating air or if placed in contact with sulphites, the coin will acquire a glossy brown surface. In between the brilliant and glossy brown stages it will be part red and part brown.

An Uncirculated coin with full original mint brilliance, usually slightly subdued in coloration, is typically described as Brilliant Uncirculated (our example here is for a typical Uncirculated or MS-60 coin); a choice piece would be called Choice Brilliant Uncirculated, and so on. One which is part way between brilliant and brown surface hues would be called Red and Brown Uncirculated. Specimens with brownish surfaces can be called Brown Uncirculated. Particularly valuable coins can have the coloration described in more detail. Generally, in any category of grading, the more explanation given, the more accurate is the description.

Brilliant Proof (with mirrorlike fields) copper and bronze coins are pale orange when first struck. Over a period of time they, like Uncirculated pieces of the same metal, tend to tone brown. Often attractive iridescent hues will develop in the intermediate stages. A Proof copper coin can be described as Brilliant Proof (if the surfaces are still "bright"), Red and Brown Proof, or Brown Proof.

Matte Proofs were made at the Philadelphia Mint in the Lincoln cent series from 1909 to 1916. When first introduced, these were stored in yellow tissue paper which tended to tone them quickly to shades varying from deep reddish-brown to dark brown with iridescent tones. This surface coloration is normal today for a Matte Proof bronze coin and should be expected. Most "bright" Matte Proofs have been cleaned or dipped.

Early copper and bronze coins with full original mint brilliance are more valuable than Red and Brown Uncirculated pieces. The more original mint brilliance present, the more valuable a coin will be. The same is true of Proofs.

Circulated copper coins are never fully Brilliant, but are toned varying shades of brown. Certain early large cents and half cents often tone black because of the presence of impurities in the original metal.

Nickel. Uncirculated nickel (actually an alloy of copper and nickel) coins when first minted are silver-gray in appearance, not as bright as silver but still with much brilliance. Over a period of time nickel coins tend to tone a hazy gray, gray, or golden coloration, sometimes with bluish overtones. Proof nickel coins will tone in the same manner.

The presence or absence of attractive toning does not affect an Uncirculated or Proof nickel coin's value. Many collectors, particularly those with great experience, will actually prefer and will sometimes pay a premium for very attractive light toning. Very dull, heavily toned, or spotted coins are considered less valuable. Circulated nickel coins have a gray appearance.

Silver. When first minted, silver coins have a bright silvery-white surface. Over a period of time silver, a chemically active metal, tends to tone deep brown or black. Uncirculated and Proof silver pieces often exhibit very beautiful multi-colored iridescent hues after a few years. The presence or absence of attractive toning does not affect a silver coin's value one way or the other. Old timers and museums will often prefer attractively toned coins. Beginners sometimes think that "brilliant is best." Circulated silver coins often have a dull gray appearance, sometimes with deep gray or black areas.

Gold. When first struck, gold coins are a bright yellow-orange color. As gold coins are not pure gold but are alloyed with copper and traces of other substances, they do not tend to tone over a period of time. Over a period of decades, a gold coin will normally acquire a deep orange coloration, sometimes with light brown or orange-brown toning "stains" or streaks in areas (resulting from improperly mixed copper traces in the alloy). Light toning does not affect the value of a gold coin.

Very old gold coins, particularly those in circulated grades, will sometimes show a red oxidation. Gold coins which have been recovered from treasure wrecks after centuries at the sea bottom will sometimes have a minutely porous surface because of the corrosive action of sea water. Such pieces sell for less then specimens which have not been so affected. Care must be taken to distinguish these from cast copies which often have a similar surface.

Handling and Storing Numismatic Treasures

Some handling and storage methods are known to contribute to the deterioration of coins, lowering values considerably along the way. If you don't want the shock of someday discovering that a half dollar bought at MS-65 must be seriously downgraded because of treatment received from you, read this chapter carefully. It could save you much mental anguish later on.

Firstly, never handle an unprotected coin any other way except by its edges. If your fingers come in contact with either one of its sides, small amounts of oil and acid in the skin could be left behind. Always place a soft surface below the coin in case it should accidentally slip from your grasp. There will be a lesser risk of damage by doing so. Do not allow any collectible coin to come in contact with other coins or hard objects. Any bump or scrape could leave scratches. By no means should a person scoot a valuable coin along any surface, no matter how soft or slick the surface is.

The best way to protect and store your coins is to keep them in special holders or albums available through coin dealers and bookstores. Not all containers are of equal quality, so it's best to get advice before you place your most valuable coins in any of them.

Never use paper envelopes for storing coins. Most paper products contain sulfur, which can cause an ugly black or yellow tone to appear on your coins. If a coin is shipped to you in a paper envelope, be certain to remove it right away. As an additional precaution, maintain separate storage facilities for your important papers and your numismatic investments.

Some types of coin holders, one kind in particular called a "flip," contains a chemical know as polyvinyl chloride (PVC) which is the agent that keeps plastic soft and pliable. PVC sometimes breaks down and leaves a filmy deposit on the surface of a coin and tarnishes it. To test if your coin holder contains PVC, take a small copper wire and heat it in a flame. Place the wire on a piece of the plastic so that a small portion melts onto the wire. Reheating the wire will produce a blue-green flame if the plastic contains PVC. Plastics not containing PVC will produce a yellow or colorless flame. If you think that your coins are in the initial phases of PVC corrosion, a dip in a trichlorotrifluroethane solution (TO) will wash away the contaminants and neutralize the coin's surface. You ought to be able to purchase some TO from your coin dealer or the local science store.

The most common holder today for single coins is the 2"x2" or 1½"x1½" cardboard square with the centrally located round window through which the coin can be viewed. An inert (meaning non-reactive) material called mylar is used to cover the hole, and the coin is sandwiched in between two cardboard squares and stapled shut. Unfortunately, some problems have been reported with the cardboard holders. The mylar can get contaminated with the cardboard dust, which can migrate to the coin itself, causing sulfur contamination. Luckily there are other alternatives better suited to your needs.

Any coin container composed of the following materials is acceptable for holding coins over a long period of time: polyethylene, polypropylene, polystyrene, polymethyl methacrlate (brand names Plexiglas and Lucite), and polyethylene terephthalate (brand name Mylar). All of these compounds are inert and therefore have no agents that will react with the metal in your coins. One common brand name holder made of polyethylene is called "Saflips." Saflips resemble vinyl flips but are much stiffer since there are no plasticizers, and are relatively inexpensive. Like anything else relating to numismatics, Saflips can most easily be found at coin stores.

Another coin holder that has been met with good reviews is a product called "Kointains." Kointains are two piece capsules that form a shell around the coin, touching it only along the edges. Made of unbending, transparent plastic, this is a desirable holder for long term storage.

For your most valuable coins, you should consider a holder made of lucite or some acrylic material. These offer maximum protection and are the most attractive containers available today. A company called Capitol Plastics, Inc. is the largest marketer of this item and is in fact virtually synonymous with the subject of lucite holders. The major drawbacks of these top-of-the-line holders are that they are expensive and somewhat cumbersome.

There are only a few coin albums on the market to choose from. One type is the Whitman folder, used most often by young collectors. Each coin is forced into a slot with paper backing. There is one slot for each date and mint mark of the series. The reverses can easily tarnish from their contact with the paper, and the obverse have little if any protection. Such albums should be used only for displaying very inexpensive well circulated coins.

The Coinmaster Album by Harco is a brown-like binder containing transparent pages with see-through sliding inserts filled with coins. Coinmaster albums have always provided protection from nicks and scratches but the earlier albums contained PVC. If you've got one of the older albums, you would be wise to purchase some of the newer inserts, made of inert polyethylene and designed to fit Coinmaster albums.

Coingard Albums, made on the same design as Coinmaster, is a popular album presently. Reportedly, the inserts are completely free of PVC or any other dangerous chemicals that can attack a coin's surface.

Before you use any album, make certain it consists only of materials and chemicals that won't harm your coins. Other brands recognized as acceptable containers are Air Tite holders, American Tight Fit Coin Sheets, and Blue Ribbon Safety Flipettes. This list is by no means complete, but these are some of the industry leaders.

It almost goes without saying that slabbed coins are encased in safe, inert plastic, and have no need to be replaced in other holders. Indeed, to do so would defeat a major purpose of certifying a coin to begin with.

Atmospheric conditions can lead to the decay of your coins also. Your storage area should be dry and free from dampness and moisture of any kind. Water is one of the worst corrosion promoters of all. If some moisture is inevitable, a packet of silica gel (available in drugstores and photographic supply stores) stored with your coins will serve to absorb moisture.

Do not leave your coins exposed to sunlight, high heat, or high humidity for an extended period of time. These conditions can easily damage a coin.

The presence of industrial fumes, such as sulfur or acid, will be detrimental to your collection. Storage in an airtight container is the best solution to the problem, but if that isn't possible, you should buy a pellet or two of a product called "Metal Safe." This additive neutralizes atmospheric ions and thus prohibits deterioration. Each capsule is good for about a year and protects two to three cubic feet.

Protecting your coins from damage and subsequent value erosion should rank high on your priority list, whether you're a collector, an investor, or both. If that's not enough incentive to motivate you, consider the subject in this regard: although you technically own your coins, you are in reality only their temporary custodian, just as all the owners previous to you were. In an ethical sense, you have a responsibility to preserve your numismatic inheritance for future generations of coin enthusiasts. Someday your collection will be passed on to your children or sold to a complete stranger. In either event, the new custodians will be wholeheartedly grateful for your thoughtfulness and foresight in preserving another wonderful piece of Americana. Your coins are not only important to you, they will be important to the people of the future as well.

Collecting Coins for Fun

Anyone interested in investing in coins should consider enjoying some of the benefits derived from coin collecting as well. Coins can be fascinating to anyone with an intellectual curiosity and a fertile mind. The cold investor who is oblivious to their charms is denying himself one of the greatest profits in buying coins.

Collecting, by definition, implies that coins are being assembled in a non-random manner with a basic purpose or goal in mind, as opposed to simply accumulating coins. The pursuit of this objective offers a form of relaxation and enjoyment to ease the tensions and pressures of everyday life. Hopefully, that's what any hobby will do for its participants.

Many collectors get a kick out of owning pieces of history. Knowing that the 1863 Indian Head cent in your collection actually could have been in Abraham Lincoln's pocket as he delivered the Gettysburg Address is an exciting thought, or perhaps the 1917 nickel resting in your Buffalo nickel album was once donated by a New York school child to help our doughboys fighting over in Europe during World War I. Unlikely, but indeed possible. If you let your imagination run wild, the possibilities are endless. Legendary figures come alive or nostalgic eras can be revisited. Visualize being towed in a boat by horses along the old Erie Canal, for maybe your 1824 quarter was once upon a time used to pay the toll. It could be that an 1814 dime in your possession was spent by a drunken sailor in Baltimore for a mug of rum the night Francis Scott Key wrote "Oh, say can you see..." In a sense, coins are visitors from the past. If only they could relive their travels with us!

Often collectors are drawn because of the intellectual aspect coins offer. How were coins minted in the 1790's and who designed them? How were certain artistic patterns selected and why? Why were some denominations accepted by the public while others were rejected? There are countless coin related topics to research and study, with many,

many fine references available for anyone aspiring to embark on any such endeavor.

It's easy to be both a collector and investor. Actually, many successful investors are collectors too. Learn about the coins you've bought or plan to buy. Get acquainted with the facts and legacies associated with your coins. Not only can you build an investment program of extraordinary potential, you can also assemble a true numismatic treasure filled with enjoyment and pride.

There are several things you can do to increase your activity as a collector. Join the local coin club if you have the opportunity. You'll meet people who have similar interests and develop new friendships. Attend coin shows and conventions. There you'll see a wide display of coins and have a chance to talk with dealers and other collectors one-on-one. Start up a numismatic library, purchasing books to educate you about the workings of the industry and coins that have special interest to you. Subscribe to at least one of the hobby's periodical publications. You'll soak in a lot of valuable information by reading them.

As an investor of coins, you owe it to yourself to at least try to get involved with the hobby for the sake of pleasure. Not only will you improve your status as an investor, you'll experience certain other advantages that don't register on the bottom line of your balance sheet. Enjoy coins and take part in the world's greatest hobby!

Closing Comments

Ten years from now (or probably less), investors will be muttering to themselves "if only I had bought that coin back in 1993 when I had the chance..." Because collecting and investing in coins has been, and will continue to be popular for a very long time, we can rightfully conclude that obtaining certain, well chosen coins today, will post impressive gains in the years to come. This is the essence of the coin market. Investors who have enough insight to get involved with numismatics will most likely be the ones to reap the nicest returns.

Hopefully, this publication will better enable you to seize upon the finest opportunities presently offered. Having read the preceding chapters, you understand basically what makes a coin valuable. You also now have some exposure to the slabbed coin market and the collector's market, and how they interrelate with each other. You know that you cannot take a random approach to buying coins, or subscribe to the theory of acquiring whatever is hot at the moment. Work only with reputable coin professionals and carefully plan each addition to your collection and protect it from all harm. Become a hobbyist and enjoy the leisure side of numismatics. Take your time, be judicious and let each experience heighten your interest and skills and guide you to your next decision. Do all this, and the chances are excellent that you will do very well by investing coins.

The American Numismatic Association

At this point we would like to recommend that the reader consider becoming a member of the American Numismatic Association. The A.N.A. is a nonprofit educational association that was founded in 1891 and chartered by an act of Congress in 1912. It welcomes all persons eleven years of age and over who have a sincere interest in numismatics, whether they collect coins, paper money, tokens or medals, whether advanced collectors or those only generally interested in the subject without being collectors. The association has over 30,000 members from every state in the Union and many foreign countries.

A.N.A. membership makes it easier for you, as a collector, to make a serious study of the area of numismatics that interests you—to build up a real knowledge of your specialty while you are building your collection. Benefits of membership include a subscription to THE NUMISMATIST, the Association's official magazine, which is mailed free to all members except associates. There are many informative articles in this magazine which usually has 224 pages or more. Advertising in THE NUMISMATIST is accepted from members only who must agree to abide by a very strict code of ethics. The A.N.A. also maintains the largest circulating numismatic library in the world, consisting of about 7,000 books in addition to over 15,000 periodicals and catalogs. Books and other library items are loaned to members without charge other than postage. In addition to these benefits, there is a museum, conventions, seminars, coin clubs, programs for young numismatists and other programs. There is also a certification and grading service which, for a fee, will examine coins submitted to it and issue certificates of authentification for those determined to be genuine, and grade the coin expertly.

To get more information about the A.N.A. and an application form, write to:

AMERICAN NUMISMATIC ASSOCIATION
818 N. Cascade Avenue
Colorado Springs, Colorado 80903-3279

Investor's Tips
....

HALF CENTS 1793-1857

KEY DATES	BEST BETS
1793	• All half cents in Mint State are very
1796	desirable, particularly those with original "mint red" color

LARGE CENTS 1793-1857

KEY DATES	BEST BETS
1793 All Types	• All Pre-1816 large cents in Fine or better
1799	• 1816-1857 large cents in Extremely Fine to Mint state
1804	

SMALL CENTS 1856-TO DATE

KEY DATES	BEST BETS
1856	• MS-60 to MS-63 Indian cents with original color
1877	• MS-65 Lincoln cents
1901 S Indian	
1909 S Lincoln	
1909 S VDB	
1914 D	
1922 D (no D)	
1931 S	

Investor's Tips

TWO CENT PIECES 1864-1873

KEY DATES	BEST BETS
1864 SM	• MS-60 to MS-65 problem free
1872	
1873	

THREE CENT PIECES SILVER 1851-1873

KEY DATES	BEST BETS
1855	• MS-65 Uncirculated - well struck
1863 to 1873	• Proof 65 - well struck

THREE CENT PIECES NICKEL 1865-1889

KEY DATES	BEST BETS
1877	• MS-65 Uncirculated - well struck
1878	• Proof 65 - well struck
1883 to 1887	

HALF DIMES 1794-1873

KEY DATES	BEST BETS
1802	• All Pre-1805 dates in F - EF
1870 S	• 1846 in all conditions
	• 1838-1873 in Very Fine and better
	• 1839 to 1852 New Orleans mint MS-63 to MS-65

NICKELS 1867-TO DATE

KEY DATES	BEST BETS
1867 with rays	• Shield nickels in MS-60 to MS-63 Uncirculated and Proof
1877 to 1881	• Liberty nickels in MS-63 to MS-65
1885	• Uncirculated doubled die and Proof
1916	• Buffalo nickels in MS-60 to MS-65+
1918/7-D	• Jefferson nickels in MS-65+ with full steps
1937-D 3 legs	

DIMES 1796-TO DATE

KEY DATES	BEST BETS
1796	• 1796-1807 all grades
1798/97 13 Stars	• 1809-1837 EF to MS-60
1873 CC	• Liberty Seated dimes in AU to MS-65
1874 CC	• Barber dimes in MS-60 to MS-63
1916 D	• Mercury dimes - well struck coins with full split bands
	• Proof Mercury dimes

Investor's Tips

QUARTERS 1796-TO DATE

KEY DATES	BEST BETS
1976	• 1796 all grades
1804	• 1815-1838 in EF-40 to MS-60
1823/22	• 1838-1891 in MS-60 to MS-63
1870 CC	• Barber quarters in EF-40 to MS-63
1873 CC Arrows	• Standing Liberty in MS-60 to MS-65
1916	• Pre-1940 Washingtons in MS-63 to MS-65
1918/7-S	
1932-D	
1938-S	

HALF DOLLARS 1794-TO DATE

KEY DATES	BEST BETS
1796	• 1801-1807 in EF-40
1797	• 1807-1836 in Fine to EF
1815/12	• Liberty Seated halves in EF to MS-65
1842 O Small Date	• Barber halves in Extremely Fine to MS-65
1870 CC	• Pre-1934 Walking Liberty halves in EF to MS-65
1873 Open 3	• Common date MS-65 Walking Liberty halves
No Arrows	• Franklin halves in MS-65
1878 S	• Proof Franklins
1921 P-D-S	

SILVER DOLLARS 1794-TO DATE

KEY DATES	BEST BETS
1794	• All pre-1804 dollars
1854	• Liberty Seated dollars in all grades
1855	• Trade dollars in MS-60 to MS-65
1858	• Key and semi-key Morgans and
1871 CC	• Peace dollars in VF or better
1873 CC	• Morgans in MS-65
1878 CC	• Peace dollars in MS-65
1889 CC	• Eisenhower dollars in MS-65 and better
1893 S	
1894	
1895	
1928	

GOLD DOLLARS 1849-1889

KEY DATES	BEST BETS
1861 D	• All dates in AU and better
1855 D	• Key and semi-key dates in EF and better
1856 D	
1860 D	
1861 D	
1875	

Investor's Tips

QUARTER EAGLES 1796-1929 ($2.50 GOLD PIECES)

KEY DATES	BEST BETS
1796	• Both Types Classic Head Type in EF and AU
1804 13 Stars	• Low mintage Coronet Type in EF and better grades
1808	• Common date MS-60 to MS-63 Corone and Indian Head Types
1838 C	• Key dates in VF and better
1848 CAL.	• All dates in MS-60 to MS-65
1854 S	
1856 D	
1864	
1875	
1854 D	
1873 Closed 3	
1875	
1876	

HALF EAGLES 1795-1929 ($5.00 GOLD PIECES)

KEY DATES	BEST BETS
1798 Sm. Eagle	• All early dates
1815	• Classic Head Type in EF to MS-63
1819	• Coronet Type—
1827	Charlotte, North carolina (C Mint)
1842 C	Dahlonega, Georgia (D Mint)
1861 D	New Orleans, Louisiana (O Mint)
1832 S	Carson City, Neveda (CC Mint)
1864 S	• Coronet Type MS-60 to MS-63 Uncirculated
1870 CC	• Indian Head Type MS-60 to MS-65
1878 CC	

EAGLES 1795-1933 ($10.00 GOLD PIECES)

KEY DATES	BEST BETS
1795 9 Leaves	• 1795-1804 all grades
1798	• No Motto Coronet Type in EF and Better
1858	• Indian Head Type in MS-60 to MS-65
1860 S	• All keys and semi-keys, EF and better
1862 S	
1863	
1864 S	
1873	
1876	
1877	
1920 S	

The Coin Market Insider / Robert S. Riemer

The Right Way to Ship Coins Through the Mail

Since I am a dealer in rare U.S. coins, and most of my dealings with the general public as well as other dealers is transacted through the U.S. Mail, I am always asked: "Can I trust the Mail with my coins?"

The United States Postal Service (USPS) has several services for people to ship merchandise through its system while protecting items of value from theft.

Many of you may have purchased this edition of Edmund's Coin Prices with the intention of finding the value of your coin holdings, and selling them. People call me daily asking approximately what I would pay for a group of coins. When I explain that I have to see them to arrive at a true grade, and thus price for the coins, some are taken aback when I tell them to ship the coins through the mail. "Oh, I can't do that!" they say.

The "Hope" Diamond Was Shipped Through the Postal Service?!

Many years ago, I heard a story that the rare multi-million dollar "Hope Diamond" was transported, not by armored car, not by armed guard, but by the U.S. Postal Service! No, not placed in an envelope with a ten-cent stamp, but by one of the safest methods known to mankind - Registered Mail!

Now mind you, I haven't done the research to validate the above story, but I do know that vast amounts of rare coins, stamps, antiques, and even cash are transported daily by U.S. Registered Mail. So, as far as its' being safe? Nothing is absolute, but its' record of security is second to none, if rated by the sheer number of daily letters and parcels handled that arrive safe and sound.

Registered Mail - How Does It Work?

The best way to package coins for shipment by Registered Mail, is to wrap large quantity groups of lower value items in paper or plastic tubes. Higher value coins should be placed in individual coin holders. All the coins should then be placed in a sturdy box, using bubble-plastic or paper to protect the contents from moving and shifting once sealed. The box should be sealed using paper brown tape. The reason for the use of paper tape, is so the Postal Service can "plug" or postmark the outside of the box, to prevent tampering. Your package of coins then travels in sealed Postal bags, and is signed for by every postal employee who handles the package.

How Much Does Registered Mail Cost?

For insured Registered Mail the fees are as follows:

$0.00 to $100. .... $ 4.50
$100.01 to $500. .... $ 4.85
$500.01 to $1000. .... $ 5.25
Each additional $1000. in coverage, add .45¢

The maximum value of insured Registered Mail is $25,000. But what about that "Hope Diamond", you may say, it was worth millions?! For items worth over $25,000.,the Postal Service will accept the package only with private insurance. One more point to remember, the above charges only cover insurance; all Registered Mail also has to go via first class or priority mail, and additional charges may apply depending on weight.

As an example of what you may expect to pay: a 2-pound Registered package with a value of $2,000. will cost $8.60. Not at all excessive for the service and security.

What About Lower Value Packages?

For coins worth under $500. Insured Mail is less expensive, and just as fast. The security is not as good, as the coins travel in the main stream of mail. But the cost is less, so it might be a consideration for the lower value coin packages.

I hope that this makes you feel a bit more secure about sending that package of coins to that dealer for their offer. Just make sure the dealer is knowledgeable, and has been in the business for a while. Publications like this would be a great start for finding reputable dealers.

If you have questions on any coin topics for future articles please feel free to write.

Robert S. Riemer has been a dealer of rare U.S. coins, buying and selling coins for over 20 years. He is a member of two national coin trading teletypes, and a member of the American Numismatic Association (a national dealer/collector organization) since 1970. He can be reached at: Robert S. Riemer, Box 33, Brooklyn, NY 11230. His phone number is: 718-253-5031.

United States Regular Issue Coins

EARLY COPPER COINS

Half cent coins were produced intermittently from 1793 to 1857 and are the smallest face value piece ever minted by the United States. Die tooling wasn't precise back then, resulting in numerous varieties of half cent coins, making this, along with the large cents, one of the more interesting series in U.S. coinage. "Variety" means a slight difference or abnormality in a coin from the normal strike, involving the planchet or die. Mint errors fall under this category. A change in design type, on the other hand, results in the introduction of an entirely new pattern coinciding with the retirement of the previous one. There are many varieties of half cents and large cents, and the most notable varieties recognized by numismatic scholars are included in this text.

For investors with a small budget, buy pieces in Good to Very Fine condition dated 1802 or older. For coins dated 1803 to 1811, you ought to be able to afford specimens grading at least Fine, although many Good and Very Good coins of that age have a respectable track record also. Obtain uncirculated examples of later issues, if at all possible.

For those able to spend more, the most valuable half cent dates are 1793 and the varieties of 1796. The 1793 coin has always been expensive because it is a single year type coin, being the only Liberty Cap type with the head facing left. Pressure from type collectors has resulted in many years of healthy appreciation. The 1796 half cent is so valuable because it is very rare and difficult to find. Other than those damaged, these coins are desirable in any condition.

Much of what was said about the half cents holds true for the large cents. There are many varieties to study with dates ranging from 1793 to 1857 continuously, with the exception of 1815.

The most expensive large cents are the 1793 Flowing Hair varieties, the 1799 and the 1804. Like the 1793 half cent, the 1793 large cent is a single year type coin sought after by type collectors. The 1799 and 1804 coins are rarities that have always been elusive to date collectors. All three have done very well in all grades at times in the past, including most recently, as have some of the other earlier large cents. The sharp increases over the last several years or so may indicate that they have already reached their full potential for now. However, for an investor in the game for the long run, these key dates are sure winners.

Uncirculated cents older than 1814 are exceedingly rare and seldom encountered. Should you be able to locate one for sale and can afford to part with many thousands of dollars, you will probably be able to resell at a substantial profit five years or so down the road.

Avoid low circulated grades for most of the large cents, especially those dated 1816 and later—historically very sluggish advancers. A good bargain with promising investment potential are Extremely Fine or Uncirculated coins which are much scarcer than low grades, but still easily within the reach of many investors.

HALF CENTS
1793-1857

LIBERTY CAP TYPE
1793-1797

DIAMETER—
  1793 - 22mm
  1794-1797 - 23.5mm
WEIGHT—
  1793-1795 6.74 Grams
  1795-1797 5.44 Grams
COMPOSITION—Copper
DESIGNER—
  1793 Adam Eckfeldt,
  1794-Robert Scot,
  1795-John S. Gardner
EDGE—1793-1795,
TWO HUNDRED FOR DOLLAR:
  1795-1797 Plain

DATE	MINTAGE	G-4	VG-8	F-12	VF-20	EF-40	MS-60
1793 Head Left	35,334	1650.	2200.	4400.	6700.	10,500.	—
1794 Head Right	81,600	275.	400.	700.	1300.	2200.	—
1795 Lettered Edge, Pole	25,600	250.	375.	600.	1100.	2000.	—
1795 Lettered Edge Punctuated Date	Inc. Above	250.	375.	600.	1100.	2200.	—
1795 Plain Edge, No Pole	109,000	240.	350.	575.	1000.	1800.	—
1795 Plain Edge, Punctuated Date	Inc. Above	250.	350.	575.	1000.	1900.	—
1796 With Pole	5,090	4000.	5400.	8000.	12,000.	20,000.	—
1796 No Pole	1,390			VERY RARE			
1797 Plain Edge	119,215	280.	400.	625.	1100.	2000.	—
1797 Lettered Edge	Inc. Above	900.	1500.	2400.	4750.	—	—
1797 1 Above 1	Inc. Above	250.	350.	575.	1000.	1800.	—

DRAPED BUST TYPE
1800-1808

DIAMETER—23.5mm
WEIGHT—5.44 Grams
COMPOSITION—Copper
DESIGNER—Robert Scot
EDGE—Plain

DATE	MINTAGE	G-4	VG-8	F-12	VF-20	EF-40	MS-60
1800	211,530	35.00	40.00	60.00	140.	325.	—
1802/0 Rev. 1800	14,366	5000.	8750.	12,500.	—	—	—
1802/0 Rev. 1802	Inc. Above	400.	950.	2200.	4000.	9500.	—
1803	97,900	30.00	40.00	52.50	125.	325.	—

DATE	MINTAGE	G-4	VG-8	F-12	VF-20	EF-40	MS-60
1804 Plain 4, Stemless	1,055,312	30.00	40.00	50.00	65.00	180.	1000.
1804 Plain, 4, Stems	Inc. Above	30.00	40.00	50.00	70.00	200.	1000.
1804 Cross 4, Stemless	Inc. Above	30.00	40.00	50.00	70.00	200.	1000.
1804 Cross 4, Stems	Inc. Above	30.00	40.00	50.00	70.00	200.	1000.
1804 Spiked Chin	Inc. Above	30.00	40.00	50.00	65.00	180.	—
1805 Small 5, Stemless	814,464	30.00	40.00	55.00	75.00	220.	—
1805 Small 5, Stems	Inc. Above	450.	950.	2200.	3000.	3750.	—
1805 Large 5, Stems	Inc. Above	30.00	40.00	50.00	75.00	220.	—
1806 Small 6, Stems	356,000	180.	300.	425.	750.	1600.	—
1806 Small 6, Stemless	Inc. Above	30.00	40.00	50.00	65.00	180.	1000.
1806 Large 6, Stems	Inc. Above	30.00	40.00	50.00	65.00	180.	1000.
1807	476,000	30.00	40.00	50.00	75.00	275.	1000.
1808 Over 7	400,000	55.00	100.	180.	600.	—	—
1808	Inc. Above	30.00	40.00	50.00	75.00	300.	1000.

CLASSIC HEAD TYPE
1809-1836

DIAMETER—23.5mm
WEIGHT—5.44 Grams
COMPOSITION—Copper
DESIGNER—John Reich
EDGE—Plain

DATE	MINTAGE	G-4	VG-8	F-12	VF-20	EF-40	MS-60
1809 Over 6	1,154,572	25.00	32.50	37.50	52.50	75.00	525.
1809	Inc. Above	25.00	32.50	37.50	50.00	70.00	500.
1810	215,000	30.00	37.50	50.00	100.	180.	1700.
1811	63,140	75.00	120.	300.	850.	1800.	—
1811 Restrike Rev. Of 1802							6400.
1825	63,000	27.50	32.50	42.50	65.00	115.	1000.
1826	234,000	27.50	32.50	40.00	55.00	80.00	750.
1828 13 Stars	606,000	25.00	27.50	32.50	45.00	62.50	300.
1828 12 Stars	Inc. Above	20.00	22.00	27.50	45.00	65.00	500.
1829	487,000	25.00	27.50	32.50	45.00	67.50	600.
1831 Original	2,200	—	—	—	3500.	4500.	7500.
1832 Restrike Lg. Berries, Rev Of 1836						PROOF ONLY	5800.
1831 Restrike Sm. Berries, Rev Of 1840-1857						PROOF ONLY	7000.
1832	154,000	25.00	27.50	32.50	45.00	65.00	300.
1833	120,000	25.00	27.50	32.50	45.00	62.50	300.
1834	141,000	25.00	27.50	32.50	45.00	62.50	300.
1835	398,000	25.00	27.50	32.50	45.00	62.50	375.
1836 Original						PROOF ONLY	6500.
1836 Restrike Rev. Of 1840-1857						PROOF ONLY	6500.

BRAIDED HAIR TYPE
1840-1857

DIAMETER—23mm
WEIGHT—5.44 Grams
COMPOSITION—Copper
DESIGNER—Christian Gobrecht
EDGE—Plain

DATE	MINTAGE	Prf-60
1840 Original	PROOF ONLY	4000.
1840 Restrike	PROOF ONLY	3400.
1841 Original	PROOF ONLY	4000.
1841 Restrike	PROOF ONLY	3200.
1842 Original	PROOF ONLY	4000.
1842 Restrike	PROOF ONLY	3400.
1843 Original	PROOF ONLY	4000.
1843 Restrike	PROOF ONLY	3400.
1844 Original	PROOF ONLY	4000.
1844 Restrike	PROOF ONLY	3400.
1845 Original	PROOF ONLY	4000.
1845 Restrike	PROOF ONLY	3400.
1846 Original	PROOF ONLY	4000.
1846 Restrike	PROOF ONLY	3400.
1847 Original	PROOF ONLY	4000.
1847 Restrike	PROOF ONLY	3400.
1848 Original	PROOF ONLY	4000.
1848 Restrike	PROOF ONLY	3400.
1849 Original Small Date	PROOF ONLY	4000.
1849 Restrike Small Date	PROOF ONLY	3400.

DATE	MINTAGE	G-4	VG-8	F-12	VF-20	EF-40	MS-60
1849 Large Date	39,864	37.50	40.00	45.00	57.50	80.00	425.
1850	39,812	35.00	37.50	42.50	55.00	75.00	450.
1851	147,672	31.00	35.00	40.00	50.00	67.50	175.
1852					PROOF ONLY		4200.
1853	129,694	31.00	35.00	40.00	50.00	67.50	175.
1854	55,358	31.00	35.00	40.00	50.00	70.00	175.
1855	56,500	31.00	35.00	40.00	50.00	70.00	175.
1856	40,430	35.00	37.50	42.50	55.00	75.00	275.
1857	35,180	45.00	47.50	52.50	62.50	85.00	300.

LARGE CENTS
1793-1857

FLOWING HAIR TYPE
1793

DIAMETER—26-27mm
WEIGHT—13.48 Grams
COMPOSITION—Copper
DESIGNER—Henry Voight
EDGE—Bars and Vine with Leaves

DATE	MINTAGE	G-4	VG-8	F-12	VF-20	EF-40	MS-60
1793 Chain AMERI	36,103	2500.	4000.	5800.	10,000.	26,000.	—
1793 Chain AMERICA	Inc. Above	2300.	3750.	5500.	9500.	24,000.	—

Aug. 1980 Auction Sale MS-65 $120,000.

DIAMETER—26-28mm
WEIGHT—13.48 Grams
COMPOSITION—Copper
DESIGNER—Adam Eckfeldt
EDGE—Vine and Bars or Lettered
ONE HUNDRED FOR A DOLLAR

DATE	MINTAGE	G-4	VG-8	F-12	VF-20	EF-40	MS-60
1793 Wreath	63,353	1000.	1300.	2000.	3500.	7250.	—

LIBERTY CAP TYPE
1793-1796

DIAMETER—29mm
WEIGHT—1793-1795 –13.48 Grams
   1795-1798 –10.89 Grams
COMPOSITION—Copper
DESIGNER—1793-1795 Joseph Wright
   1795-1796 John S. Gardner
EDGE—1793-1795 ONE HUNDRED FOR A DOLLAR
   1795-1796 Plain

DATE	MINTAGE	G-4	VG-8	F-12	VF-20	EF-40	MS-60
1793 Liberty Cap	11,056	2500.	3250.	4500.	6000.	—	—
1794	918,521	160.	240.	425.	800.	1400.	—
1794 Head Of 1793	Inc. Above	325.	500.	1100.	2000.	—	—
1795	501,500	160.	250.	425.	700.	1375.	—
1795 Lettered Edge	37,000	185.	275.	450.	725.	1375.	—
1796 Liberty Cap	109,825	175.	265.	425.	850.	1600.	—

DRAPED BUST TYPE
1795-1807

DIAMETER—29mm
WEIGHT—10.89 Grams
COMPOSITION—Copper
DESIGNER—Robert Scot
EDGE—Plain

DATE	MINTAGE	G-4	VG-8	F-12	VF-20	EF-40	MS-60
1796	363,375	70.00	110.	160.	325.	750.	—
1797	897,510	37.50	60.00	125.	325.	750.	—
1797 Stemless	Inc. Above	70.00	125.	200.	1500.	2250.	—
1798	979,700	35.00	50.00	120.	325.	675.	—
1798/97	Inc. Above	65.00	110.	180.	450.	800.	—
1799	904,585	950.	1750.	4000.	6000.	—	—
1800	2,822,175	30.00	45.00	100.	300.	650.	3500.
1801	1,362,837	30.00	45.00	100.	300.	650.	3500.
1801 3 Errors Rev.	Inc. Above	30.00	50.00	135.	300.	675.	—
1802	3,435,100	22.50	35.00	95.00	275.	650.	3400.
1803	2,471,353	22.50	35.00	95.00	275.	650.	3400.
1804	756,838	625.	1000.	1750.	3400.	5000.	—
1805	941,116	27.50	40.00	100.	300.	650.	3400.
1806	348,000	40.00	65.00	100.	275.	750.	—
1807	727,221	30.00	45.00	110.	300.	650.	3400.

CLASSIC HEAD TYPE
1808-1814

DIAMETER—29mm
WEIGHT—10.89 Grams
COMPOSITION—Copper
DESIGNER—John Reich
EDGE—Plain

DATE	MINTAGE	G-4	VG-8	F-12	VF-20	EF-40	MS-60
1808	1,109,000	2.50	55.00	175.	500.	1050.	3200.
1809	222,867	80.00	150.	225.	650.	1500.	—
1810	1,458,500	30.00	42.00	170.	500.	1050.	3200.
1811	218,025	65.00	100.	260.	625.	1100.	—
1812	1,075,500	30.00	50.00	175.	525.	1150.	3200.
1813	418,000	45.00	75.00	200.	600.	1200.	—
1814	357,830	30.00	50.00	170.	550.	1150.	3200.

CORONET HEAD TYPE
1816-1839

DIAMETER—28-29mm
WEIGHT—10.89 Grams
COMPOSITION—Copper
DESIGNER—Robert Scot
EDGE—Plain

DATE	MINTAGE	G-4	VG-8	F-12	VF-20	EF-40	MS-60
1816	2,820,982	12.00	17.50	30.00	50.00	125.	300.
1817	3,948,400	11.00	12.50	20.00	40.00	100.	275.
1817 15 Stars	Inc. Above	12.00	20.00	30.00	65.00	160.	450.
1818	3,167,000	10.00	12.50	20.00	40.00	100.	325.
1819	2,671,000	11.00	12.50	20.00	40.00	100.	275.
1820	4,407,550	11.00	12.50	20.00	40.00	100.	275.
1821	389,000	17.50	30.00	45.00	100.	250.	—
1822	2,072,339	11.00	15.00	25.00	47.50	140.	400.
1823	Inc. 1824	35.00	55.00	90.00	225.	650.	—
1823/22	Inc. 1824	27.50	42.50	65.00	170.	340.	1900.
1824	1,262,000	11.00	15.00	30.00	52.50	80.00	1100.
1824/22	Inc. Above	20.00	60.00	100.	225.	265.	1650.
1825	1,461,100	10.00	14.00	23.00	55.00	145.	375.
1826	1,517,425	11.00	14.00	23.00	47.50	130.	325.
1826/25	Inc. Above	17.50	30.00	60.00	115.	250.	550.
1827	2,357,732	10.00	12.50	20.00	42.50	110.	325.
1828	2,260,624	11.00	14.00	20.00	47.50	110.	325.
1829	1,414,500	10.00	12.50	22.00	42.50	115.	375.
1830	1,711,500	10.00	12.50	20.00	37.50	105.	325.
1831	3,359,260	9.00	11.00	20.00	32.50	95.00	340.
1832	2,362,000	9.00	11.00	17.50	37.50	95.00	340.
1833	2,739,000	9.00	11.00	17.50	32.50	95.00	325.
1834	1,855,100	9.00	11.00	17.50	37.50	95.00	315.
1835	3,878,400	9.00	11.00	17.50	37.50	95.00	300.
1836	2,111,000	9.00	11.00	17.50	37.50	90.00	300.
1837	5,558,300	9.00	11.00	17.50	30.00	85.00	275.
1838	6,370,200	9.00	11.00	17.50	30.00	80.00	275.
1839	3,128,661	9.00	11.00	17.50	40.00	95.00	375.
1839/36	Inc. Above	160.	325.	700.	1400.	---	—

BRAIDED HAIR TYPE
1840-1857

DIAMETER—27.5mm
WEIGHT—10.89 Grams
COMPOSITION—Copper
DESIGNER—Christian Gobrecht
EDGE—Plain

DATE	MINTAGE	G-4	VG-8	F-12	VF-20	EF-40	MS-60
1840 Small Date	2,462,700	9.00	10.00	12.00	20.00	57.50	250.
1840 Large Date	Inc. Above	9.00	10.00	12.00	20.00	57.50	250.
1841	1,597,367	9.00	11.00	13.00	22.50	67.50	300.
1842 Small Date	2,383,390	9.00	10.00	12.00	20.00	55.00	250.
1842 Large Date	Inc. Above	9.00	10.00	12.00	20.00	55.00	250.
1843	2,425,342	10.00	12.00	16.00	25.00	65.00	225.
1843 Head Of 1840, Large Letters Rev	Inc. Above	10.00	20.00	40.00	50.00	80.00	375.
1844	2,398,752	9.00	11.00	12.00	17.50	50.00	175.
1844/81	Inc. Above	12.00	20.00	30.00	60.00	125.	425.
1845	3,894,804	9.00	10.00	12.00	15.00	40.00	175.
1846	4,120,800	9.00	10.00	12.00	15.00	40.00	175.
1847	6,183,669	9.00	10.00	12.00	15.00	42.50	175.
1848	6,415,799	9.00	10.00	12.00	15.00	42.50	175.
1849	4,178,500	9.00	10.00	12.00	17.00	42.50	175.
1850	4,426,844	9.00	10.00	12.00	15.00	45.00	175.
1851	9,889,707	9.00	10.00	12.00	15.00	42.50	175.
1851/81	Inc. Above	10.00	12.50	17.50	35.00	90.00	375.
1852	5,063,094	9.00	10.00	12.00	15.00	42.50	175.
1853	6,641,131	9.00	10.00	12.00	15.00	42.50	175.
1854	4,236,156	9.00	10.00	12.00	15.00	42.50	175.
1855 Upright 5's	1,574,829	9.00	10.00	12.00	15.00	42.50	175.
1855 Slanting 5's	Inc. Above	9.00	10.00	12.00	15.00	42.50	175.
1856 Upright 5's	2,690,463	9.00	10.00	12.00	15.00	42.50	175.
1856 Slanting 5's	Inc. Above	9.00	10.00	12.00	15.00	42.50	175.
1857 Large Date	333,456	22.50	27.50	35.00	47.50	65.00	300.
1857 Small Date	Inc. Above	25.00	30.00	40.00	55.00	70.00	325.

Small Cents 1856 To Date

The year 1856 saw the introduction of the Flying Eagle small cent, although it wasn't until the following year that the small cent type was released for general circulation. Because Flying Eagle cents were discontinued after a few short years of production, they are always included in any album displaying Indian head cents, and are usually mentioned in any discussion concerning the Indians.

Always appreciated by collectors, the Flying Eagle and Indian head cents rode a crest of popularity in the 1950's and early 1960's, and have shown signs of life within the last 12 months, after many years of dormancy. Part of the reason they fell out of favor was because of an infestation of cleaned and whizzed coins being passed off as "uncirculated." In view of today's attractive prices, there are several exciting investment possibilities with small cents, but you've got to get familiar with grading standards in order to spot the tampered coins.

The inaugural small cent, the 1856 Flying Eagle, had a mintage of only 1,000. It was meant to be a trial run for the smaller cent and is properly termed a pattern coin. For large scale investors, the addition of an 1856 cent in any acceptable condition would be a prudent buy. Even though the coin has appreciated sharply in the recent past, it probably hasn't yet approached its legitimate value, being that it is "necessary" to complete a small cent collection, but available only in extremely small quantities. Carefully inspect any 1856 Flying Eagle Cent you're contemplating buying for authenticity. If the lower part of the six is thick it is likely an altered 1858 cent. More discernible is the fact that the figure five slants slightly to the right on a genuine 1856, with the vertical bar pointing to the center of the ball immediately below in the curved part of the number. On the 1858, this bar points outside the five.

The rarest Indians in terms of mintage are the 1877, 1908-S, and 1909-S. With a few minor corrections, the 1877 has been a consistent winner due to collector demand, but the latter two coins are far from being common coins (the 1909-S has a mintage of only 309,000, making it the lowest regular production cent since 1811), yet prices are minimal in relation to their scarcity. Perhaps especially true of this statement are the specimens grading Extremely Fine and better. Some dealers report specimens in this category are increasingly difficult to locate. In the future when the true value of both key dates are recognized, prices in 1993 will seem ridiculously low.

The 1869 over 9 overdate variety is probably a far greater rarity than previously realized and has a bright investment future in any grade. At the current price levels you can't go too far wrong. Your biggest problem will be locating examples of this variety, attesting to its actual scarcity.

Typical Uncirculated (MS-60) and MS-63 Flying Eagles and Indian head cents have escaped speculator pressure and can still be had at modest prices. These represent excellent potential within the next several years, as they are seriously undervalued in comparison to the MS-65 representatives. Don't settle for coins without full original color or sharp strikes and stay away from pieces with corrosion problems or which have been cleaned. Since copper is the most chemically reactive of all metals used in coins, not many have survived in true mint state form, not even at the MS-60 range. With some searching, you should be able to find such coins at uninflated prices.

While cents in Fine or Extremely Fine will always rise in value because of the collector factor, late date Indians in lower grades are very common and have little or no investment future.

Lincoln cents are perhaps the most widely collected series of United States coins. Like Indian head cents, they too were most popular twenty-five and thirty years ago, before the cleaning and overgrading problem set in. Also like the Indians, there have been some upward price movements in the Lincolns as of late, but picky buyers are still left with plenty of good opportunities for appreciation in the coming years.

The key dates for the Lincoln series are the 1909-S, the 1909-S VDB, the 1914-D, and the 1931-S. Even in lower grades, these coins have experienced regular and steady value increases and are likely to retain their positions as the most valuable in the series.

Some dealers and collectors nowadays prefer to include the 1922-D (no D) cent on their lists of important Lincolns. Currently, collector demand is beginning to outstrip dealer supply. Be especially wary of who you do business with. Some 1922-D examples have had their mintmarks removed by hucksters in order to resemble authentic missing D specimens.

The most undervalued of the Lincolns may be the 1955 double die variety. Some small cent experts contend there exist no more than a few thousand of these coins, and thus should be valued far higher than their current levels.

With the exception of the key dates and a few semi-keys, avoid buying any Lincoln cents for investment purposes below uncirculated condition. Most uncirculated Lincolns are easily affordable, even in MS-65 condition. In fact, it is advisable you purchase MS-65 quality Lincolns, especially those dated 1934 onward, but if this is not financially possible, insist on obtaining MS-60 cents free of corrosion and well struck. It's a good bet that issues from the San Francisco mint will be the most sought after. Be patient and look for the best, because future years will see all Lincolns in trouble-free uncirculated condition attract a lot of interest as their popularity continues to increase.

Some experts contend that Lincoln cent matte proofs of 1909 to 1916 are genuine sleepers (matte proof is a different manufacturing process than that used for later Lincoln proofs). By studying population reports, the survivorship of these pieces is relatively low, but current prices do not reflect this. These gems can be had for about $600, a price that could easily double in the next five to ten years.

If you like to gamble, take a look at the 1970-S small date variety and the 1972 double die version of the Lincoln cent. No one knows how many of these actually exist, but we can be certain that they always will be heartily welcomed by every collector of Lincoln cents now and in the future.

Don't make plans to sell your Lincoln cent collection anytime soon. This series is not going to skyrocket in the next few years like certain other issues will, but you can bank on consistent upward price movements because of the popularity of the Lincoln cent as a collectible and the ease in buying for people of all means.

SMALL CENTS
1856- DATE

FLYING EAGLE TYPE
1856-1858

DIAMETER—19mm
WEIGHT—4.67 Grams
COMPOSITION—.880 Copper .120 Nickel
DESIGNER— James B. Longacre
EDGE—Plain

DATE	MINTAGE	G-4	VG-8	F-12	VF-20	EF-40	AU-50	MS-60	MS-65	Prf-65
1856.............................Est. 1000	2750.	3000.	3250.	3600.	4000.	4500.	5000.	15,500.	21,000.
1857..........................17,450,000	9.00	10.00	12.00	25.00	75.00	150.	250.	2800.	17,000.
1858 Large Letters 24,600,000	9.00	10.00	13.50	27.50	75.00	150.	250.	2800.	17,000.
1858 Small Letters ....Inc. Above	9.00	10.00	13.50	27.50	75.00	150.	250.	2800.	17,000.

INDIAN HEAD TYPE
1859-1909

1859

DIAMETER—19mm
WEIGHT—1859-1864 4.67 Grams
   1864-1909 3.11 Grams
COMPOSITION —1859-1864 .880 Copper
  .120 Nickel
  .1864-1909 .950 Copper
  .050 Tin and Zinc
DESIGNER—James B. Longacre
EDGE—Plain

1860-1909

COPPER-NICKEL

DATE	MINTAGE	G-4	VG-8	F-12	VF-20	EF-40	AU-50	MS-60	MS-65	Prf-65
1859..........................36,400,000	5.25	6.50	10.00	22.00	57.50	130.	200.	2250.	5000.
1860..........................20,566,000	3.75	5.00	8.00	14.00	25.00	42.50	140.	950.	1900.
1861..........................10,100,000	8.50	11.00	18.00	25.00	45.00	75.00	210.	950.	1900.
1862..........................28,075,000	3.25	4.00	6.50	9.50	21.00	40.00	100.	900.	1900.
1863..........................49,840,000	3.00	4.00	5.50	8.50	19.50	35.00	100.	900.	1900.
1864..........................13,740,000	7.50	8.50	13.50	20.00	35.00	50.00	140.	900.	2000.

BRONZE

DATE	MINTAGE	G-4	VG-8	F-12	VF-20	EF-40	AU-50	MS-60	MS-65	Prf-65
1864..........................39,233,714	3.25	4.75	8.25	17.00	27.50	33.00	95.00	425.	2200.
1864 L.....................Inc. Above	25.00	30.00	52.50	85.00	125.	200.	340.	1100.	32,000.
1865..........................35,429,286	3.00	3.50	7.00	18.00	27.50	50.00	80.00	400.	650.
1866..........................9,826,500	20.00	24.00	32.50	52.50	85.00	115.	175.	800.	750.
1867..........................9,821,000	20.00	24.00	32.50	52.50	85.00	115.	175.	925.	850.
1868..........................10,266,500	20.00	24.00	32.50	52.50	85.00	115.	175.	800.	650.
1869/8 6,420,000	70.00	95.00	210.	300.	475.	675.	1000.	2400.	—
1869..........................Inc. Above	27.50	35.00	60.00	100.	150.	190.	400.	1000.	875.

DATE	MINTAGE	G-4	VG-8	F-12	VF-20	EF-40	AU-50	MS-60	MS-65	Prf-65
1870	5,275,000	21.00	30.00	52.50	75.00	120.	150.	285.	1000.	1000.
1871	3,929,500	29.00	37.00	60.00	80.00	110.	150.	325.	1100.	1100.
1872	4,042,000	40.00	50.00	80.00	115.	160.	225.	400.	1500.	1500.
1873	11,676,500	7.25	9.00	18.00	28.00	45.00	65.00	175.	600.	580.
1874	14,187,500	7.25	9.00	16.00	27.00	42.00	60.00	175.	475.	500.
1875	13,528,000	7.25	9.00	16.00	28.00	42.00	65.00	175.	600.	600.
1876	7,944,000	11.00	14.50	24.00	34.00	55.00	75.00	200.	625.	625.
1877	852,500	300.	350.	500.	600.	750.	950.	1700.	4700.	4000.
1878	5,799,850	11.00	14.50	27.50	45.00	60.00	80.00	215.	600.	475.
1879	16,231,200	3.50	4.50	8.50	14.00	22.00	27.00	85.00	400.	475.
1880	38,964,955	1.35	2.25	4.50	6.25	17.00	22.00	80.00	350.	475.
1881	39,211,575	1.35	2.25	3.75	6.25	17.00	22.00	80.00	275.	450.
1882	38,581,100	1.35	2.25	3.75	6.25	17.00	22.00	80.00	275.	450.
1883	45,589,109	1.35	2.25	3.75	6.25	17.00	22.00	80.00	275.	450.
1884	23,261,742	2.25	3.25	7.00	12.00	20.00	33.00	85.00	325.	450.
1885	11,765,384	3.50	6.50	10.00	20.00	33.00	45.00	95.00	500.	475.
1886	17,654,290	2.50	3.50	7.00	12.00	27.50	40.00	85.00	500.	475.
1887	45,226,483	1.15	1.35	2.75	3.75	12.00	18.00	75.00	250.	450.
1888	37,494,414	1.15	1.35	2.75	3.75	12.00	18.00	75.00	350.	475.
1889	48,869,361	1.15	1.35	2.75	3.75	12.00	16.00	40.00	250.	450.
1890	57,182,854	.90	1.35	2.50	3.50	12.00	16.00	40.00	250.	500.
1891	47,072,350	.90	1.35	2.50	3.50	12.00	16.00	40.00	250.	450.
1892	37,649,832	.90	1.35	2.50	3.50	12.00	16.00	40.00	250.	525.
1893	46,642,195	.90	1.35	2.50	3.50	12.00	16.00	40.00	250.	650.
1894	16,752,132	2.00	4.50	8.00	12.00	22.00	30.00	75.00	365.	600.
1895	38,343,636	.90	1.15	2.00	4.00	8.00	16.00	40.00	170.	525.
1896	39,057,293	.90	1.15	2.00	4.00	8.00	16.00	40.00	165.	550.
1897	50,466,330	.90	1.15	1.75	3.25	8.00	16.00	40.00	165.	450.
1898	49,823,079	.90	1.15	1.75	3.25	8.00	16.00	40.00	165.	450.
1899	53,600,031	.90	1.15	1.75	3.25	8.00	16.00	40.00	165.	450.
1900	66,833,764	.60	.70	1.00	1.50	7.50	14.00	25.00	130.	425.
1901	79,611,143	.60	.70	1.00	1.50	7.50	14.00	25.00	130.	425.
1902	87,376,722	.60	.70	1.00	1.50	7.50	14.00	25.00	130.	425.
1903	85,094,493	.60	.70	1.00	1.50	7.50	14.00	25.00	130.	450.
1904	61,328,015	.60	.70	1.00	1.50	7.50	14.00	25.00	130.	450.
1905	80,719,163	.60	.70	1.00	1.50	7.50	14.00	25.00	130.	450.
1906	96,022,255	.60	.70	1.00	1.50	7.50	14.00	25.00	130.	425.
1907	108,138,618	.60	.70	1.00	1.50	7.50	14.00	25.00	130.	450.
1908	32,327,987	.60	.70	1.00	1.50	7.50	14.00	25.00	130.	425.
1908 S	1,115,000	22.50	24.00	25.00	30.00	40.00	100.	140.	450.	—
1909	14,370,645	1.25	1.75	2.25	3.50	9.00	17.00	65.00	130.	475.
1909 S	309,000	125.	165.	180.	200.	250.	300.	400.	675.	—

LINCOLN TYPE, WHEAT EARS REVERSE
1909-1958

DIAMETER—19mm
WEIGHT—3.11 Grams
  1943 2.70 Grams
COMPOSITION—1909-1942, 1947-1958 .950 Copper,
  .050 Tin and Zinc
  1943 Zinc Coated Steel, 1944-1946 .950 Copper, .050 Zinc
DESIGNER—Victor D. Brenner
EDGE—Plain

DATE	MINTAGE	G-4	VG-8	F-12	VF-20	EF-40	AU-50	MS-60	MS-65	Prf-65
1909 VDB	27,995,000	1.65	2.00	2.25	2.50	3.25	5.50	15.00	70.00	3000.
1909 S VDB	484,000	240.	260.	325.	375.	400.	450.	525.	1600.	—
1909	72,702,618	.35	.45	.55	.65	1.35	5.00	20.00	90.00	475.
1909 S	1,825,000	40.00	42.50	45.00	47.50	60.00	80.00	160.	300.	—
1910	146,801,218	.15	.25	.35	.55	1.65	4.25	16.00	95.00	525.
1910 S	6,045,000	5.75	6.50	8.00	10.00	14.00	32.50	90.00	240.	—
1911	101,177,787	.15	.35	.65	1.35	2.25	7.50	20.00	175.	750.
1911 D	12,672,000	2.75	3.75	5.00	10.00	19.00	40.00	80.	675.	—
1911 S	4,026,000	9.50	10.50	12.00	15.00	24.00	48.00	125.	1150.	—
1912	68,153,060	.25	.50	1.75	4.00	6.50	14.00	25.00	165.	375.
1912 D	10,411,000	2.75	3.25	4.75	11.00	22.00	42.50	125.	900.	—
1912 S	4,431,000	8.50	9.50	10.50	14.00	18.00	42.50	125.	1150.	—
1913	76,532,352	.15	.35	1.35	2.25	6.00	7.50	25.00	185.	375.
1913 D	15,804,000	1.50	1.75	4.00	8.00	19.00	40.00	85.00	900.	—
1913 S	6,101,000	6.00	6.50	7.00	8.00	17.00	38.00	115.	2100.	—
1914	75,238,432	.25	.40	1.35	3.25	5.00	15.00	55.00	220.	375.
1914 D	1,193,000	90.00	95.00	115.	165.	300.	500.	850.	4000.	—
1914 S	4,137,000	6.50	7.00	8.00	10.00	22.00	70.00	180.	3400.	—
1915	29,092,120	.55	1.10	4.50	10.00	27.00	37.50	100.	365.	375.
1915 D	22,050,000	.55	.85	1.15	5.50	12.50	24.00	45.00	440.	—
1915 S	4,833,000	5.50	6.00	6.50	8.50	18.00	42.50	100.	1350.	—
1916	131,833,677	.15	.20	.40	.80	3.25	6.25	10.00	130.	650.
1916 D	35,956,000	.30	.50	1.00	1.65	6.00	26.00	52.00	750.	—
1916 S	22,510,000	.60	.75	1.25	1.65	6.00	24.00	60.00	1250.	—
1917	196,429,785	.15	.25	.35	.65	2.25	5.50	11.00	110.	—
1917 D	55,120,000	.25	.50	.70	3.00	4.75	24.00	50.00	600.	—
1917 S	32,620,000	.25	.50	.70	2.75	4.25	28.00	62.00	1500.	—
1918	288,104,624	.15	.25	.40	.65	2.25	5.50	11.00	130.	—
1918 D	47,830,000	.25	.50	.65	2.50	5.50	26.00	52.00	800.	—
1918 S	34,680,000	.25	.50	.65	2.50	5.50	23.00	60.00	1725.	—
1919	392,021,000	.15	.25	.35	.60	2.00	5.25	9.00	100.	—
1919 D	57,154,000	.20	.35	.70	3.00	5.50	16.50	47.50	500.	—
1919 S	139,760,000	.20	.35	.45	.85	2.25	14.50	30.00	750.	—
1920	310,165,000	.15	.20	.35	.55	2.00	5.50	10.00	110.	—
1920 D	49,280,000	.15	.25	.60	1.50	4.50	23.50	52.00	500.	—
1920 S	46,220,000	.15	.25	.55	1.50	4.50	16.50	60.00	1350.	—
1921	39,157,000	.20	.30	.55	1.20	4.75	13.50	40.00	250.	—
1922 D	7,160,000	4.25	4.75	6.00	8.00	13.50	32.50	85.00	360.	—
1922	Inc. Above	165.	200.	250.	375.	1450.	2750.	4000.	17,500.	—
1921 S	15,274,000	.65	.80	1.15	2.50	10.00	80.00	130.	2500.	—
1923	74,723,000	.15	.20	.35	.65	2.25	4.50	10.00	115.	—

DATE	MINTAGE	G-4	VG-8	F-12	VF-20	EF-40	AU-50	MS-60	MS-65	Prf-65
1923 S	8,700,000	1.75	2.00	2.50	4.50	11.50	85.00	190.	2500.	—
1924	75,178,000	.15	.25	.40	.65	3.75	11.50	24.00	130.	—
1924 D	2,520,000	8.50	9.50	12.00	14.00	38.00	105.	240.	2150.	—
1924 S	11,696,000	.55	.80	1.15	2.50	7.00	42.50	115.	2400.	—
1925	139,949,000	.15	.20	.35	.65	2.75	4.25	9.00	85.00	—
1925 D	22,580,000	.25	.40	.60	1.25	4.50	15.00	48.00	775.	—
1925 S	26,380,000	.15	.25	.45	1.15	3.25	15.00	62.00	2250.	—
1926	157,088,000	.15	.20	.40	.60	2.25	4.50	7.50	50.00	—
1926 D	28,020,000	.20	.25	.50	.90	3.25	24.50	47.00	1100.	—
1926 S	4,550,000	3.00	3.50	5.00	6.50	10.50	65.00	100.	3000.	—
1927	144,440,000	.15	.20	.30	.45	2.25	4.50	7.50	95.00	—
1927 D	27,170,000	.15	.20	.30	.45	2.75	14.50	30.00	925.	—
1927 S	14,276,000	.25	.40	.55	1.85	4.25	27.00	65.00	1250.	—
1928	134,116,000	.15	.20	.35	.45	1.65	4.50	7.50	67.00	—
1928 D	31,170,000	.20	.25	.35	.65	1.65	13.00	20.00	335.	—
1928 S	17,266,000	.25	.30	.40	.70	2.25	21.00	48.00	1225.	—
1929	185,262,000	.15	.20	.30	.45	1.35	3.75	6.00	70.00	—
1929 D	41,730,000	.15	.20	.30	.45	1.35	6.50	17.00	145.	—
1929 S	50,148,000	.15	.20	.30	.45	1.35	5.00	8.00	130.	—
1930	157,415,000	.10	.15	.20	.35	1.15	3.25	4.50	36.00	—
1930 D	40,100,000	.10	.15	.20	.45	1.15	5.50	12.50	95.00	—
1930 S	24,266,000	.10	.15	.20	.45	1.15	3.75	7.50	60.00	—
1931	19,396,000	.20	.25	.35	.45	1.75	7.50	17.00	170.	—
1931 D	4,480,000	2.50	2.75	3.00	4.00	5.25	29.00	52.00	270.	—
1931 S	866,000	30.00	32.50	35.00	40.00	42.50	55.00	75.00	165.	—
1932	9,062,000	1.35	1.65	1.95	2.25	3.00	8.00	18.00	58.00	—
1932 D	10,500,000	.70	.80	1.35	2.25	2.75	8.00	15.00	65.00	—
1933	14,360,000	.55	.65	.75	1.00	2.25	8.00	17.00	65.00	—
1933 D	6,200,000	2.00	2.15	2.45	3.00	4.50	8.00	25.00	72.00	—
1934	219,080,000	.10	.15	.20	.35	.55	.80	4.50	15.00	—
1934 D	28,446,000	.15	.20	.25	.35	1.15	7.50	34.00	58.00	—
1935	245,338,000	—	.10	.15	.20	.25	.55	2.40	8.00	—
1935 D	47,000,000	.15	.20	.25	.30	.50	1.35	4.50	16.00	—
1935 S	38,702,000	.15	.20	.25	.30	.50	2.75	10.00	58.00	—
1936	309,637,569	—	.10	.15	.20	.25	.55	1.50	3.00	725.
1936 D	40,620,000	.15	.20	.25	.30	.35	.55	2.00	5.50	—
1936 S	29,130,000	.15	.20	.25	.30	.35	.80	2.25	5.50	—
1937	309,179,320	—	—	.10	.15	.20	.50	1.75	4.75	300.
1937 D	50,430,000	—	.10	.15	.20	.25	.60	1.75	4.50	—
1937 S	34,500,000	—	.10	.15	.20	.25	.80	1.60	3.50	—
1938	156,696,734	—	—	—	.10	.15	.40	1.50	3.00	200.
1938 D	20,010,000	.15	.20	.25	.30	.55	.80	2.00	6.00	—
1938 S	15,180,000	.20	.30	.40	.50	.65	1.10	2.65	5.50	—
1939	316,479,520	—	—	—	.10	.15	.35	1.10	2.00	190.
1939 D	15,160,000	.30	.40	.55	.65	.80	1.90	4.00	9.00	—
1939 S	52,070,000	—	.10	.15	.20	.25	.95	1.90	3.75	—
1940	586,825,872	—	—	—	.10	.15	.35	1.15	3.25	170.
1940 D	81,390,000	—	—	—	.10	.15	.40	1.40	3.25	—
1940 S	112,940,000	—	—	—	.10	.15	.30	1.00	2.25	—
1941	887,039,100	—	—	—	.10	.15	.30	.85	2.25	170.
1941 D	128,700,000	—	—	—	.10	.15	1.10	2.75	5.00	—

DATE	MINTAGE	VF-20	EF-40	AU-50	MS-60	MS-65	Prf-65
1941 S	92,360,000	.10	.15	1.35	3.75	11.00	—
1942	657,828,600	.10	.15	.25	.50	1.75	170.
1942 D	206,698,000	.10	.15	.25	.65	1.75	—
1942 S	85,590,000	.15	.25	1.65	4.25	10.00	—
1943 Steel	684,628,670	.15	.20	.30	.65	.80	—
1943 D Steel	217,660,000	.25	.30	.40	1.15	1.35	—
1943 S Steel	191,550,000	—	.30			2.15	—
1944	1,435,400,000	—	.10			.30	—
1944 D	430,578,000	—	.10			.30	—
1944 D D/S	Inc Above	50.00	70.00	100.	210.	225.	—
1944 S	282,760,000	—	.15			.40	—
1945	1,040,515,000	—	.10			.35	—
1945 D	226,268,000	—	.10			.80	—
1945 S	181,770,000	—	.15			.60	—
1946	991,655,000	—	.10			.35	—
1946 D	315,690,000	—	.10			.30	—
1946 S	198,100,000	—	.15			.65	—
1947	190,555,000	—	.15			.65	—
1947 D	194,750,000	—	.10			.35	—
1947 S	99,000,000	—	.15			.80	—
1948	317,570,000	—	.10			.55	—
1948 D	172,637,000	—	.10			.35	—
1948 S	81,735,000	—	.15			.95	—
1949	217,775,000	—	.10			.80	—
1949 D	153,132,000	—	.10			.65	—
1949 S	64,290,000	—	.20			1.85	—
1950	272,686,386	—	.10			.45	45.00
1950 D	334,950,000	—	.10			.35	—
1950 S	118,505,000	—	.15			.55	—
1951	295,633,500	—	.10			1.75	40.00
1951 D	625,355,000	—	.10			.25	—
1951 S	136,010,000	—	.15			.95	—
1952	186,856,980	—	.10			.55	37.00
1952 D	746,130,000	—	.10			.25	—
1952 S	137,800,004	—	.15			.70	—
1953	256,883,800	—	.10			.25	24.00
1953 D	700,515,000	—	.10			.25	—
1953 S	181,835,000	—	.20			.40	—
1954	71,873,350	—	.20			.35	11.00
1954 D	251,552,500	—	.10			.25	—
1954 S	95,190,000	—	.15			.30	—
1955 Double Die	Inc. Below	375.	400.	500.	700.	3250.	—
1955	330,958,000	—	.10			.25	10.00
1955 D	563,257,500	—	.10			.25	—
1955 S	44,610,000	—	.40			.55	—
1956	421,414,384	—				.15	2.50
1956 D	1,098,201,000	—	—			.15	—
1957	283,787,952	—	—			.15	1.75
1957 D	1,051,342,000	—	—			.15	—
1958	253,400,652	—	—			.15	2.00
1958 D	800,953,300	—	—			.15	—

LINCOLN TYPE MEMORIAL REVERSE
1959 TO DATE

DIAMETER—19mm
WEIGHT—1959-1982 3.11 Grams
  1983-Date 2.5 Grams
COMPOSITION— 1959-1962 .950 Copper
  .050 Tin and Zinc,
  1962-1982 .950 Copper, .050 Zinc
  1982-Date .976 Zinc, .024 Copper
DESIGNER—Obv. V.D. Brenner
  Rev., Frank Gasparro
EDGE—Plain

DATE	MINTAGE	MS-60	MS-65	Prf-65
1959	610,864,291		.15	1.25
1959 D	1,279,760,000		.15	—
1960 Large Date	588,096,602		.10	1.25
1960 Small Date	Inc. Above		4.00	15.00
1960 D Large Date	1,580,884,000		.15	—
1960 D Small Date	Inc. Above		.25	—
1961	756,373,244		.10	.75
1961 D	1,753,266,700		.10	—
1962	609,263,019		.10	.75
1962 D	1,793,148,400		.10	—
1963	757,185,645		.10	.75
1963 D	1,774,020,400		.10	—
1964	2,652,525,762		.10	.75
1964 D	3,799.071,500		.10	—
1965	1,497,224,900		.15	—
1966	2,188,147,783		.15	—
1967	3,048,667,100		.15	—
1968	1,707,880,970		.15	—
1968 D	2,886,269,600		.15	—
1968 S	261,311,510		.15	.75
1969	1,136,910,000		.25	—
1969 D	4,002,832,200		.15	—
1969 S	547,309,631		.15	.75
1970	1,898,315,000		.15	—
1970 D	2,891,438,900		.15	—
1970 S	693,192,814		.15	.90
1970 S Small Date	Inc. Above	10.00	12.00	150.
1971	1,919,490,000		.15	—
1971 D	2,911,045,600		.15	—
1971 S	528,354,192		.15	.75
1972	2,933,255,000		.15	—
1972 Double Die	Inc. Above	300.	400.	—
1972 D	2,665,071,400		.15	—
1972 S	380,200,104		.15	.75
1973	3,728,245,000		.10	—
1973 D	3,549,576,588		.10	—
1973 S	319,937,634		.15	.75
1974	4,232,140,523		.10	—
1974 D	4,235,098,000		.10	—
1974 S	412,039,228		.15	.85
1975	5,451,476,142		.10	—
1975 D	4,505,245,300		.10	—
1975 S	PROOF ONLY		—	5.00
1976	4,674,292,426		.10	—
1976 D	4,221,592,455		.10	—
1976 S	PROOF ONLY		—	2.50
1977	4,469,930,000		.10	—
1977 D	4,149,062,300		.10	—
1977 S	PROOF ONLY		—	2.50

DATE	MINTAGE	MS-65	Prf-65
1978	5,558,605,000	.10	—
1978 D	4,280,233,400	.10	—
1978 S	PROOF ONLY	—	3.00
1979	6,018,515,000	.10	—
1979 D	4,280,233,400	.10	—
1979 S	PROOF ONLY	—	3.00
1980	7,414,705,000	.10	—
1980 D	5,140,098,660	.10	—
1980 S	PROOF ONLY	—	1.75
1981	7,491,750,000	.10	—
1981 D	5,373,235,677	.10	—
1981 S	PROOF ONLY	—	2.00
1982	9,125,280,000	.10	—
1982 D	6,012,979,368	.10	—
1982 S	PROOF ONLY	—	3.00
1983	7,752,355,000	.10	—
1983	6,467,199,428	.10	—
1983 S	PROOF ONLY	—	4.50
1984	8,151,079,000	.10	—
1984 D	5,569,238,906	.10	—
1984 S	PROOF ONLY	—	5.00
1985	5,648,489,887	.10	—
1985 D	5,287,399,926	.10	—
1985 S	PROOF ONLY	—	4.50
1986	4,491,395,493	.10	—
1986 D	4,442,866,698	.10	—
1986 S	PROOF ONLY	—	8.00
1987	4,682,466,931	.10	—
1987 D	4,879,389,514	.10	—
1987 S	PROOF ONLY	—	4.50
1988	6,092,810,000	.10	—
1988 D	5,253,740,443	.10	—
1988 S	PROOF ONLY	—	5.00
1989	7,261,535,000	.10	—
1989 D	5,345,467,111	.10	—
1989 S	PROOF ONLY	—	6.00
1990	6,851,765,000	.10	—
1990 D	4,922,894,533	.10	—
1990 S	PROOF ONLY	—	6.00
1991	5,165,940,000	.10	—
1991 D	4,158,442,076	.10	—
1991 S	PROOF ONLY	—	6.00
1992	—	.10	—
1992 D	—	.10	—
1992 S	PROOF ONLY	.—	6.00
1993	—	.10	—
1993 D	—	.10	—
1993 S	PROOF ONLY	—	7.50

Two Cent Pieces 1864-1873

In the long history of United States coin production, there have been some rather strange denominations, namely the two cent, three cent and the twenty cent coins. Seldom being publicly supported in their time these oddball coins disappeared from circulation relatively soon after their implementation. Over the last few years, these denominations have commanded about as much respect as they did during their production years, resulting in some negative price appreciation; now indicating that there are several attractive options here for an investor.

There are three rarities in the series. Both varieties of the 1873 piece, available only in proof condition because there were no business strikes issued that year, have performed admirably as an investment vehicle, as have all proof specimens of the two cent group. Even though this series is not a particularly popular one with collectors, coins of this quality have been in strong demand from the investment sector, usually resulting in higher and higher prices.

Another rarity, the 1872, has done better than average for the series, especially in the upper grades. With a mintage of only 65,000, this coin would be priced in the thousands of dollars if it belonged to a more heavily collected series. Someday if the two cent coins were to become popular, you would see the 1872 register impressive gains in all conditions.

The sleeper of the series is the 1864 small motto variety. At one time ranked in value alongside the 1872 and the proofs, the 1864 small motto coin has not enjoyed the same degree of appreciation, a situation which could correct itself in the future. Unblemished coins of all dates in uncirculated conditions hold much promise as well.

TWO CENT PIECES
1864-1873

DIAMETER—23mm
WEIGHT—6.22 Grams
COMPOSITION—.950 Copper .050 Tin and Zinc
DESIGNER—James B. Longacre
EDGE—Plain

DATE	MINTAGE	G-4	VG-8	F-12	VF-20	EF-40	AU-50	MS-60	MS-65	Prf-65
1864 Small Motto	19,847,500	50.00	75.00	100.	150.	260.	325.	575.	2000.	28,000.
1864 Large Motto	Inc. Above	5.50	6.50	8.00	14.00	30.00	55.00	95.00	400.	1500.
1865	13,640,000	4.50	5.00	7.00	14.00	30.00	55.00	95.00	400.	1300.
1866	3,177,000	5.00	5.50	8.00	14.00	32.50	55.00	95.00	525.	1300.
1867	2,938,750	5.00	5.50	7.00	14.00	32.50	70.00	110.	400.	1300.
1868	2,803,750	5.25	6.00	7.00	14.00	32.50	80.00	165.	450.	1300.
1869	1,546,500	6.00	7.00	9.50	16.00	37.50	90.00	165.	425.	1300.
1870	861,250	7.00	8.50	18.50	30.00	50.00	115.	225.	675.	1300.
1871	721,250	8.50	12.00	18.50	32.50	55.00	150.	275.	750.	1300.
1872	65,000	80.00	110.00	165.	265.	375.	500.	750.	2800.	1600.
1873	Est. 1,100						PROOF ONLY			3000.

Three Cent Pieces

Three cent coins were struck in both silver and nickel, each bearing a distinctively different design. The silver three cent coin, originally called a trime, is the smallest of all United States silver coins. There are three types of trimes, occurring because of subtle design changes periodically. Type I was minted from 1851 through 1853, Type II came out in 1854 continuing until 1858, and Type III ran from 1859 to 1873.

From an investor's viewpoint, the 1855 trime holds the most promise. Turned out in a quantity of only 139,000 pieces, it is the lowest mintage for all Type I and Type II style trimes. The price of MS-65 Uncirculated and MS-65 Proof trimes is presently very low, as are examples in higher circulated grades.

Carefully consider Type III trimes in all grades from AU to MS-65 and proof conditions. They have low production figures, with the trimes of 1863 onward being exceedingly rare. Because of the increased value of silver in 1863, only a few thousand were minted that year and each year thereafter, while many of those were melted down for bullion or exported shortly after leaving the mint. This explains why seldom does one encounter circulated trimes dated 1863 through 1872. Type III trimes dated 1863 to 1872 have moved in well-defined price cycles. It appears that in 1993, values for coins of this description have also hit rock bottom, meaning their "up" cycle is ahead of us and not behind.

The increase in silver value in 1863 brought a new three cent coin onto the scene with basic composition materials of copper and nickel. Beginning in 1865, three cent nickel coins were issued until 1889. The basic demand for three cent nickel pieces has traditionally come from type set collectors. There are several coins in the series that warrant attention, these being the ones dated 1876, 1879, 1880, 1882, 1888, and 1889. Top grade uncirculated and proof examples exploded in value in the late 1970's and again in the mid 1980's. Prices in 1993 have fallen dramatically from earlier highs.

THREE CENT PIECES (SILVER)
1851-1873

VARIETY ONE - NO OUTLINES TO STAR
1851-1853

DIAMETER—14mm
WEIGHT—.80 Grams
COMPOSITION—.750 Silver
.250 Copper
DESIGNER— James B. Longacre
EDGE—Plain

DATE	MINTAGE	G-4	VG-8	F-12	VF-20	EF-40	AU-50	MS-60	MS-65	Prf-65
1851	5,477,400	12.00	15.00	17.50	30.00	60.00	120.	160.	1800.	1500.
1851 O	720,000	17.00	22.50	32.50	65.00	120.	240.	400.	4400.	—
1852	18,663,500	9.50	11.00	14.00	30.00	65.00	120.	180.	1800.	1500.
1853	11,400,000	9.50	11.00	14.00	30.00	60.00	120.	160.	1800.	1500.

VARIETY TWO - THREE OUTLINES TO STAR
1854-1858

DIAMETER—14mm
WEIGHT—.75 Gram
COMPOSITION—.900 Silver
  .100 Copper
DESIGNER— James B. Longacre
EDGE—Plain

DATE	MINTAGE	G-4	VG-8	F-12	VF-20	EF-40	AU-50	MS-60	MS-65	Prf-65
1854	671,000	11.50	16.00	22.50	42.50	115.	220.	325.	8000.	—
1855	139,000	17.00	27.50	45.00	85.00	175.	450.	450.	15,000.	26,000.
1856	1,458,000	11.00	15.00	22.50	42.50	90.00	220.	275.	8750.	26,000.
1857	1,042,000	11.00	15.00	22.50	42.50	90.00	220.	325.	8000.	11,000.
1858	1,604,000	11.00	15.00	22.50	42.50	90.00	220.	275.	8000.	11,000.

VARIETY THREE - TWO OUTLINES TO STAR
1859-1873

DIAMETER—14mm
WEIGHT—.75 Gram
COMPOSITION—.900 Silver,
  .100 Copper
DESIGNER— James B. Longacre
EDGE—Plain

DATE	MINTAGE	G-4	VG-8	F-12	VF-20	EF-40	AU-50	MS-60	MS-65	Prf-65
1859	365,000	14.00	17.50	22.50	32.50	70.00	125.	150.	1400.	3000.
1860	287,000	14.00	17.50	22.50	32.50	70.00	125.	150.	1400.	3000.
1861	498,000	14.00	17.50	22.50	32.50	70.00	125.	150.	1400.	2600.
1862	343,550	14.00	17.50	22.50	32.50	70.00	125.	150.	1400.	2800.
1863	21,460	—	—	—	—	600.	700.	950.	3000.	2700.
1864	12,470	—	—	—	—	490.	550.	700.	2750.	2700.
1865	8,500	—	—	—	—	500.	550.	725.	3250.	2700.
1866	22,725	—	—	—	—	400.	480.	700.	2900.	2700.
1867	4,625	—	—	—	—	525.	620.	750.	5200.	2700.
1868	4,100	—	—	—	—	525.	620.	750.	7400.	2700.
1869	5,100	—	—	—	—	525.	620.	750.	5400.	2700.
1870	4,000	—	—	—	—	525.	620.	750.	6600.	2700.
1871	4,360	—	—	—	—	525.	620.	750.	2700.	2700.
1872	1,950	—	—	—	—	650.	775.	950.	6600.	2700.
1873	600						PROOF	ONLY		2800.

THREE CENT PIECES (NICKEL)
1865-1889

DIAMETER—17.9mm
WEIGHT—1.94 Grams
COMPOSITION—.750 Copper
.250 Nickel
DESIGNER—James B. Longacre
EDGE—Plain

DATE	MINTAGE	G-4	VG-8	F-12	VF-20	EF-40	AU-50	MS-60	MS-65	Prf-65
1865	11,382,000	5.50	6.50	7.50	10.00	20.00	37.50	80.00	950.	1700.
1866	4,801,000	5.50	6.50	7.50	10.00	20.00	37.50	80.00	950.	1100.
1867	3,915,000	5.50	6.50	7.50	10.00	20.00	37.50	80.00	950.	1000.
1868	3,252,000	5.50	6.50	7.50	10.00	20.00	37.50	80.00	950.	1000.
1869	1,604,000	6.50	7.50	8.50	11.00	20.00	37.50	90.00	950.	1000.
1870	1,335,000	6.50	7.50	9.00	12.00	20.00	40.00	95.00	950.	1000.
1871	604,000	6.50	7.50	9.50	12.50	20.00	50.00	100.	950.	1000.
1872	862,000	6.50	7.50	9.50	12.50	20.00	50.00	100.	1250.	900.
1873	1,173,000	6.50	7.50	9.00	12.00	20.00	40.00	95.00	2500.	925.
1874	790,000	6.50	7.50	9.50	12.50	20.00	50.00	110.	2100.	900.
1875	228,000	7.50	10.00	14.00	19.50	27.50	90.00	170.	950.	1100.
1876	162,000	11.00	14.00	17.00	22.50	30.00	90.00	185.	2200.	900.
1877	Est. 900							PROOF ONLY		1800.
1878	2,350							PROOF ONLY		1000.
1879	41,200	39.00	45.00	50.00	57.50	67.50	180.	260.	950.	800.
1880	24,955	47.50	52.50	60.00	75.00	85.00	180.	280.	950.	800.
1881	1,080,575	5.50	6.50	7.50	10.00	17.50	50.00	165.	950.	800.
1882	25,300	42.50	45.00	55.00	60.00	72.50	160.	265.	1050.	825.
1883	10,609	80.00	95.00	115.	140.	165.	200.	380.	3000.	800.
1884	5,642	150.	165.	180.	200.	235.	270.	575.	4750.	800.
1885	4,790	215.	235.	255.	280.	315.	375.	750.	2000.	850.
1886	4,290							PROOF ONLY		1000.
1887/6	7,961							PROOF ONLY		1000.
1887	Inc. Above	175.	190.	205.	230.	260.	315.	525.	1200.	850.
1886	41,083	34.00	37.50	40.00	45.00	55.00	140.	285.	950.	800.
1889	21,561	42.50	45.00	55.00	62.50	75.00	150.	275.	950.	800.

Five Cent Coins

Half-dimes were minted from 1794 through 1873, and carried a face value of five cents. No half-dimes were produced after 1805 until 1829. There were five basic design changes in the history of the half-dime, although technically there are eight types in all, if you consider the addition or omission of stars or arrows in the Liberty Seated theme.

Collector demand for half-dimes comes from type set numismatists. Assembling an entire set is too costly for the average collector, although there are no special or key rarities as in so many other denominations.

If you take pleasure in collecting half-dimes for your type set, maybe you should consider some of the investment angles as you plot a course of action. First of all, there is a group of very rare half-dimes minted in Philadelphia during the 1860's that appreciated enormously throughout most of the 1980's, but have fallen off in the 1990's. Try to acquire at least one of these coins in any collectible grade, for in all likelihood they will resume their steep rise in the coming years. If you have an opportunity to purchase MS-63 to MS-65 Uncirculated half-dimes of this caliber, then go for it. Although values have increased about 10% from last year, this could be just the beginning of what is to come.

The 1846 looks like a real sleeper in any condition. With a relatively small mintage for post-1829 half-dimes of 27,000, this coin was one of the more prized half-dimes in the 1950's and 1960's. Having achieved some healthy price hikes during the 1980's in relation to most of the other half-dimes, it still isn't what it used to be. Look for the 1846 to someday reassume its position as one of the most valuable of all late half-dimes.

For investors with big wallets, this paragraph and the next contain interesting tidbits: some numismatic experts contend that half-dimes in nice uncirculated condition struck at the New Orleans mint during the years 1839 through 1852 are far rarer than their already expensive prices would indicate. If you have an opportunity to purchase MS-63 to MS-65 Uncirculated half dimes of this caliber, then go for it. Although values have increased about 10% from last year, this could only be the beginning of what is to come.

All early half-dimes (minted in 1805 or before) are headed on a one-way street going uphill. As all of them are rare, they are a desirable purchase in all grades listed. If affordable, zero in on Fine to Extremely Fine condition.

For investors with more limited capital, there are the common date specimens. Most of these have performed only mildly in lower grades, while some have done quite well in grades Very Fine or better. If you want to buy common date half-dimes for investment purposes, purchase them only in conditions Very Fine or above.

The Shield nickel was the first non-silver five cent coin, approved as a substitute for the silver half-dime in 1866 when silver prices reveled in a state of chaos. The introduction of the "nickel" brought on the demise of the silver five cent piece. The Shield nickel was produced every year following its initial release until 1883.

Few of the Shield nickels in heavily circulated conditions have provided satisfactory returns as investments. As usual, Uncirculated and Proof grades performed very well, with current MS-60 and MS-63 prices for both Uncirculated and Proof examples being truly advantageous to the buyer.

The rarest business strikes in the Shield nickel are the 1879, 1880, and 1881 coins. These prices multiplied in value at least tenfold from 1975 to the early 1980's. There's every reason to expect them to take off again in rampant fashion sometime in the 1990's. The values of these coins in all conditions cannot go much lower than they presently are.

Liberty nickels, also known as the "V" nickels, entered the scene in 1883 and were regularly produced until 1912. There are a large number of Liberty nickels that could fetch a tidy profit in the near future if bought today. The 1885 piece is without a doubt the key date in the set, but has not advanced in value over the last several years like it should. Look for this situation to reverse itself in the near future.

The 1912-S has by far the lowest mintage of any regular Liberty nickel, with only 238,000 pieces issued. After increasing in value incredibly in the 1950's and 60's, the only San Francisco mint Liberty nickel struggled for much of the next fifteen years. After some good years in the 1980's, it has been dormant since. Appreciation in all grades reminiscent of the 50's and 60's may occur soon, as investors and collectors notice what a true 20th century rarity the 1912-S Liberty nickel really is. For the buyer looking for serious bargains, take a close look at all Proofs and Uncirculated Liberty nickels grading MS-63 to MS-65. Retail values have plummeted nearly 40% in many cases, indicating that at this time they are underpriced in relation to their actual scarcity. These coins are true sleepers, just waiting for the alarm clock to sound!

Buffalo nickels, sometimes called the Indian head nickels, were minted from 1913 to 1938. This series is characterized by frequent poor strikes and changes in surface design, making grading more difficult than usual. As always, grading is critical, but in many instances with Buffalo nickels, values literally multiply each grade up after Very Fine, so be sure to absorb as much information as you can regarding the grading of these coins.

Buffalo nickels belong to a highly volatile market. They have been bouncing back and forth in price in all conditions for many years. It is especially important with Buffalo nickels to study each date separately, because these coins change in value independently of each other, more so than other series of United States coins. Although interest in the series has been increasing, there are many fine opportunities at surprisingly affordable prices. Among the best are scarce dates grading in the Extremely Fine to Almost Uncirculated range.

One of the classic American coins is the 1937-D three-legged Buffalo nickel variety, apparently due to an overpolished or clogged die. We've seen all grades increase sharply in value over the last year, but as a long term investment, a buyer cannot go wrong in acquiring this rarity, owing to its tremendous following from collectors. Beware of altered coins.

Another Buffalo head nickel popular with collectors is the 1918/7-D issue. Already this coin will set you back hundreds (if not thousands) of dollars, but we can look for consistent pressure from collectors to keep values moving in a positive direction. Because the 1918/7-D is so difficult to find in Extremely Fine and better, many buyers will pay a premium above book value to land one.

A darkhorse candidate is the 1938-D/S variety. This was the first mint mark overstrike ever discovered on a United States coin and has some worthwhile potential because of that distinction. Priced anywhere from $7.50 in Very Fine to $180 in MS-65, the 1938-D/S fell steadily from 1965 to 1992, and is now finally on the upswing. Being the first of its kind, dramatic rises will occur when collectors realize the obvious significance of this coin. Try to purchase the highest quality possible. At these low prices this is one bargain too good to pass up.

Carefully study the values of the MS-60 Uncirculated coins. Many of them have declined in value since 1980 and are now poised for near term price hikes. Unlike so many other series, MS-65 Buffalos are not priced out of sight as yet. In fact, there have been some price corrections recorded in the last several years. You'll discover some Buffalo nickels in MS-65 can now be had for under $100, indicating that strong price surges can be expected within the next few years. If you can afford to do so, purchase early Buffalos grading higher than MS-65. Grading service population reports suggest these nickels are extremely rare, but their present day price tags do not agree.

The familiar Jefferson nickel has been with us now since 1938. Once popularly collected, Jefferson nickels have been in the doldrums for many years, with complete sets now available for little more than what they were selling for 25 years ago; therefore, Jefferson nickels are a very solid investment area, especially attractive to low budget collectors, with virtually no downside risk.

The Jefferson nickels minted during World War II had 35% silver content. During the last big silver boom, war nickels suffered heavy melting, which someday could result in war nickel shortages. With the dead Jefferson nickel market, this scenario hasn't yet manifested itself, but with heightened popularity in the series, this situation will change.

For a modern series, the Jefferson nickel group includes a large number of error varieties. The most widely identified error coins are the 1939 doubled MONTICELLO, 1943-P 3/2, 1949-D/S, and the 1954-S/D. Although interesting pieces indeed, they have never taken off in value (with the exception of the 1939 doubled MONTICELLO), but with the inevitable return of interest in the Jeffersons, you can look for these coins to have a bright future ahead. At these low current prices, push for the absolute highest obtainable grade.

The key coin in the Jefferson nickel series has been the 1950-D. A well-storied item in its own right, the 1950-D was the rave of the numismatic world twenty-five years ago. Even non-collectors were scouring through pocket change searching for the highly publicized coin. In spite of a series-low mintage of 2,630,030, the 1950-D nickel has done nothing for over twenty years, and may never return to its former glory days. However, at these extremely low prices, this coin is a handsome and affordable addition to anyone's collection.

As modest as prices are today, it is recommended to purchase Jefferson nickels grading no less than MS-65, if possible. You should also be very selective. Look for sharp strikes, particularly at the center of the reverse. Examine the steps of Monticello under magnification. Only on well struck coins can you plainly see all six steps leading up to the door of Jefferson's home. The "Full Step" occurrence has not currently gained full widespread acceptance as a grading criterion contributing to increased value, but there is a definite shift in that direction. Insist on acquiring only Full Step Jeffersons today and tomorrow you'll probably be rewarded with an impressive premium for your foresight.

HALF DIMES
1794-1873

FLOWING HAIR TYPE
1794-1795

DIAMETER—16.5mm
WEIGHT—1.35 Grams
COMPOSITION—.8924 Silver
 .1076 Copper
DESIGNER—Robert Scot
EDGE—Reeded

DATE	MINTAGE	G-4	VG-8	F-12	VF-20	EF-40	MS-60
1794	86,416	1100.	1250.	2000.	2700.	4500.	8750.
1795	Inc. Above	650.	750.	1000.	1500.	2750.	6000.

DRAPED BUST TYPE
SMALL EAGLE REVERSE
1796-1797

DIAMETER—16.5mm
WEIGHT—1.35 Grams
COMPOSITION—.8924 Silver
.1076 Copper
DESIGNER—Robert Scot
EDGE—Reeded

DATE	MINTAGE	G-4	VG-8	F-12	VF-20	EF-40	MS-60
1796	10,320	850.	950.	1250.	2100.	3400.	5750.
1796 LIBERTY	Inc. Above	850.	950.	1250.	2100.	3400.	—
1796/5	Inc. Above	1250.	1450.	1700.	2500.	3600.	9000.
1797 13 Stars	44,527	900.	1000.	1325.	2200.	3400.	12,000.
1797 15 Stars	Inc. Above	850.	950.	1250.	2100.	3400.	5750.
1797 16 Stars	Inc. Above	850.	950.	1250.	2100.	3400.	5750.

DRAPED BUST TYPE
HERALDIC EAGLE REVERSE
1800-1805

DATE	MINTAGE	G-4	VG-8	F-12	VF-20	EF-40	MS-60
1800	24,000	700.	900.	1150.	1500.	2500.	5200.
1800 LIBERTY	Inc. Above	700.	900.	1150.	1500.	2500.	5200.
1801	33,910	700.	950.	1150.	1600.	2850.	10,000.
1802	13,010	10,000.	12,500.	24,000.	32,500.	45,000.	
1803	37,850	650.	850.	1100.	1500.	2500.	5200.
1805	15,600	1000.	1150.	1500.	2000.	3500.	—

CAPPED BUST TYPE
1829-1837

DIAMETER—15.5mm
WEIGHT—1.35 Grams
COMPOSITION—.8924 Silver
.1076 Copper
DESIGNER—William Kneass
EDGE—Plain

DATE	MINTAGE	G-4	VG-8	F-12	VF-20	EF-40	AU-50	MS-60	MS-65
1829	1,230,000	14.00	17.50	25.00	48.00	125.	240.	325.	3600.
1830	1,240,000	14.00	17.50	25.00	48.00	125.	240.	325.	3600.
1831	1,242,700	14.00	17.50	25.00	48.00	125.	240.	325.	3600.
1832	965,000	14.00	17.50	25.00	48.00	125.	240.	325.	3600.
1833	1,370,000	14.00	17.50	25.00	48.00	125.	240.	325.	3600.
1834	1,480,000	14.00	17.50	25.00	48.00	125.	240.	325.	3600.
1835 Lg. Date, Lg. 5C	2,760,000	14.00	17.50	25.00	48.00	125.	240.	325.	3600.
1835 Lg. Date, Sm. 5C	Inc. Above	14.00	17.50	25.00	48.00	125.	240.	325.	3600.
1835 Sm. Date, Lg. 5C	Inc. Above	14.00	17.50	25.00	48.00	125.	240.	325.	3600.
1835 Sm. Date, Sm. 5C	Inc. Above	14.00	17.50	25.00	48.00	125.	240.	325.	3600.
1836 Large 5C	1,900,000	14.00	17.50	25.00	48.00	125.	240.	325.	3600.
1836 Small 5C	Inc. Above	14.00	17.50	25.00	48.00	125.	240.	325.	3600.
1837 Large 5C	2,276,000	14.00	17.50	25.00	48.00	125.	240.	325.	3600.
1837 Small 5C	Inc. Above	22.50	30.00	55.00	85.00	150.	375.	1300.	8750.

LIBERTY SEATED TYPE
1837-1873

VARIETY ONE - NO STARS ON OBVERSE
1837-1873

DIAMETER—15.5mm
WEIGHT—1.34 Grams
COMPOSITION—.900 Silver,
.100 Copper
DESIGNER—Christian Gobrecht
EDGE—Reeded

DATE	MINTAGE	G-4	VG-8	F-12	VF-20	EF-40	MS-60
1837 Sm. Date	Inc. Above	25.00	30.00	55.00	125.	250.	800.
1837 Lg. Date	Inc. Above	25.00	30.00	55.00	125.	250.	600.
1838 O	70,000	120.	165.	250.	450.	750.	4000.

VARIETY TWO - STARS ON OBVERSE
1838-1853

DIAMETER—15.5mm
WEIGHT—1.34 Grams
COMPOSITION—.900 Silver
.100 Copper
DESIGNER—Christian Gobrecht
EDGE—Reeded

DATE	MINTAGE	G-4	VG-8	F-12	VF-20	EF-40	MS-60
1838 O No Drapery	2,255,000	7.50	10.00	12.00	25.00	80.00	350.
1838 O Sm. Stars	Inc. Above	25.00	42.50	60.00	120.	250.	1250.
1839 O No Drapery	1,069,150	7.50	10.00	12.00	20.00	55.00	350.
1839 O No Drapery	1,034,039	16.00	19.00	27.50	50.00	85.00	700.
1840 O No Drapery	1,344,085	7.50	10.00	12.00	20.00	50.00	475.
1840 O No Drapery	935,000	16.00	22.50	32.50	55.00	90.00	750.
1840 O Drapery	Inc. Above	25.00	35.00	60.00	80.00	175.	1850.
1840 O Drapery	Inc. Above	35.00	55.00	90.00	125.	225.	1850.
1841	1,150,000	11.00	16.00	22.50	37.50	45.00	200.
1841 O	815,000	13.50	19.00	27.50	42.50	75.00	650.
1842	815,000	11.00	16.00	22.50	37.50	45.00	200.
1842 O	350,000	30.00	50.00	75.00	150.	400.	—
1843	1,165,000	11.00	16.00	22.50	22.50	45.00	200.
1844	430,000	11.00	16.00	22.50	37.50	65.00	200.
1844 O	220,000	75.00	100.	175.	400.	1000.	—
1845	1,564,000	11.00	16.00	22.50	37.50	47.50	200.
1846	27,000	125.	200.	300.	450.	850.	—
1847	1,274,000	11.00	16.00	22.50	37.50	45.00	200.
1848 Medium Date	668,000	11.00	16.00	22.50	37.50	65.00	200.
1848 Large Date	Inc. Above	16.00	22.50	32.50	65.00	90.00	525.
1848 O	600,000	16.00	22.50	32.50	65.00	90.00	650.
1849/8	1,309,000	20.00	27.50	32.50	50.00	75.00	525.
1849/6	Inc. Above	13.50	20.00	27.50	45.00	70.00	450.
1849	Inc. Above	11.00	16.00	22.50	37.50	50.00	625.
1849 O	140,000	27.50	37.50	70.00	265.	475.	—
1850	955,000	11.00	16.00	22.50	27.50	45.00	425.
1850 O	690,000	16.00	22.50	32.50	50.00	90.00	775.
1851	781,000	11.00	16.00	22.50	27.50	45.00	425.
1851 O	860,000	13.50	20.00	43.50	55.00	85.00	775.
1852	1,000,500	11.00	16.00	22.50	27.50	45.00	200.
1852 O	260,000	32.50	37.50	65.00	100.	215.	—
1853	135,000	16.00	27.50	55.00	80.00	135.	775.
1853 O	160,000	125.	150.	265.	400.	800.	—

VARIETY THREE - ARROWS AT DATE
1853-1855

DIAMETER—15.5mm
WEIGHT—1.24 Grams
COMPOSITION—.900 Silver
  .100 Copper
DESIGNER—Christian Gobrecht
EDGE—Reeded

DATE	MINTAGE	G-4	VG-8	F-12	VF-20	EF-40	MS-60	Prf-65
1853	13,210,020	6.50	8.50	10.00	16.50	50.00	225.	19,000.
1853 O	2,200,000	6.50	8.50	11.50	17.50	60.00	350.	—
1854	5,740,000	6.50	8.50	10.00	16.50	50.00	275.	18,000.
1854 O	1,560,000	8.50	13.50	16.50	37.50	80.00	750.	—
1855	1,750,000	6.50	8.50	10.00	16.50	50.00	275.	18,000.
1855 O	600,000	16.00	22.50	32.50	55.00	90.00	1050.	—

VARIETY TWO - RESUMED
1856-1859

DATE	MINTAGE	G-4	VG-8	F-12	VF-20	EF-40	MS-60	Prf-65
1856	4,880,000	8.50	13.00	17.50	22.50	45.00	200.	20,000.
1856 O	1,100,000	11.00	16.00	22.50	32.50	65.00	575.	—
1857	1,280,000	8.50	13.00	17.50	22.50	50.00	200.	6000.
1857 O	1,380,000	11.00	16.00	22.50	32.50	65.00	575.	—
1858	3,500,000	8.50	13.00	17.50	22.50	50.00	200.	9500.
1858/Inverted Date	Inc. Above	32.50	37.50	75.00	125.	200.	675.	—
1858 O	1,660,000	11.00	16.00	22.50	32.50	65.00	575.	—
1859	340,000	16.00	27.50	52.50	70.00	95.00	275.	6000.
1859 O	560,000	16.00	22.50	32.50	42.50	75.00	725.	—

VARIETY FOUR - LEGEND ON OBVERSE
1860-1873

DIAMETER—15.5mm
WEIGHT—1.24 Grams
COMPOSITION—.900 Silver
 .100 Copper
DESIGNER—Christian Gobrecht
EDGE—Reeded

DATE	MINTAGE	G-4	VG-8	F-12	VF-20	EF-40	MS-60	Prf-65
1860	799,000	8.00	12.00	14.00	25.00	45.00	200.	2250.
1860 O	1,060,000	8.00	14.00	18.00	30.00	45.00	375.	—
1861	3,361,000	8.00	10.00	12.00	18.00	35.00	200.	2250.
1862	1,492,550	8.00	10.00	12.00	18.00	35.00	200.	2250.
1863	18,460	65.00	75.00	110.	165.	225.	775.	3600.
1863 S	100,000	17.50	22.50	32.50	50.00	110.	900.	—
1864	48,470	235.	275.	350.	425.	625.	1250.	3600.
1864 S	90,000	27.50	37.50	80.00	150.	275.	1250.	—
1865	13,500	115.	150.	200.	225.	300.	875.	3600.
1865 S	120,000	17.50	22.50	32.50	70.00	110.	950.	—
1866	10,725	125.	155.	210.	250.	325.	1000.	3600.
1866 S	120,000	17.50	22.50	32.50	55.00	135.	950.	—
1867	8,625	165.	215.	265.	325.	425.	1050.	3600.
1867 S	120,000	17.50	22.50	37.50	75.00	165.	900.	—
1868	89,200	22.50	32.50	42.50	80.00	165.	575.	3600.
1868 S	280,000	10.00	16.50	20.00	30.00	60.00	475.	—
1869	208,600	11.00	17.50	27.50	37.50	70.00	450.	3600.
1869 S	230,000	10.00	16.50	20.00	32.50	65.00	475.	—
1870	536,600	8.00	10.00	12.00	20.00	40.00	425.	2250.
1870 S	Unique	One Known, Uncirculated, 1980 Private Sale $425,000.						
1871	1,873,960	6.00	8.00	10.00	18.00	32.50	400.	2250.
1871 S	161,000	16.50	32.50	52.50	80.00	135.	650.	—
1872	2,947,950	6.00	8.00	10.00	18.00	35.00	400.	2250.
1872 S MM in Wreath	837,000	6.00	8.00	10.00	18.00	35.00	400.	—
1872 S MM Below Wreath	Inc. Above	6.00	8.00	10.00	18.00	35.00	425.	—
1873	712,600	6.00	7.00	12.00	20.00	35.00	375.	2750.
1873 S	324,000	8.00	10.00	15.00	25.00	42.50	375.	—

NICKEL FIVE CENT PIECES
1866 TO DATE

SHIELD TYPE
1866-1883

**FIRST REVERSE
RAYS BETWEEN STARS
1866-1867**

**SECOND REVERSE
WITHOUT RAYS
1867-1883**

DIAMETER—20.5mm
WEIGHT—5 Grams
COMPOSITION—.750 Copper
  .250 Nickel
DESIGNER— James B. Longacre
EDGE—Plain

DATE	MINTAGE	G-4	VG-8	F-12	VF-20	EF-40	AU-50	MS-60	MS-65	Prf-65
1866	14,742,500	15.00	17.50	25.00	35.00	110.	165.	175.	4000.	4500.
1867 With Rays	2,019,000	13.00	16.50	27.50	40.00	125.	260.	325.	4400.	30,000.
1867 Without Rays	28,890,500	6.00	8.00	10.00	16.00	30.00	60.00	125.	875.	1200.
1868	28,817,000	6.00	8.00	10.00	16.00	30.00	55.00	100.	875.	1175.
1869	16,395,000	6.00	8.00	10.00	16.00	30.00	57.50	125.	925.	950.
1870	4,806,000	11.00	12.50	16.00	22.50	37.50	60.00	110.	1000.	1250.
1871	561,000	35.00	40.00	45.00	60.00	90.00	170.	325.	1500.	1000.
1872	6,036,000	11.00	12.50	16.00	22.50	37.50	65.00	125.	950.	950.
1873	4,550,000	6.50	12.50	16.00	22.50	37.50	65.00	135.	975.	1000.
1874	3,538,000	11.00	13.00	17.50	25.00	40.00	70.00	135.	1175.	950.
1875	2,097,000	13.00	16.00	22.50	30.00	47.50	85.00	170.	2700.	1150.
1876	2,530,000	12.00	15.00	20.00	27.50	45.00	80.00	135.	1450.	1000.
1877	Est. 500						PROOF ONLY			2500.
1878	2,350						PROOF ONLY			1500.
1879	29,100	235.	285.	385.	450.	550.	600.	650.	2000.	850.
1880	19,995	275.	350.	400.	475.	600.	650.	675.	4000.	850.
1881	72,375	220.	260.	325.	375.	450.	550.	550.	1250.	850.
1882	11,476,600	8.00	10.00	14.00	20.00	32.50	47.50	100.	900.	850.
1883	1,456,919	11.00	12.00	14.00	20.00	32.50	47.50	110.	900.	850.
1883/2	Inc. Above	75.00	100.	120.	150.	180.	250.	375.	3200.	—

LIBERTY HEAD TYPE
1883-1913

**VARIETY ONE
WITHOUT CENTS
1883 ONLY**

**VARIETY ONE
WITH CENTS
1883 -1913**

DIAMETER—21.2mm
WEIGHT—5 Grams
COMPOSITION—.750
  .250 Nickel
DESIGNER— Charles E. Barber
EDGE—Plain

DATE	MINTAGE	G-4	VG-8	F-12	VF-20	EF-40	AU-50	MS-60	MS-65	Prf-65
1883 No Cents	5,479,519	2.25	3.25	4.00	7.00	10.00	12.00	35.00	475.	1000.
1883 With Cents	16,032,983	6.50	9.00	19.00	26.00	30.00	65.00	95.00	675.	650.
1884	11,273,942	7.50	9.50	20.00	27.50	36.00	75.00	125.	800.	650.
1885	1,476,490	155.	215.	325.	425.	625.	675.	875.	1900.	900.

DATE	MINTAGE	G-4	VG-8	F-12	VF-20	EF-40	AU-50	MS-60	MS-65	Prf-65
1886	3,330,290	50.00	60.00	100.	140.	220.	320.	525.	2000.	725.
1887	15,263,652	4.25	5.75	16.00	24.00	42.00	65.00	95.00	725.	625.
1888	10,720,483	6.50	11.00	20.00	30.00	52.50	90.00	130.	700.	625.
1889	15,881,361	4.25	5.75	16.00	24.00	40.00	65.00	95.00	675.	625.
1890	16,259,272	4.25	5.75	16.00	24.00	42.00	70.00	110.	850.	625.
1891	16,834,350	4.00	5.75	16.00	24.00	40.00	65.00	95.00	825.	625.
1892	11,699,642	4.75	7.50	18.00	27.50	45.00	75.00	110.	725.	625.
1893	13,370,195	4.50	6.50	17.00	25.00	40.00	65.00	95.00	800.	625.
1894	5,413,132	7.50	10.00	22.00	32.50	85.00	130.	190.	1150.	625.
1895	9,979,884	5.75	7.00	17.00	28.00	42.00	65.00	90.00	1100.	800.
1896	8,842,920	6.00	7.50	20.00	30.00	45.00	70.00	95.00	1100.	625.
1897	20,428,735	1.25	2.25	6.00	10.00	27.50	60.00	85.00	975.	625.
1898	12,532,087	1.50	2.50	6.50	10.50	27.50	60.00	85.00	675.	625.
1899	26,029,031	.90	2.00	4.25	8.00	22.50	55.00	85.00	675.	625.
1900	27,255,995	.80	1.50	3.75	7.50	20.00	45.00	70.00	675.	625.
1901	26,480,213	.80	1.50	3.75	7.50	20.00	45.00	70.00	675.	625.
1902	31,480,579	.80	1.35	3.50	7.00	20.00	45.00	70.00	675.	625.
1903	28,006,725	.80	1.50	3.75	7.25	20.00	45.00	70.00	675.	625.
1904	21,404,984	.85	1.65	4.00	8.00	20.00	45.00	70.00	675.	750.
1905	29,827,276	.80	1.35	3.50	7.00	20.00	45.00	70.00	675.	625.
1906	38,613,725	.70	1.10	3.25	6.50	20.00	45.00	70.00	675.	625.
1907	39,214,800	.70	1.10	3.25	6.50	20.00	45.00	70.00	675.	650.
1908	22,686,177	.80	1.25	3.75	7.50	20.00	45.00	70.00	800.	625.
1909	11,590,526	.90	1.35	4.00	8.75	22.50	50.00	85.00	750.	625.
1910	30,169,353	.70	1.10	3.25	6.50	20.00	45.00	70.00	700.	625.
1911	39,559,372	.70	1.10	3.25	6.50	20.00	45.00	70.00	675.	625.
1912	26,236,714	.75	1.25	3.50	7.00	20.00	45.00	70.00	675.	625.
1912 D	8,474,000	1.00	1.75	6.00	15.00	52.50	95.00	185.	825.	—
1912 S	238,000	50.00	60.00	75.00	200.	375.	500.	575.	2400.	—
1913	5 Known					Jan. 1985 Buss Sale $385,000.				

INDIAN HEAD OR BUFFALO TYPE
1913-1938

FIRST REVERSE
BUFFALO ON MOUND
1913 ONLY

SECOND REVERSE
BUFFALO ON LINE
1913 ONLY

DIAMETER—21.2mm
WEIGHT—5 Grams
COMPOSITION—.750 Copper,
.250 Nickel
DESIGNER—James Earle Fraser
EDGE—Plain

DATE	MINTAGE	G-4	VG-8	F-12	VF-20	EF-40	AU-50	MS-60	MS-65	Prf-65
1913 Mound Type	30,993,520	2.75	3.25	4.25	7.25	11.50	20.00	32.50	120.	2000.
1913 D Mound Type	5,337,000	5.25	6.25	9.00	11.00	21.00	40.00	55.00	325.	—
1913 S Mound Type	2,105,000	8.25	10.00	14.00	22.00	40.00	70.00	85.00	650.	—
1913 Line Type	29,858,700	3.25	3.75	4.75	7.00	13.00	22.50	30.00	275.	1200.
1913 D Line Type	4,156,000	40.00	45.00	50.00	70.00	95.00	140.	180.	750.	—
1913 S Line Type	1,209,000	60.00	65.00	80.00	100.	120.	275.	360.	2300.	—
1914	20,665,738	4.25	5.25	7.00	8.00	13.00	33.00	45.00	375.	1200.
1914 D	3,912,000	26.50	32.00	44.00	57.50	100.	175.	250.	1600.	—

DATE	MINTAGE	G-4	VG-8	F-12	VF-20	EF-40	AU-50	MS-60	MS-65	Prf-65
1914 S	3,470,000	4.25	5.25	13.00	16.50	37.50	55.00	105.	2100.	—
1915	20,987,270	2.00	2.75	4.25	5.75	11.00	22.50	45.00	300.	1200.
1915 D	7,569,500	6.00	6.50	12.50	32.50	52.50	80.00	150.	2400.	—
1915 S	1,505,000	10.00	12.50	20.00	47.50	85.00	150.	275.	2600.	—
1916	63,498,066	.65	.90	1.25	2.50	6.50	22.50	38.00	250.	2200.
1916 Dbld. Die Obv.	Inc. Above	1500.	3400.	4850.	6800.	9000.	12,000.	13,500.	50,000.	—
1916 D	13,333,000	4.25	5.50	9.50	20.00	42.50	75.00	200.	2700.	—
1916 S	11,860,000	3.25	4.25	7.00	16.50	40.00	75.00	160.	2800.	—
1917	51,424,029	.85	1.10	1.65	3.25	10.00	30.00	50.00	500.	—
1917 D	9,910,800	3.75	5.50	10.00	42.50	85.00	110.	235.	3100.	—
1917 S	4,193,000	4.75	5.50	9.50	62.50	37.50	115.	275.	3500.	—
1918	32,086,314	.75	1.50	2.75	5.50	15.00	40.00	60.00	1000.	—
1918 D/17	8,362,000	400.	525.	825.	2250.	4000.	6000.	9500.	57,000.	—
1918 D	Inc. Above	3.75	6.50	11.00	62.50	85.00	170.	335.	3100.	—
1918 S	4,882,000	3.75	5.25	10.00	37.50	80.00	135.	285.	11,000.	—
1919	60,868,000	.50	.75	1.25	3.25	7.50	17.00	45.00	420.	—
1919 D	8,006,000	3.25	6.50	16.50	75.00	110.	185.	360.	3400.	—
1919 S	7,521,000	2.75	5.50	11.50	47.50	80.00	135.	320.	7000.	—
1920	63,093,000	.45	.70	1.25	3.25	7.50	18.50	45.00	600.	—
1920 D	9,418,000	2.75	4.50	9.50	52.50	100.	175.	335.	4000.	—
1920 S	9,689,000	2.25	3.25	7.50	27.00	85.00	125.	220.	13,500.	—
1921	10,663,000	.65	1.00	2.75	6.50	17.00	42.50	90.00	540.	—
1921 S	1,557,000	8.50	16.50	32.50	77.50	210.	350.	900.	4000.	—
1923	35,715,000	.40	.55	1.15	3.25	7.50	20.00	45.00	440.	—
1923 S	6,142,000	1.35	2.75	5.25	24.00	57.50	90.00	175.	9600.	—
1924	21,620,000	.40	.55	1.15	3.25	9.50	22.50	65.00	580.	—
1924 D	5,258,000	2.75	3.75	8.00	42.50	77.50	130.	235.	2200.	—
1924 S	1,437,000	4.25	6.75	16.50	90.00	200.	375.	1000.	4400.	—
1925	25,565,100	.45	.65	1.15	2.50	16.50	47.50	37.50	245.	—
1925 D	4,450,000	3.75	6.50	13.00	52.50	85.00	175.	300.	3825.	—
1925 S	6,256,000	2.50	4.25	7.50	24.00	47.50	115.	230.	16,500.	—
1926	44,693,000	.35	.45	.85	2.25	5.50	14.00	40.00	135.	—
1926 D	5,638,000	2.25	4.25	9.00	35.00	47.50	95.00	160.	2550.	—
1926 S	970,000	5.50	8.50	17.50	325.	875.	1050.	1500.	20,000.	—
1927	37,981,000	.35	.45	.85	1.75	5.25	14.00	37.50	235.	—
1927 D	5,730,000	.85	1.50	3.00	12.00	40.00	60.00	100.	2200.	—
1927 S	3,430,000	1.15	1.75	4.50	14.00	57.50	90.00	170.	11,000.	—
1928	23,411,000	.35	.45	.85	2.25	4.00	15.00	37.50	265.	—
1928 D	6,436,000	.55	.85	2.25	4.25	12.00	26.50	45.00	800.	—
1928 S	6,936,000	.55	.80	1.50	2.75	11.00	32.50	75.00	4400.	—
1929	36,446,000	.35	.45	.85	1.75	3.75	9.00	30.00	225.	—
1929 D	8,370,000	.50	.60	1.15	3.75	10.00	24.00	60.00	1050.	—
1929 S	7,754,000	.45	.55	.85	1.75	8.50	20.00	45.00	300.	—
1930	22,849,000	.35	.55	.85	1.75	3.75	10.00	32.50	120.	—
1930 S	5,435,000	.55	.65	1.15	2.00	7.00	20.00	45.00	440.	—
1931 S	1,200,000	3.25	3.50	4.00	5.50	13.50	30.00	50.00	215.	—
1934	20,213,003	.35	.45	.70	1.75	3.75	12.00	30.00	325.	—
1934 D	7,480,000	.50	.60	.95	1.75	4.25	26.50	40.00	1400.	—
1935	58,264,000	.35	.40	.50	.90	1.75	8.50	20.00	82.00	—
1935 D	12,092,000	.40	.50	.70	2.00	2.75	24.00	30.00	425.	—
1935 S	10,300,000	.40	.45	.60	1.10	2.25	14.00	27.50	240.	—

DATE	MINTAGE	G-4	VG-8	F-12	VF-20	EF-40	AU-50	MS-60	MS-65	Prf-65
1936........................119,001,420		.35	.40	.50	.90	1.75	9.00	15.00	45.00.	1000.
1936 D 24,814,000		.35	.45	.60	1.10	2.25	11.00	17.50	75.00	—
1936 S........................14,930,000		.35	.45	.60	1.10	2.00	13.00	16.00	75.00	—
1937........................79,485,769		.35	.40	.50	.90	1.75	9.50	14.00	40.00.	1000.
1937 D 17,826,000		.35	.45	.65	1.10	2.00	10.00	14.00	45.00	—
1937 D 3 Leg................Inc. Above		190.	225.	250.	345.	400.	525.	800.	12,000.	—
1937 S........................5,635,000		.45	.50	.55	1.10	1.75	10.00	14.00	45.00	—
1938 D 7,020,000		.45	.50	.60	1.10	1.75	7.50	14.00	40.00	—
1938 D/S....................Inc. Above		—	—	6.25	7.50	10.00	16.50	27.50	180.	—

JEFFERSON TYPE
1938 TO DATE

DIAMETER—21.2mm
WEIGHT—5 Grams
COMPOSITION—1938-1942
   1946-Date .750 Copper,.250 Nickel
   1942-1945, .560 Copper
   .350 Silver .090 Manganese
DESIGNER—Felix Schlag
EDGE—Plain
PURE SILVER CONTENT—1942-1945, .05626 Tr. Oz.

DATE	MINTAGE	G-4	VG-8	F-12	VF-20	EF-40	MS-60	Prf-65
1938 19,515,365		—	.35	.50	1.00	1.50	3.75	50.00
1938 D 5,376,000		1.20	1.35	1.65	1.95	2.65	5.00	—
1938 S 4,105,000		2.25	2.40	2.75	3.00	3.50	6.00	—
1939 120,627,535		—	—	—	.20	.40	1.75	60.00
1939 Double Monticello................Inc. Above		—	8.00	12.00	27.50	52.50	210.	—
1939 D 3,514,000		2.75	3.25	3.75	4.25	7.00	37.50	—
1939 S 6,630,000		.50	.70	.80	1.10	2.25	22.50	—
1940 176,499,158		—	—	—	.15	.25	1.15	50.00
1940 D 43,540,000		—	—	—	.20	.35	2.50	—
1940 S 39,690,000		—	—	—	.25	.55	2.25	—
1941 203,283,720		—	—	—	—	.20	.80	50.00
1941 D 53,432,000		—	—	—	.20	.40	2.75	—
1941 S 43,445,000		—	—	—	.20	.40	4.00	—
1942 49,818,600		—	—	—	.20	.40	1.75	32.50
1942 D 13,938,000		.20	.25	.35	.45	2.25	18.00	—

WARTIME ALLOY, LARGE MINTMARK ABOVE DOME
1942-1945

DATE	MINTAGE	G-4	VG-8	F-12	VF-20	EF-40	MS-60	Prf-65
1942 P 57,900,000		—	—	—	1.00	3.35	11.00	130.
1942 S 32,900,000		—	—	—	1.00	1.50	10.00	—
1943 P 271,165,000		—	—	—	1.00	1.50	4.00	—
1943 P 3/2 ....Inc. Above		22.50	32.50	50.00	75.00	125.	275.	—
1943 D 15,294,000		—	—	—	1.00	1.75	3.50	—
1943 S 104,060,000		—	—	—	1.00	1.50	4.00	—

DATE	MINTAGE	G-4	VG-8	F-12	VF-20	EF-40	MS-60	Prf-65
1944 P	119,150,000	—	—	—	1.00	1.50	4.75	—
1944 D	32,309,000	—	—	—	1.00	1.50	8.00	—
1944 S	21,640,000	—	—	—	1.00	1.50	7.50	—
1945 P	119,408,100	—	—	—	1.00	1.50	5.00	—
1945 D	37,158,000	—	—	—	1.00	1.50	4.50	—
1945 S	58,939,000	—	—	—	1.00	1.50	3.75	—

PRE-WAR COMPOSITION RESUMED
1946 TO DATE

DATE	MINTAGE	VG-8	F-12	VF-20	EF-40	MS-60	Prf-65
1946	161,116,000	—	—	—	.15	.45	—
1946 D	45,292,200	—	—	—	.20	.80	—
1946 S	13,560,000	—	—	—	.40	.65	—
1947	95,000,000	—	—	—	.15	.45	—
1947 D	37,822,000	—	—	—	.30	.70	—
1947 S	24,720,000	—	—	.25	.40	.60	—
1948	89,348,000	—	—	—	.15	.40	—
1948 D	44,734,000	—	—	—	.30	1.10	—
1948 S	11,300,000	—	.20	.30	.50	1.10	—
1949	60,652,000	—	—	—	.15	.80	—
1949 D	36,498,000	—	—	.25	.30	1.10	—
1949 D/S	Inc. Above	—	26.50	32.50	70.00	180.	—
1949 S	9,716,000	.25	.30	.40	.80	2.10	—
1950	9,847,386	.30	.40	.50	.95	2.00	40.00
1950 D	2,630,030	7.75	8.00	8.25	8.50	18.00	—
1951	28,609,500	—	—	—	.35	1.10	35.00
1951 D	20,460,000	—	—	—	.30	1.35	—
1951 S	7,776,000	.35	.40	.50	.95	2.75	—
1952	64,069,980	—	—	—	.15	.60	34.00
1952 D	30,638,000	—	—	—	.70	1.60	—
1952 S	20,572,000	—	—	—	.20	.70	—
1953	46,772,800	—	—	—	—	.40	32.00
1935 D	59,878,600	—	—	—	—	.35	—
1953 S	19,210,900	—	—	—	.40	.55	—
1954	47,917,350	—	—	—	—	.25	17.50
1954 D	117,136,560	—	—	—	—	.35	—
1954 S	29,384,000	—	—	—	—	.40	—
1954 S/D	Inc. Above	—	4.00	7.25	12.00	27.50	—
1955	8,266,200	.35	.40	.50	.65	.80	10.00
1955 D	74,464,100	—	—	—	—	.25	—
1956	35,885,384	—	—	—	—	.30	1.75
1956 D	67,222,940	—	—	—	—	.25	—
1957	39,655,952	—	—	—	—	.30	1.75
1957 D	136,828,900	—	—	—	—	.25	—
1958	17,963,652	—	.20	.25	.25	.35	1.50
1958 D	168,249,120	—	—	—	—	.25	—
1959	28,397,291	—	—	—	—	.25	1.25
1959 D	160,738,240	—	—	—	—	.15	—
1960	57,107,602	—	—	—	—	.15	1.00
1960 D	192,582,180	—	—	—	—	.15	—
1961	76,668,244	—	—	—	—	.15	1.00

DATE	MINTAGE	VG-8	F-12	VF-20	EF-40	MS-60	Prf-65
1961 D	229,342,760	—	—	—	—	.15	—
1962	100,602,019	—	—	—	—	.15	1.00
1962 D	280,195,720	—	—	—	—	.15	—
1963	178,851,645	—	—	—	—	.15	1.00
1963 D	276,829,460	—	—	—	—	.15	—
1964	1,028,622,762	—	—	—	—	.15	1.00
1964 D	1,787,297,160	—	—	—	—	.15	—

DATE	MINTAGE	MS-65	Prf-65
1965	136,131,380	.15	—
1966	156,208,283	.15	—
1967	107,325,800	.15	—
1968	—	—	—
1968 D	91,227,880	.15	—
1968 S	103,437,510	.15	.40
1969	—	—	—
1969 D	202,807,500	.15	—
1969 S	123,099,631	.15	.40
1970	—	—	—
1970 D	515,485,380	.15	—
1970 S	241,464,814	.15	.65
1971	106,884,000	.15	—
1971 D	316,144,800	.15	—
1971 S	PROOF ONLY	—	.90
1972	202,036,000	.15	—
1972 D	351,694,600	.15	—
1972 S	PROOF ONLY	—	.90
1973	384,396,000	.15	—
1973 D	261,405,400	.15	—
1973 S	PROOF ONLY	—	1.00
1974	601,752,000	.15	—
1974 D	277,373,000	.15	—
1974 S	PROOF ONLY	—	1.25
1975	181,772,000	.15	—
1975 D	401,875,300	.15	—
1975 S	PROOF ONLY	—	1.25
1976	367,124,000	.15	—
1976 D	563,964,147	.15	—
1976 S	PROOF ONLY	—	.50
1977	585,376,000	.15	—
1977 D	297,313,460	.15	—
1977 S	PROOF ONLY	—	.50
1978	391,308,000	.15	—
1978 D	313,092,780	.15	—
1978 S	PROOF ONLY	—	.60
1979	463,188,000	.15	—
1979 D	325,867,672	.15	—

DATE	MINTAGE	MS-65	Prf-65
1979 S PROOF ONLY	—	.75
1980 P 593,004,000	.15	—
1980 D 502,323,448	.15	—
1980 S PROOF ONLY	—	.50
1981 P 657,504,000	.15	—
1981 D 364,801,843	.15	—
1981 S PROOF ONLY	—	.50
1982 P 292,355,000	.15	—
1982 D 373,726,544	.15	—
1982 S PROOF ONLY	—	2.00
1983 P 561,615,000	.15	—
1983 D 536,726,276	.15	—
1983 S PROOF ONLY	—	1.50
1984 P 746,769,000	.15	—
1984 D 517,675,146	.15	—
1984 S PROOF ONLY	—	1.25
1985 P 647,114,962	.15	—
1985 D 459,747,446	.15	—
1985 S PROOF ONLY	—	1.50
1986 P 536,883,483	.15	—
1986 D 361,819,140	.15	—
1986 S PROOF ONLY	—	1.50
1987 P 371,499,481	.15	—
1987 D 410,590,604	.15	—
1987 S PROOF ONLY	—	1.50
1988 P 771,360,000	.15	—
1988 D 663,771,652	.15	—
1988 S PROOF ONLY	—	1.50
1989 P 898,812,000	.15	—
1989 D 570,842,474	.15	—
1989 S PROOF ONLY	—	1.50
1990 P 661,636,000	.15	—
1990 D 663,938,503	.15	—
1990 S PROOF ONLY	—	1.50
1991 P 614,104,000	.15	—
1991 D 436,496,678	.15	—
1991 S PROOF ONLY	—	1.50
1992 P —	.15	—
1992 D —	.15	—
1992 S PROOF ONLY	—	1.50
1993 P —	.15	—
1993 D —	.15	—
1993 S PROOF ONLY	—	1.50

Dimes 1796 to Date

Dimes have been minted continuously since 1796, providing numismatists with a vast array of dates and mint marks to study. The designs of the various dime series parallel those of the half-dimes through part of the Liberty Seated pattern. In all, there are eleven distinct types of dimes.

Excellent investment potential exists in all the Draped Bust dimes, owing to the fact that these coins are very rare and have always been on a brisk rise, with little chance of coming to a permanent halt. Unfortunately, the price tags of the earlier dimes confine purchasing mainly to well-off investors.

The Capped Bust type of 1809-1837 is more easily affordable in lower conditions, but offers opportunities to investors of all means. This is so because Capped Bust dimes in MS-60 have tumbled by as much as 50% from their 1989 levels. Included in this group are the 1814 (small date), 1830 (over 29), and the 1835. These are being offered at basement prices, and will make a fine addition to anyone's collection.

The most expensive coin in the series is the 1822. Having a history of large price leaps followed by long periods of inactivity, the 1822 is fully priced at the moment. On the other hand, it is a sure bet if purchased with long term investment in mind. Take a close look at the 1809, 1811/9 (as all 1811's are), and the 1828 large date variety, and all coins of comparable mintage to the 1822. Back in 1965, these issues were valued near the top of the heap of Capped dimes, alongside the 1822, and own similar appreciation records until recently. The 1822 has advanced enormously in value, while the other three have not. It is only a matter of time before the "left behind" Capped Dimes catch up with their 1822 brother and take on "normal" price differentials again.

The Liberty Seated dime was first introduced in 1837 along with the Liberty Seated half-dime. There are many dimes among the Liberty Seated series that have fallen in the last few years and are currently undervalued, including slabbed coins in MS-60 to MS-65 Uncirculated condition. On a general note, the reader should not equate the precipitous plunge of Liberty Seated material with that of generic coins. High grade Liberty Seated coins and their contemporaries, unlike generic coins, are legitimately scarce. At today's depressed prices, they have excellent potential and should be among the best performers in the next market boom. This fact will be borne out repeatedly in the pages to follow.

A few typical examples of MS-60 Liberty Seated dimes costing anywhere from 10% to 30% less now than a few years ago are the 1837, 1838-0, 1838 (small stars), and the 1853 (no arrows). It is interesting to note that the Liberty Seated 1837 in MS-60 has act-ually dipped below its 1975 levels! Seldom will a 19th century coin of mid-range scarcity be found with the uncirculated value equaling less than that of nearly two decades ago.

The Barber dime series went into production in 1892 and ran through 1916, in conjunction with a matching design on the front side of the quarter and half dollar. There is a wide spectrum of exciting opportunities awaiting Barber dime buyers, no matter if you have only a little or a lot to spend.

A good profit opportunity exists in MS-60 and MS-63 Uncirculateds, whose prices remain lower than those seen during the 1979-1980 explosion. Although demand has pushed price levels higher over the last year or so, especially for MS-63, they still represent nice values for the buyer. Barber dimes in Extremely Fine to Almost Uncirculated should also perform superbly, most notably for the better dates. Common date Barber dimes grading less than Fine have jumped upward in price at past intervals too, but only on the basis of their silver content and not because of their collectible value. Try to stick with the better grades for these particular coins.

One of the most popular collector coins has been the Mercury dime. To assemble a complete set a collector must locate pieces dating from 1916 to 1945. In reality, the woman figure on the coin's obverse is a rendition of Miss Liberty, with wings crowning her cap to symbolize freedom of thought. The American public incorrectly saw Miss Liberty and her wings as the Greek god Mercury, hence the dime became regularly known as the "Mercury" dime.

In the latter part of the 1980's the series stagnated, with values of MS-60 and below examples plunging dramatically. Those same coins have rebounded nicely in the 1990's, but it is still not too late to add them to your collection at bargain prices. It would be to your advantage to land a few MS-63's and MS-65's also, since many of them are not overpriced and have fantastic investment potential.

For only a few hundred dollars, you can obtain proof Mercury dimes. Doing so may be a challenge, as they were produced from 1936 to 1942, in relatively small quantities (less than 80,000 total). Indeed, these are scarce "type" coins, but they are not priced as such.

The undisputed key Mercury is the 1916-D. Aside from concern over purchasing an altered coin, don't worry about losing ground with a 1916-D Mercury. It will be in demand from collectors for a very long time to come.

Well struck Mercury dimes sometimes have a distinct separation of the horizontal bands on the fasces design on the reverse, described as "Full Split Bands" (abbreviated FSB). Prices for FSB Uncirculated dimes are routinely listed beside normal Uncirculated dimes and always carry a premium. Buy FSB Mercury dimes if the premium to be paid isn't too far above the value of similar quality Uncirculated dimes without the FSB. Be sure the bands are not only clearly separated, but are also fully raised and rounded. Many beginners mistake flattened split bands for truly full split bands, which may be a costly error.

Roosevelt dimes began production in 1946 following the death of Franklin D. Roosevelt, to honor him for his stout leadership through two of the most ominous events to ever confront the American nation. Other than their bullion value, very few of the Roosevelt dimes have ever advanced substantially over a short period of time. This lack of movement can only be interpreted as an absence of interest by collectors and investors. Although the Roosevelt dime market probably won't come alive anytime soon, the long range investor with small working capital will find this to be one of the better areas for investment.

Even in the uppermost grades, Roosevelt dimes are easily affordable. Purchase a complete set of Roosevelt dimes, including proofs, in nothing less than MS-60 condition, although MS-65 coins have greater potential. With such a minor price difference, you really shouldn't pass up the MS-65 dimes, as there could be a much greater gap between the two grades in ten years or so, which is the route so many other series have gone in the past. Buy them now and put them away for long term growth.

DIMES
1796 to DATE

DRAPED BUST TYPE, SMALL EAGLE REVERSE
1796-1797

DIAMETER—19mm
WEIGHT—2.70 Grams
COMPOSITION—.8924 Silver, .1076 Copper
DESIGNER—Robert Scot
EDGE—Reeded

DATE	MINTAGE	G-4	VG-8	F-12	VF-20	EF-40	MS-60
1796	22,135	1000.	1250.	1600.	2500.	4250.	7500.
1797 13 Stars	25,261	1000.	1250.	1600.	2500.	4400.	7500.
1797 16 Stars	Inc. Above	1000.	1250.	1600.	2500.	4250.	7500.

DRAPED BUST TYPE HERALDIC EAGLE REVERSE
1798-1807

DIAMETER—19mm
WEIGHT—2.70 Grams
COMPOSITION—.8924 Silver
  .1076 Copper
DESIGNER—Robert Scot
EDGE—Plain

DATE	MINTAGE	G-4	VG-8	F-12	VF-20	EF-40	MS-60
1798	27,550	600.	725.	1000.	1400.	2000.	6250.
1798/97 13 Stars	Inc. Above			VERY RARE			
1798/97 16 Stars	Inc. Above	600.	750.	950.	1400.	2000.	4000.
1798 Small 8	Inc. Above			RARE			
1800	21,760	600.	725.	1100.	1550.	1900.	5500.
1801	34,640	600.	725.	1100.	1550.	1800.	5500.
1802	10,975	800.	1150.	1650.	2800.	4800.	5750.
1803	33,040	600.	725.	950.	1400.	1800.	5750.
1804 13 Stars	8,265	1100.	1500.	2400.	3750.	7000.	—
1804 14 Stars	Inc. Above	1000.	1300.	2200.	3250.	5800.	—
1805 4 Berries	120,780	500.	550.	900.	1200.	1750.	4000.
1805 5 Berries	Inc. Above	500.	550.	900.	1200.	1850.	4750.
1807	165,000	500.	550.	900.	1200.	1750.	4000.

CAPPED BUST TYPE
1809-1837

DIAMETER—18.8mm
WEIGHT—2.70 Grams
COMPOSITION—.8924 Silver, .1076 Copper
DESIGNER—John Reich
EDGE—Reeded

VARIETY ONE - LARGE SIZE *1809-1828*

DATE	MINTAGE	G-4	VG-8	F-12	VF-20	EF-40	MS-60
1809	.51,065	75.00	100.	150.	225.	750.	4400.
1811/9	.65,180	45.00	65.00	85.00	150.	475.	4250.
1814 Sm. Date	.421,500	25.00	35.00	52.50	90.00	450.	850.
1814 Lg. Date	.Inc. Above	25.00	30.00	45.00	80.00	345.	850.
1820 Lg. O	.942,587	22.50	27.50	40.00	95.00	325.	850.
1820 Sm. O	.Inc. Above	22.50	27.50	40.00	95.00	325.	850.
1821 Lg. Date	.1,186,512	22.50	27.50	40.00	100.	325.	850.
1821 Sm. Date	.Inc. Above	22.50	30.00	45.00	100.	375.	850.
1822	.100,000	350.	575.	900.	1250.	2400.	6000.
1823/2 Large E's	.440,000	22.50	27.50	40.00	100.	300.	850.
1823/2 Small E's	.Inc. Above	22.50	27.50	40.00	100.	375.	850.
1824/2	.510,000	22.50	27.50	40.00	100.	450.	850.
1825	.Inc. Above	20.00	26.00	37.50	95.00	300.	850.
1827	.1,215,000	20.00	25.00	32.50	95.00	300.	850.
1828 Lg. Date	.125,000	35.00	45.00	70.00	120.	450.	3200.

VARIETY TWO - DIAMETER SLIGHTLY REDUCED *1828-1837*

DATE	MINTAGE	G-4	VG-8	F-12	VF-20	EF-40	MS-60
1828 Sm. Date	.Inc. Above	25.00	30.00	40.00	85.00	300.	1000.
1829 Lg. 10C	.770,000	22.50	27.50	37.50	75.00	300.	675.
1829 Med. 10C	.Inc. Above	14.00	16.50	20.00	50.00	275.	675.
1829 Sm. 10C	.Inc. Above	14.00	16.50	20.00	50.00	200.	675.
1830 Lg. 10C	.510,000	14.00	16.50	20.00	50.00	200.	675.
1830 Sm. 10C	.Inc. Above	14.00	16.50	20.00	50.00	225.	675.
1830/29	—	80.00	135.	215.	270.	1100.
1831	.771,350	14.00	16.50	20.00	50.00	200.	600.
1832	.522,500	14.00	16.50	20.00	50.00	200.	600.
1833	.485,000	14.00	16.50	20.00	50.00	200.	600.
1833 High 3	.Inc. Above	14.00	16.50	20.00	50.00	200.	600.
1834 Large 4	.635,000	14.00	16.50	20.00	50.00	200.	600.
1834 Small 4	.Inc. Above	14.00	16.50	20.00	50.00	200.	600.
1835	.1,410,000	14.00	16.50	20.00	50.00	200.	600.
1836	.1,190,000	14.00	16.50	20.00	50.00	200.	600.
1837	.1,042,000	14.00	16.50	20.00	50.00	200.	675.

LIBERTY SEATED TYPE
1837-1891

VARIETY ONE - NO STARS ON OBVERSE
1837-1838

DIAMETER—17.9mm
WEIGHT—2.67 Grams
COMPOSITION—.900 Silver, .100 Copper
DESIGNER—Christian Gobrecht
EDGE—Reeded

DATE	MINTAGE	G-4	VG-8	F-12	VF-20	EF-40	MS-60
1837 Sm. Date	Inc. Above	25.00	36.00	50.00	135.	325.	1150.
1837 Lg. Date	Inc. Above	25.00	36.00	50.00	135.	325.	1150.
1838 O	406,034	47.50	55.00	85.00	200.	500.	3750.

VARIETY TWO - STARS ON OBVERSE
1838-1853

DIAMETER—17.9mm
WEIGHT—2.67 Grams
COMPOSITION—.900 Silver, .100 Copper
DESIGNER—Christian Gobrecht
EDGE—Reeded

DATE	MINTAGE	G-4	VG-8	F-12	VF-20	EF-40	MS-60
1838 Sm. Stars	1,992,500	22.50	32.50	42.50	85.00	275.	2000.
1838 Lg. Stars	Inc. Above	11.50	16.00	22.50	42.50	80.00	875.
1838 Part Drapery	Inc. Above	42.50	70.00	90.00	120.	375.	1450.
1839	1,053,115	11.50	13.50	19.00	37.50	75.00	300.
1839 O	1,323,000	13.50	17.50	22.50	65.00	110.	1000.
1840	1,358,580	8.50	9.50	11.50	37.50	60.00	300.
1840 O	1,175,000	16.50	32.50	47.50	70.00	110.	1600.
1840 Drapery	Inc. Above	45.00	70.00	150.	225.	475.	—
1841	1,622,500	8.50	11.50	16.50	37.50	65.00	225.
1841 O	2,007,500	16.50	22.50	32.50	52.50	140.	1600.
1842	1,887,500	8.50	11.50	16.50	37.50	65.00	225.
1842 O	2,020,000	16.50	22.50	32.50	65.00	130.	—
1843	1,370,000	8.50	11.50	16.50	37.50	65.00	225.
1843 O	150,000	52.50	70.00	135.	270.	675.	—
1844	72,500	27.50	42.50	75.00	160.	325.	2150.
1845	1,755,000	8.50	11.50	16.50	25.00	45.00	225.
1845 O	230,000	16.50	32.50	80.00	160.	525.	—
1846	31,300	78.00	90.00	150.	275.	525.	—
1847	245,000	16.50	27.50	52.50	80.00	140.	1250.
1848	451,500	11.50	13.50	25.00	35.00	70.00	775.
1849	839,000	8.50	11.50	17.50	25.50	55.00	750.
1849/8	Inc. Above	52.50	80.00	150.	225.	400.	—
1849 O	300,000	16.50	22.50	37.50	90.00	200.	—
1850	1,931,500	8.50	11.50	15.00	20.00	45.00	225.
1850 O	510,000	13.50	17.50	32.50	45.00	85.00	1050.
1851	1,026,500	8.50	11.50	15.00	20.00	45.00	225.

DATE	MINTAGE	G-4	VG-8	F-12	VF-20	EF-40	MS-60
1851 O	400,000	13.50	17.50	25.00	50.00	95.00	1450.
1852	1,535,500	8.50	11.50	15.00	20.50	45.00	225.
1852 O	430,000	16.50	22.50	42.50	90.00	225.	1750.
1853	95,000	60.00	75.00	100.	175.	300.	1050.

VARIETY THREE - ARROWS AT DATE
1853-1855

DIAMETER—17.9mm
WEIGHT—2.49 Grams
COMPOSITION—.900 Silver, .100 Copper
DESIGNER—Christian Gobrecht
EDGE—Reeded

DATE	MINTAGE	G-4	VG-8	F-12	VF-20	EF-40	MS-60	Prf-65
1853	12,078,010	6.50	9.50	13.50	22.50	50.00	325.	24,000.
1853 O	1,100,000	8.50	16.50	27.50	42.50	100.	950.	—
1854	4,470,000	6.50	11.50	16.50	27.50	50.00	325.	24,000.
1854 O	1,770,000	6.50	13.50	22.50	37.50	80.00	700.	—
1855	2,075,000	6.50	9.50	16.50	25.00	50.00	375.	24,000.

VARIETY TWO - RESUMED
1856-1860

DATE	MINTAGE	G-4	VG-8	F-12	VF-20	EF-40	MS-60	Prf-65
1856 Sm. Date	5,780,000	6.50	9.50	13.50	20.00	35.00	360.	24,000.
1856 Lg Date	Inc. Above	11.50	16.50	22.50	30.00	65.00	360.	—
1856 O	1,180,000	7.50	12.50	15.50	27.50	65.00	360.	—
1856 S	70,000	100.	125.	175.	275.	425.	—	—
1857	5,580,000	6.50	9.50	13.50	17.00	35.00	270.	5700.
1857 O	1,540,000	7.50	12.50	15.50	20.00	55.00	360.	—
1858	1,540,000	6.50	9.50	13.50	17.00	35.00	270.	5700.
1858 O	290,000	15.00	20.00	30.00	50.00	130.	825.	—
1858 S	60,000	90.00	110.	140.	250.	425.	1350.	—
1859	430,000	6.50	9.50	13.50	20.00	55.00	360.	5700.
1859 O	480,000	6.50	11.50	16.50	25.00	75.00	575.	—
1859 S	60,000	125.	150.	185.	300.	475.	—	—
1860 S	140,000	16.50	25.00	35.00	70.00	165.	—	—

VARIETY FOUR - LEGEND ON OBVERSE
1860-1873

DIAMETER—17.9mm
WEIGHT—2.49 Grams
COMPOSITION—.900 Silver, .100 Copper
DESIGNER—Christian Gobrecht
EDGE—Reeded

DATE	MINTAGE	G-4	VG-8	F-12	VF-20	EF-40	MS-60	Prf-65
1860	607,000	6.50	13.50	20.00	25.00	45.00	550.	2250.
1860 O	40,000	425.	525.	750.	1150.	1750.	—	—
1861	1,884,000	6.50	11.50	16.50	20.00	32.50	525.	2250.
1861 S	172,500	22.50	27.50	47.50	70.00	150.	—	—
1862	847,550	5.50	11.50	16.50	20.00	40.00	525.	2250.
1862 S	180,750	22.50	27.50	42.50	80.00	160.	—	—
1863	14,460	110.	150.	200.	245.	350.	1250.	2250.
1863 S	157,500	22.50	37.50	47.50	80.00	185.	1150.	—
1864	11,470	95.00	140.	190.	225.	325.	1250.	2250.
1864 S	230,000	16.50	22.50	32.50	55.00	150.	1175.	—
1865	10,500	125.	165.	215.	300.	375.	1050.	2250.
1865 S	175,000	16.50	27.50	32.50	65.00	150.	—	—
1866	8,725	135.	190.	245.	350.	425.	1250.	4000.
1866 S	135,000	16.50	27.50	32.50	60.00	160.	1500.	—
1867	6,625	185.	240.	325.	400.	475.	1750.	4000.
1867 S	140,000	16.50	27.50	32.50	60.00	160.	1150.	—
1868	464,600	6.50	11.50	27.50	55.00	135.	675.	2250.
1868 S	260,000	11.50	16.50	27.50	95.00	200.	975.	—
1869	256,600	6.50	11.50	27.50	80.00	150.	750.	2250.
1869 S	450,000	8.50	13.50	20.00	52.50	105.	850.	—
1870	71,500	6.50	11.50	20.00	52.50	110.	450.	2250.
1870 S	50,000	150.	170.	220.	325.	500.	2700.	—
1871	907,710	6.50	10.00	14.00	22.50	40.00	375.	2250.
1871 CC	20,100	325.	425.	800.	1000.	2100.	—	—
1871 S	320,000	16.50	27.50	42.50	80.00	150.	975.	—
1872	2,396,450	6.50	10.00	14.00	22.50	27.50	375.	2250.
1872 CC	35,480	215.	325.	475.	625.	1250.	—	—
1872 S	190,000	27.50	42.50	85.00	135.	225.	1150.	—
1873 Closed 3	1,568,600	8.00	10.00	12.00	20.00	35.00	375.	2250.
1873 Open 3	Inc. Above	27.50	47.50	70.00	110.	160.	—	—
1873 CC	12,400	UNIQUE-ELIASBERG COLLECTION						

VARIETY FIVE - ARROWS AT DATE
1873-1874

DIAMETER—17.9mm
WEIGHT—2.50 Grams
COMPOSITION—.900 Silver, .100 Copper
DESIGNER—Christian Gobrecht
EDGE—Reeded

DATE	MINTAGE	G-4	VG-8	F-12	VF-20	EF-40	MS-60	Prf-65
1873	2,378,500	12.50	20.00	30.00	47.50	125.	500.	9,000.
1873 CC	18,791	525.	750.	1100.	1600.	2750.	14,000.	—
1873 S	455,000	17.50	22.50	35.00	65.00	135.	1600.	—
1874	2,940,700	12.50	20.00	30.00	47.50	125.	500.	9,000.
1874 CC	10,817	950.	1400.	2000.	2600.	4250.	—	—
1874 S	240,000	25.00	37.50	75.00	110.	185.	1600.	—

VARIETY FOUR - RESUMED
1875-1891

DATE	MINTAGE	G-4	VG-8	F-12	VF-20	EF-40	MS-60	Prf-65
1875	10,350,700	3.00	4.00	7.00	10.00	25.00	150.	4750.
1874 CC Above Bow	4,645,000	6.00	7.00	9.00	12.50	30.00	170.	—
1875 CC Below Bow	Inc. Above	6.00	7.00	9.00	12.50	40.00	170.	—
1875 S Above Bow	9,070,000	6.00	7.00	9.00	12.50	30.00	500.	—
1875 S Below Bow	Inc. Above	6.00	7.00	9.00	12.50	25.00	150.	—
1876	11,461,150	3.00	4.00	7.00	10.00	25.00	150.	2250.
1876 CC	8,270,000	3.00	4.00	7.00	15.00	30.00	150.	—
1876 S	10,420,000	3.00	4.00	7.00	10.00	25.00	150.	—
1877	7,310,510	3.00	4.00	7.00	10.00	25.00	150.	2250.
1877 CC	7,700,000	3.00	4.00	7.00	15.00	30.00	150.	—
1877 S	2,340,000	3.00	4.00	7.00	10.00	30.00	160.	—
1878	1,678,800	3.00	4.00	7.00	10.00	35.00	150.	2250.
1878 CC	200,000	50.00	75.00	120.	165.	240.	950.	—
1879	15,100	170.	200.	250.	300.	400.	750.	2250.
1880	37,335	120.	150.	185.	235.	300.	700.	2250.
1881	24,975	140.	170.	200.	250.	350.	700.	2250.
1882	3,911,100	3.00	4.00	7.00	10.00	25.00	150.	2250.
1883	7,675,712	3.00	4.00	7.00	10.00	25.00	150.	2250.
1884	3,366,380	3.00	4.00	7.00	10.00	25.00	150.	2250.
1884 S	564,969	11.50	16.50	22.50	37.50	70.00	475.	—
1885	2,533,427	3.00	4.00	7.00	10.00	25.00	150.	2250.
1885 S	43,690	200.	225.	275.	400.	550.	3150.	—
1886	6,377,570	3.00	4.00	7.00	10.00	25.00	150.	2250.
1886 S	206,524	16.50	22.50	40.00	65.00	95.00	525.	—
1887	11,283,939	3.00	4.00	7.00	10.00	25.00	150.	2250.
1887 S	4,454,450	3.00	4.00	7.00	10.00	25.00	150.	—
1888	5,496,487	3.00	4.00	7.00	10.00	25.00	150.	2250.
1888 S	1,720,000	3.00	4.00	7.00	10.00	25.00	150.	—
1889	7,380,711	3.00	4.00	7.00	10.00	25.00	150.	2250.
1889 S	972,678	11.50	16.50	22.50	27.50	55.00	500.	—
1890	9,911,541	3.00	4.00	7.00	10.00	25.00	150.	2250.
1890 S	1,423,076	10.00	16.50	22.50	27.50	50.00	500.	—
1891	15,310,600	3.00	4.00	7.00	10.00	25.00	150.	2250.
1891 O	4,540,000	3.00	4.00	7.00	10.00	25.00	500.	—
1891 S	3,196,116	3.00	4.00	7.00	10.00	25.00	525.	—

BARBER TYPE
1892-1916

DIAMETER—17.9mm
WEIGHT—2.50 Grams
COMPOSITION—.900 Silver, .100 Copper
DESIGNER—Charles E. Barber
EDGE—Reeded
PURE SILVER CONTENT—.07234 Tr. Oz.

DATE	MINTAGE	G-4	VG-8	F-12	VF-20	EF-40	AU-50	MS-60	MS-65	Prf-65
1892	12,121,245	3.50	4.25	8.00	16.50	37.50	60.00	185.	950.	1800.
1892 O	3,841,700	4.75	9.25	16.50	24.00	42.50	70.00	200.	2600.	—

DATE	MINTAGE	G-4	VG-8	F-12	VF-20	EF-40	AU-50	MS-60	MS-65	Prf-65
1892 S	990,710	32.00	50.00	70.00	95.00	125.	215.	240.	6000.	—
1893	3,340,792	5.00	10.00	18.00	30.00	50.00	85.00	190.	950.	1800.
1893 O	1,760,000	13.50	22.50	35.00	47.50	85.00	125.	200.	4500.	—
1893 S	2,491,401	6.00	10.00	20.00	35.00	55.00	95.00	225.	3700.	—
1894	1,330,972	6.50	12.50	25.00	37.50	70.00	115.	200.	1400.	1800.
1894 O	720,000	27.50	50.00	85.00	120.	235.	550.	900.	9250.	—
1894 S	24				January 1990 Stack's Sale PROOF-65 $275,000.					
1895	690,880	52.50	90.00	115.	175.	250.	350.	500.	2750.	1800.
1895 O	440,000	175.	200.	500.	650.	1100.	1250.	1600.	10,500.	—
1895 S	1,120,000	15.00	25.00	42.50	60.00	95.00	150.	200.	6200.	—
1896	2,000,762	7.75	13.00	27.50	45.00	65.00	100.	195.	2250.	1800.
1896 O	610,000	40.00	67.50	100.	150.	215.	350.	525.	6200.	—
1896 S	575,056	40.00	65.00	95.00	140.	210.	325.	375.	6200.	—
1897	10,869,264	2.50	3.50	12.00	20.00	40.00	65.00	185.	950.	1800.
1897 O	666,000	35.50	62.50	95.00	135.	215.	315.	550.	6750.	—
1897 S	1,342,844	7.75	13.50	27.50	55.00	85.00	125.	225.	7250.	—
1898	16,320,735	2.50	3.00	8.50	15.00	37.50	55.00	185.	950.	1800.
1898 O	2,130,000	4.50	8.50	24.00	40.00	75.00	120.	280.	5850.	—
1898 S	1,702,507	4.00	8.00	15.00	27.00	45.00	67.50	225.	7200.	—
1899	19,580,846	2.50	3.00	7.50	15.00	35.00	52.50	185.	950.	1800.
1899 O	2,650,000	4.25	9.00	22.50	35.00	65.00	100.	275.	5850.	—
1899 S	1,867,493	4.00	8.00	15.00	30.00	50.00	75.00	210.	6500.	—
1900	17,600,912	2.00	3.00	7.50	15.00	35.00	52.50	185.	950.	1800.
1900 O	2,010,000	5.57	9.50	22.50	40.00	72.50	110.	300.	5500.	—
1900 S	5,168,270	2.00	3.50	8.00	15.00	35.00	52.50	195.	2250.	—
1901	18,860,478	2.00	3.50	6.00	12.50	32.50	50.00	185.	1300.	1800.
1901 O	5,620,000	2.00	3.50	7.50	20.00	50.00	100.	275.	3700.	—
1901 S	593,022	42.50	65.00	105.	150.	225.	375.	625.	5600.	—
1902	21,380,777	2.00	2.50	6.00	12.50	30.00	47.50	185.	950.	1800.
1902 O	4,500,000	3.00	4.25	8.00	20.00	42.50	65.00	200.	5200.	—
1902 S	2,070,000	3.50	8.50	20.00	32.50	65.00	100.	235.	4800.	—
1903	19,500,755	2.00	3.00	6.50	15.00	32.50	50.00	185.	950.	1800.
1903 O	8,180,000	2.00	3.50	7.50	20.00	40.00	60.00	200.	7000.	—
1903 S	613,300	35.00	55.00	70.00	115.	210.	325.	525.	5600.	—
1904	14,601,027	2.00	3.00	7.00	15.00	32.50	50.00	185.	4100.	1800.
1904 S	800,000	25.00	47.50	65.00	110.	185.	290.	475.	5500.	—
1905	14,552,350	2.00	3.00	6.00	15.00	32.50	50.00	185.	950.	1800.
1905 O	3,400,000	2.25	5.25	16.50	30.00	60.00	95.00	200.	4300.	—
1905 S	6,855,199	2.00	3.25	9.00	20.00	40.00	60.00	225.	1350.	—
1906	19,958,406	1.75	2.50	5.00	12.50	30.00	45.00	185.	950.	1800.
1906 D	4,060,000	2.15	3.75	9.00	20.00	42.50	65.00	215.	2500.	—
1906 O	2,610,000	3.25	5.75	17.50	30.00	52.50	80.00	225.	1350.	—
1906 S	3,136,640	2.50	3.75	9.00	22.00	42.50	67.50	230.	950.	—
1907	22,220,575	1.75	2.50	5.00	12.50	30.00	45.00	185.	950.	1800.
1907 D	4,080,000	2.15	3.75	9.00	20.00	42.50	65.00	200.	4900.	—
1907 O	5,058,000	2.00	3.00	8.50	20.00	42.50	62.50	190.	2850.	—
1907 S	3,178,470	2.25	4.00	8.50	17.50	37.50	70.00	240.	4400.	—
1908	10,600,545	1.85	3.00	4.25	11.50	30.00	44.00	185.	950.	1800.
1908 D	7,490,000	2.00	3.00	4.25	11.50	30.00	45.00	190.	2400.	—
1908 O	1,789,000	3.75	7.00	13.50	23.50	40.00	72.50	240.	2400.	—
1908 S	3,220,000	2.25	3.25	7.75	17.50	36.50	67.50	230.	2750.	—

DATE	MINTAGE	G-4	VG-8	F-12	VF-20	EF-40	AU-50	MS-60	MS-65	Prf-65
1909	10,240,650	2.00	3.00	4.25	12.00	32.00	46.00	185.	950.	1800.
1909 D	954,000	3.75	6.75	16.00	32.00	57.50	95.00	240.	3200.	—
1909 O	2,287,000	2.25	3.00	7.50	18.50	37.50	67.50	210.	1350.	—
1909 S	1,000,000	4.75	9.50	20.00	37.50	62.50	120.	260.	4900.	—
1910	11,520,551	2.00	2.50	3.25	11.00	30.00	45.00	185.	950.	1800.
1910 D	3,490,000	2.25	3.00	5.75	13.00	33.50	67.50	240.	3000.	—
1910 S	1,240,000	3.25	5.00	9.00	18.50	38.50	64.00	215.	2400.	—
1911	18,870,543	1.75	2.25	2.75	9.00	29.00	43.50	185.	950.	1800.
1911 D	11,209,000	1.85	2.25	2.75	9.50	30.00	44.50	185.	950.	—
1911 S	3,520,000	2.25	3.00	4.75	15.00	37.50	65.00	215.	1500.	—
1912	19,350,000	1.75	2.25	3.00	9.00	29.00	43.50	185.	950.	1800.
1912 D	11,760,000	1.75	2.25	3.00	9.00	29.00	43.50	185.	950.	—
1912 S	3,420,000	2.00	2.50	4.00	14.00	35.00	57.50	215.	1300.	—
1913	19,760,622	1.75	2.25	3.00	9.00	29.00	43.50	185.	950.	1800.
1913 S	510,000	7.75	15.00	32.50	65.00	145.	240.	275.	1300.	—
1914	17,360,655	1.75	2.25	3.00	9.00	29.00	43.50	185.	950.	2700.
1914 D	11,908,000	1.75	2.25	3.00	9.00	29.00	43.50	185.	950.	—
1914 S	2,100,000	2.25	3.00	4.25	13.00	35.00	57.50	215.	950.	—
1915	5,620,450	2.00	2.25	4.25	10.50	33.00	52.50	240.	950.	3200.
1915 S	960,000	3.00	4.25	9.50	18.50	41.00	80.00	235.	4200.	—
1916	18,490,000	1.75	2.25	3.00	9.50	29.00	43.50	185.	950.	—
1916 S	5,820,000	1.85	2.25	3.75	12.00	33.00	48.50	190.	950.	—

MERCURY TYPE
1916-1945

DIAMETER—17.9mm
WEIGHT—2.50 Grams
COMPOSITION—.900 Silver, .100 Copper
DESIGNER—Adolph A. Weinman
EDGE—Reeded
PURE SILVER CONTENT—.07234 Tr. Oz.

DATE	MINTAGE	G-4	VG-8	F-12	VF-20	EF-40	MS-60	MS-65	FSB-65	Prf-65
1916	22,180,080	2.00	3.25	4.25	5.25	8.50	32.50	90.00	180.	—
1916 D	264,000	400.	600.	950.	1600.	2500.	3600.	11,000.	13,000.	—
1916 S	10,450,000	2.50	3.00	5.25	7.50	12.50	47.50	160.	320.	—
1917	55,230,000	—	1.75	3.25	4.25	6.50	45.00	140.	260.	—
1917 D	9,402,000	2.25	2.50	8.00	13.00	32.00	100.	825.	4600.	—
1917 S	27,330,000	1.75	2.00	3.25	5.25	8.50	55.00	900.	1850.	—
1918	26,680,000	2.00	2.50	4.00	8.50	21.00	65.00	475.	700.	—
1918 D	22,674,800	2.00	2.50	4.25	8.50	19.00	80.00	1100.	11,000.	—
1918 S	19,300,000	1.75	2.00	3.25	5.75	12.00	42.50	1250.	3900.	—
1919	35,470,000	1.75	2.00	3.25	4.75	8.00	40.00	375.	425.	—
1919 D	9,939,000	2.50	3.25	6.25	16.00	32.50	150.	1850.	4600.	—
1919 S	8,850,000	2.50	2.75	6.25	16.00	31.00	150.	1950.	3900.	—
1920	59,030,000	1.75	2.00	2.50	4.25	5.50	30.00	300.	385.	—
1920 D	19,171,000	1.75	2.00	2.50	6.25	14.00	80.00	1850.	2600.	—
1920 S	13,820,000	1.75	2.00	2.50	6.25	13.00	70.00	1150.	3850.	—
1921	1,230,000	20.00	30.00	67.50	125.	400.	750.	2750.	4100.	—
1921 D	1,080,000	30.00	45.00	95.00	180.	375.	750.	3000.	4500.	—

DATE	MINTAGE	G-4	VG-8	F-12	VF-20	EF-40	MS-60	MS-65	FSB-65	Prf-65
1923	50,130,000	1.75	2.00	2.50	3.75	5.25	20.00	250.	320.	—
1923 S	6,440,000	2.00	2.50	4.00	6.75	26.50	85.00	1850.	2750.	—
1924	24,010,000	1.75	2.00	2.50	3.75	7.50	52.00	360.	450.	—
1924 D	6,810,000	1.75	2.00	4.00	6.25	20.00	85.00	1250.	2600.	—
1924 S	7,120,000	1.75	2.00	3.25	6.25	17.50	85.00	2700.	5300.	—
1925	25,610,000	—	1.75	2.00	3.25	5.75	36.00	235.	425.	—
1925 D	5,117,000	3.50	4.75	8.00	26.50	75.00	235.	1650.	4400.	—
1925 S	5,850,000	1.75	2.00	2.50	6.25	16.00	110.	2250.	2900.	—
1926	32,160,000	—	1.75	2.00	3.25	4.75	18.00	275.	525.	—
1926 D	6,828,000	1.75	2.00	3.25	5.25	16.50	65.00	625.	1800.	—
1926 S	1,520,000	6.75	9.00	12.00	35.00	70.00	440.	3500.	5000.	—
1927	28,080,000	—	1.75	2.00	2.50	4.25	18.00	235.	300.	—
1927 D	4,812,000	2.00	2.50	5.25	13.00	31.00	160.	1250.	4200.	—
1927 S	4,770,000	1.75	2.00	2.75	5.25	16.00	90.00	1300.	2400.	—
1928	19,480,000	—	1.75	2.00	2.50	4.25	22.00	225.	275.	—
1928 D	4,161,000	1.75	2.00	4.25	13.00	32.00	120.	925.	1500.	—
1928 S	7,400,000	1.75	2.00	2.50	4.75	11.00	47.50	700.	1600.	—
1929	25,970,000	—	1.75	2.00	2.50	3.50	20.00	65.00	125.	—
1929 D	5,034,000	1.75	2.00	3.00	5.25	8.00	45.00	80.00	120.	—
1929 S	4,730,000	1.75	2.00	2.50	3.50	4.25	42.00	120.	360.	—
1930	6,770,000	1.75	2.00	2.50	3.25	4.75	20.00	120.	275.	—
1930 S	1,843,000	1.75	2.50	4.25	5.75	11.50	70.00	285.	340.	—
1931	3,150,000	—	1.75	2.25	3.25	8.50	40.00	140.	300.	—
1931 D	1,260,000	7.50	8.50	10.00	16.00	26.00	105.	260.	340.	—
1931 S	1,800,000	2.25	2.50	4.75	5.50	10.00	75.00	270.	600.	—
1934	24,080,000	—	—	—	1.75	19.00	22.00	35.00	75.00	—
1934 D	6,772,000	—	—	—	1.75	5.25	32.50	65.00	450.	—
1935	58,830,000	—	—	—	1.75	2.50	12.00	30.00	60.00	—
1935 D	10,477,000	—	—	1.75	2.25	7.50	42.00	55.00	500.	—
1935 S	15,840,000	—	—	—	1.75	2.50	25.00	45.00	220.	—
1936	87,504,130	—	—	—	1.75	2.50	13.00	25.00	65.00	1000.
1936 D	16,132,000	—	—	—	1.75	4.25	28.00	45.00	140.	—
1936 S	9,210,000	—	—	—	1.75	2.50	20.00	35.00	55.00	—
1937	56,865,756	—	—	—	1.75	2.50	13.00	25.00	45.00	400.
1937 D	14,146,000	—	—	—	1.75	2.50	25.00	45.00	120.	—
1937 S	9,740,000	—	—	—	1.75	2.50	18.50	45.00	120.	—
1938	22,198,728	—	—	—	1.75	2.50	12.50	30.00	50.00	300.
1938 D	5,537,000	—	—	—	1.75	2.50	25.00	30.00	50.00	—
1938 S	8,090,000	—	—	—	1.75	5.25	16.00	35.00	95.00	—
1939	67,749,321	—	—	—	1.75	2.50	12.00	25.00	85.00	280.
1939 D	29,394,000	—	—	—	1.75	2.50	12.00	25.00	50.00	—
1939 S	10,540,000	—	—	—	1.75	2.50	17.00	55.00	525.	—
1940	65,361,827	—	—	—	1.75	2.50	9.00	25.00	45.00	240.
1940 D	21,198,000	—	—	—	1.75	2.50	14.00	25.00	45.00	—
1940 S	21,560,000	—	—	—	1.75	2.50	9.00	25.00	50.00	—
1941	175,106,557	—	—	—	1.75	2.50	9.00	25.00	45.00	220.
1941 D	45,634,000	—	—	—	1.75	2.50	12.00	25.00	45.00	—
1941 S	43,090,000	—	—	—	1.75	2.50	13.00	30.00	45.00	—
1942/41	Unknown	200.	220.	240.	260.	320.	975.	6000.	9000.	—
1942	205,432,329	—	—	—	—	1.75	9.00	25.00	45.00	220.
1942 D	60,740,000	—	—	—	—	1.75	11.00	25.00	65.00	—

DATE	MINTAGE	G-4	VG-8	F-12	VF-20	EF-40	MS-60	MS-65	FSB-65	Prf-65
1942/41 D......................Unknown		210.	230.	250.	275.	350.	1150.	4500.	6500.	—
1942 S......................49,300,000		—	—	—	—	1.75	23.00	30.00	65.00	—
1943......................191,710,000		—	—	—	—	1.75	9.00	25.00	45.00	—
1943 D 71,949,000		—	—	—	—	1.75	9.00	30.00	45.00	—
1943 S......................60,400,000		—	—	—	—	1.75	12.00	28.00	50.00	—
1944......................231,410,000		—	—	—	—	1.75	9.00	25.00	75.00	—
1944 D 62,224,000		—	—	—	—	1.75	12.00	24.00	45.00	—
1944 S......................49,490,000		—	—	—	—	1.75	12.00	28.00	45.00	—
1945......................159,130,000		—	—	—	—	1.75	9.00	25.00	3200.	—
1945 D 40,245,000		—	—	—	—	1.75	12.00	25.00	45.00	—
1945 S......................41,920,000		—	—	—	—	1.75	12.00	28.00	110.	—
1945 S Micro S......Inc. Above		—	—	—	—	2.25	16.00	65.00	450.	—

NOTE: The listing of FSB-65 denotes a MS-65 specimen that is fully struck with fully split horizontal bands on the fasces.

ROOSEVELT TYPE
1946 TO DATE

DIAMETER—17.9mm
WEIGHT—1946-1964 2.50 Grams
  1965 To Date 2.27 Grams
COMPOSITION —1946-1964
  .900 Silver
  .100 Copper
1965 To Date Copper Clad Issue
  .750 Copper
  ..250 Nickel Outer Layers
Pure Copper Inner Core
DESIGNER—John R. Sinnock
EDGE—Reeded
PURE SILVER CONTENT -
  1946-1964 .07234 Tr. Oz.

DATE	MINTAGE	EF-40	AU-50	MS-60	MS-65	Prf-65
1946...................225,250,000		—	1.25	1.75	2.75	—
1946D..................61,043,500		—	1.25	3.25	4.75	—
1946S..................27,900,000		—	1.25	4.50	5.50	—
1947...................121,520,000		—	1.25	4.00	5.00	—
1947 D..................46,835,000		—	1.25	8.00	10.00	—
1947 S..................34,840,000		—	1.25	4.50	5.50	—
1948...................74,950,000		—	1.25	4.00	6.00	—
1948 D..................52,841,000		1.75	2.00	7.50	10.00	—
1948 S..................35,520,000		—	1.25	7.00	9.50	—
1949...................30,940,000		4.00	7.25	22.00	30.00	—
1949 D..................26,034,000		1.50	2.25	10.00	13.00	—
1949 S..................13,510,000		5.25	7.75	47.50	55.00	—
1950...................50,181,500		—	1.15	3.75	4.75	30.00
1950 D..................46,803,000		—	1.15	4.00	4.75	—
1950 S..................20,440,000		—	4.00	20.00	35.00	—
1951...................102,937,602		—	.90	2.25	3.50	26.00
1951 D..................56,529,000		—	.90	2.00	3.50	—
1951 S..................31,630,000		—	2.75	14.00	25.00	—
1952...................99,122,073		—	.90	2.50	3.50	27.50
1952 D..................122,100,000		—	.90	3.00	4.00	—
1952 S..................44,419,500		—	1.25	5.50	7.00	—
1953...................53,618,920		—	.90	2.50	3.75	26.00
1953 D..................136,433,000		—	.90	2.00	3.50	—
1953 S..................39,180,000		—	.90	1.50	2.25	—
1954...................114,243,503		—	.90	1.35	2.25	10.00
1954 D..................106,397,000		—	.90	1.50	2.25	—
1954 S..................22,860,000		—	1.50	1.65	2.25	—
1955...................12,828,381		—	1.15	2.00	2.75	9.00
1955 D..................13,959,000		—	1.25	1.75	2.50	—
1955 S..................18,510,000		—	1.15	1.50	2.50	—
1956...................109,309,384		—	.90	1.40	2.00	3.00
1956 D..................108,015,100		—	.90	1.25	2.00	—
1957...................101,407,952		—	.90	1.25	1.50	2.50
1957 D..................113,354,330		—	.90	1.25	1.50	—
1958...................32,785,652		—	.90	1.50	1.75	3.00
1958 D..................136,564,600		—	.90	1.25	1.75	—
1959...................86,929,291		—	.90	1.25	1.50	2.00

DATE	MINTAGE	EF-40	AU-50	MS-60	MS-65	Prf-65
1959 D	164,919,790	—	.90	1.15	1.50	—
1960	72,081,602	—	.90	1.00	1.25	2.00
1960 D	200,160,400	—	—	1.00	1.25	—
1961	96,758,244	—	—	1.00	1.25	2.00
1961 D	209,146,550	—	—	1.00	1.25	—
1962	75,668,019	—	—	1.00	1.25	2.00
1962 D	334,948,380	—	—	1.00	1.25	—
1963	126,725,645	—	—	1.00	1.25	2.00
1963 D	421,476,530	—	—	1.00	1.25	—
1964	933,310,762	—	—	1.00	1.25	2.00
1964 D	1,357,517,180	—	—	1.00	1.25	—

COPPER-NICKEL CLAD COINAGE

DATE	MINTAGE	MS-60	MS-65	Prf-65
1965	1,652,140,570	—	.20	—
1966	1,382,734,540	—	.20	—
1967	2,244,007,320	—	.20	—
1968	424,470,000	—	.20	—
1968 D	480,748,280	—	.20	—
1968 S	PROOF ONLY	—	—	.75
1969	145,790,000	—	.20	—
1969 D	563,323,870	—	.20	—
1969 S	PROOF ONLY	—	—	.75
1970	345,570,000	—	.20	—
1970 D	754,942,100	—	.20	—
1970 S	PROOF ONLY	—	—	.60
1971	162,690,000	—	.20	—
1971 D	377,914,240	—	.20	—
1971 S	PROOF ONLY	—	—	.60
1972	431,540,000	—	.20	—
1972 D	330,290,000	—	.20	—
1972 S	PROOF ONLY	—	—	.70
1973	315,670,000	—	.20	—
1973 D	455,032,426	—	.20	—
1973 S	PROOF ONLY	—	—	.50
1974	470,248,000	—	.20	—
1974 D	571,083,000	—	.20	—
1974 S	PROOF ONLY	—	—	.60
1975	585,673,900	—	.20	—
1975 D	313,705,300	—	.20	—
1975 S	PROOF ONLY	—	—	.60
1976	568,760,000	—	.20	—
1976 D	695,222,774	—	.20	—
1976 S	PROOF ONLY	—	—	.40
1977	796,930,000	—	.20	—
1977 D	376,607,228	—	.20	—
1977 S	PROOF ONLY	—	—	.40
1978	663,980,000	—	.20	—
1978 D	282,847,540	—	.20	—
1978 S	PROOF ONLY	—	—	.60

DATE	MINTAGE	MS-60	MS-65	Prf-65
1979	315,440,000	—	.20	—
1979 D	390,921,184	—	.20	—
1979 S	PROOF ONLY	—	—	.70
1980 P	735,170,000	—	.20	—
1980 D	719,354,321	—	.20	—
1980 S	PROOF ONLY	—	—	.50
1981 P	676,650,000	—	.20	—
1981 D	712,284,143	—	.20	—
1981 S	PROOF ONLY	—	—	.60
1982 P	519,475,000	—	.20	—
1982 D	542,713,584	—	.20	—
1982 S	PROOF ONLY	—	—	.70
1983 P	647,025,000	—	.20	—
1983 D	730,129,224	—	.20	—
1983 S	PROOF ONLY	—	—	1.25
1984 P	856,669,000	—	.20	—
1984 D	704,803,976	—	.20	—
1984 S	PROOF ONLY	—	—	1.00
1985 P	705,200,962	—	.20	—
1985 D	587,979,970	—	.20	—
1985 S	PROOF ONLY	—	—	1.10
1986 P	682,649,693	—	.20	—
1986 D	473,326,970	—	.20	—
1986 S	PROOF ONLY	—	—	1.10
1987 P	762,709,481	—	.20	—
1987 D	653,203,402	—	.20	—
1987 S	PROOF ONLY	—	—	1.10
1988 P	1,030,550,000	—	.20	—
1988 D	962,385,489	—	.20	—
1988 S	PROOF ONLY	—	—	1.10
1989 P	1,298,400,000	—	.20	—
1989 D	896,535,597	—	.20	—
1989 S	PROOF ONLY	—	—	1.10
1990 P	1,034,340,000	—	.20	—
1990 D	839,995,824	—	.20	—
1990 S	PROOF ONLY	—	—	1.10
1991 P	927,220,000	—	.20	—
1991 D	601,241,114	—	.20	—
1991 S	PROOF ONLY	—	—	1.10
1992 P	—	—	.20	—
1992 D	—	—	.20	—
1992 S	PROOF ONLY	—	—	1.10
1993 P	—	—	.20	—
1993 D	—	—	.20	—
1993 S	PROOF ONLY	—	—	1.10

Twenty Cent Pieces

The twenty cent coin is the shortest-lived denomination of all United States coins, being minted for circulation in 1875 and 1876. In 1877 and 1878 production was limited only to Proofs. The series died a premature death because the American people complained it resembled too closely the quarter dollar.

Investors should choose coins grading Extremely Fine to MS-65. These coins have displayed consistent value growth for much of the past three decades, but at the moment, prices are only at about 70% of what they were just a few years ago. 1993 would be a most advantageous time to add one of these oddities to your collection.

TWENTY CENT PIECES
1875-1878

DIAMETER—22mm
WEIGHT—5 Grams
COMPOSITION—.900 Silver
.100 Copper
DESIGNER— William Barber
EDGE—Plain

DATE	MINTAGE	G-4	VG-8	F-12	VF-20	EF-40	AU-50	MS-60	MS-65	Prf-65
1875	39,700	50.00	62.50	100.	160.	275.	450.	1300.	9000.	12,000.
1875 S	1,155,000	32.00	45.00	55.00	85.00	160.	400.	700.	8500.	—
1875 CC	133,290	50.00	62.50	100.	160.	285.	550.	1500.	10,000.	—
1876	15,900	95.00	130.	180.	235.	375.	600.	1550.	10,000.	12,000.
1876 CC	10,000				VERY RARE				85,000.	—
1877	510					PROOF ONLY				25,000.
1878	600					PROOF ONLY				25,000.

Quarter Dollars 1796 To Date

The quarter dollar has been a part of our coinage system intermittently since 1796. All told, there are thirteen types of quarters to collect. The first type is a one-year only design, the 1796 Draped Bust with small eagle. Like so many other American coins of the 18th century, the 1796 quarter has done extremely well as an investment. Should you happen to be an investor geared toward long term growth who has a minimum of nearly $3500 to spend, this issue may be tailored for you. Since the 1796 quarter in lower grades has been red-hot for almost fifteen years, we have witnessed a cooling-off period in the 1990's similar to that of the late 1960's. However, any owner of a 1796 quarter can expect it to resume its upward climb in the not so far distant future.

The Draped Bust quarters with the heraldic (large) eagle of 1804 to 1807 have seen some serious price corrections across the board since the middle 1980's. Judging from value trends of the past, one can anticipate a steep rise within the next several years. There will probably never be a better time than 1993 to purchase these early American quarters.

The Liberty Capped series presents more opportunities for the shorter term investor. Minted from 1815 to 1838, this group of quarters has, for the most part, not participated in any price explosions as of late and should be a good place to put some of your investment dollars. As a matter of fact, a fair portion of the Liberty Capped quarters grading MS-60 have slipped by about 40% from their 1983 highs.

What these coins are worth today will pale in comparison to what we'll see in the next few years. If you think purchase of this sort fits in with your plans, give some special consideration to the 1822 quarter dollar. Even though it has one of the tiniest mintages of all the Liberty Capped quarters, it is and always has been priced in the same neighborhood as its contemporaries.

The long-running Liberty Seated pattern was in use from 1838 to 1891. There are so many opportunities in that span for investors to capitalize upon that space allows discussion of only a small percentage of the best prospects. Here again we find a steep fall off from prices realized in the 1980's. Today's prices for high grade material would suggest that these are little more than common stuff, but this is not the case. The present situation is merely a temporary abberation certain to correct itself in the not so distant future.

Most of the Liberty Seated quarters in MS-60 Uncirculated are so badly undervalued that they almost cry out for proper consideration, especially the Philadelphia minted quarters of the 1880's. Not only have they dipped in value since 1980, they are also priced in the ballpark with other Liberty Seated quarters of the identical type in MS-60 Uncirculated condition having an original mintage up to 1400 times greater. If that's not enough to grab your attention, take a peek at their appreciation records. At times in the past, quarters of the 1880's were worth much more than what the more common quarters of the 1870's sold for. In short, this equal treatment of these very rare quarters probably will not continue much longer. If you have the finances, check out some of the Liberty Seated quarters in MS-63. Price levels would indicate they too are positioned for an upsurge.

Barber quarters were coined between the years 1892 to 1916 inclusive. The items that appear most attractive in the Barber quarter series appear to be in the Extremely Fine to MS-63 Uncirculated grade range, especially those that collectors have the most difficulty acquiring in order to complete their collections. These coins have not taken part in any major bull market for years now, and have reached the point where they are far scarcer in relation to MS-65 specimens than their values would indicate. Respected authors have concluded that the Barber series of dimes, quarters and halves grading Extremely Fine to MS-63 Uncirculated should be one of the next big booms in the coin world. Publications such as these, although well-founded and factual, may actually help to perpetuate the price explosion, becoming a self-fulfilling prophecy.

You will find encouraging possibilities in key date Barber quarters, even in lower grades. These dates can be identified as the 1896-S, the 1901-S, and the 1913-S. These issues have experienced sluggish performances recently, but now there is every reason to expect a resumption of consistent growth from here, just as was exhibited throughout much of the last 40 years.

The 1914-S is starting to come alive, but it's not too late to cash in on its up-and-coming status. This issue has the fourth lowest coinage of the Barber quarter series, with only 264,000 pieces released from the San Francisco mint. Nevertheless, it is valued at only $80 in Very Good and $110 in Fine, which is a severe underestimation for a coin of this rarity. The 1914-S will probably appreciate steadily in the years to come, eventually assuming a position more appropriate in relation to the key dates in the series. According to dealers who specialize in Barbers, collector interest in their area of expertise seems to be growing. If so, then look for this rise to come faster and be stronger.

In 1916, when the Barber quarter entered into permanent retirement, the stylish Standing Liberty quarter made its debut. There were several modifications made in the following year because of public outrage to Miss Liberty's unclothed top on the premiere design. There were also three stars added below the eagle on the reverse. And so, there are two varieties of the Standing Liberty quarter to be had: Variety I being the "obscene" design of 1916-1917, and Variety II, with clothing and extra stars, from 1917 to the termination of the series in 1930.

One of two key coins in the series without question is the 1916 issue. Having a mintage of only 52,000, this coin is the most difficult link in completing the set, which has long been a favorite with collectors. Numismatic popularity explains why the 1916 Standing Liberty quarter has been such a consistent winner over time with only a few minor reversals. Prices will likely never be lower than they are at the present time, but with bargain prices starting at "only" $950 in Good condition, this investment is certainly not within reach of most buyers.

The other important date is the 1918/7-S overstrike. Even in the lowest grades, a quarter of this description has always commanded respect. In better grades, prices absolutely go through the roof. Obtain the highest affordable quality, and look for collector interest to keep pushing the value of your coin up, up, and away!

There are many excellent buys among the MS-60 to MS-65 Uncirculated pieces. In most cases MS-65 Uncirculated Standing Liberty quarters are selling 50% below 1990 prices, but possess tremendous potential for appreciation.

You should be aware of the "Full Head" evaluation for strike quality. Analogous to the

Full Split Bands in the Mercury dime, a Standing Liberty quarter with a fully detailed head is very elusive and commands much higher prices than more normal quarters with weaker strikes. Quarters bearing this quality are denoted by the abbreviation FH immediately following the grade. Naturally, most quarters of the caliber are described in Uncirculated condition, although occasionally a few Standing Liberty quarters in Almost Uncirculated are advertised as having Full Head detail.

One low cost coin in the Standing Liberty quarter series possessing some potential is the 1917 Variety I issues. If you'll remember, Variety I was in production for only two years, and since the 1916 is so rare, the 1917 quarters are really the only Variety I example readily available. For type set collectors, a specimen of a Variety I Standing Liberty quarter is essential, meaning there will likely be more pressure to bear on this coin in the future. Acquire this coin in grades Fine to MS-65 Uncirculated, according to your means. At the moment, this coin is being offered at prices lower than ten years ago.

The familiar Washington quarter has been in circulation since 1932. Originally intended to be a one year commemorative issue to mark the 200th anniversary of the birth of our first president, the Washington quarter is somewhat popular with modern day collectors, and undoubtedly will be in far greater demand in the future.

The only true rare dates in the series are the 1932-D and 1932-S. In lower grades, don't expect any big gains within the next few years. However, prices will likely multiply in the years ahead when Washington quarters become really "hot" numismatic items. Prices have been stagnant for over twenty years now, so they're already at basement levels.

Generally, buy Washington quarters in MS-63, and whenever possible in MS-65. Specimens from the 1930's and 1940's grading MS-65 have doubled in value over the last few years, but they probably haven't even begun to reach their full potential, especially the pre-1940 Washingtons. Pieces dated beyond 1950 have such a small valuation difference between the two uncirculated classifications, it's really foolish not to opt for the MS-65. While selecting quarters of this description, be sure to include the 1955-D. It's one of the rarest Washingtons, but presently is not priced accordingly. Set aside some high quality proof specimens too. If your motive is profit, self discipline here is important. Settle only for the finest examples of Washington quarters. As with the Roosevelt dimes, don't anticipate great things to happen in the next few years. However, you can rest assured that someday you'll be very pleased for adding these coins to your collection at today's prices.

On many Washington quarters, the reverse design and the rim have a tendency to be weakly struck. The most frequently affected dates are the 1934-D, 1935-D, 1935-S, 1936-D, 1936-S, 1937-D, 1937-S, 1939-D, and 1940-D. Always keep in mind poor strikes are not restricted to these dates only. Professional coin analysts report that this situation is every bit as pronounced in Washington quarters as are the Full Split Bands in Mercury dimes or Full Head in Standing Liberty quarters, although it is less studied at present. Knowing this may provide you with an additional advantage when you select Washington quarters, as any future increase in collector and/or investor activity is likely to bring strike quality to the forefront. Just as with the previously mentioned denominations, there will probably be significant premiums attached to such coins.

QUARTER DOLLARS
1796 TO DATE

DRAPED BUST TYPE
SMALL EAGLE REVERSE
1796

DIAMETER—27.5mm
WEIGHT—6.74 Grams
COMPOSITION—.8924 Silver,
 .1076 Copper
DESIGNER—Robert Scot
EDGE—Reeded

DATE	MINTAGE	G-4	VG-8	F-12	VF-20	EF-40	AU-50	MS-60	MS-65
1796	6,146	4200.	5500.	7400.	14,000.	19,000.	24,000.	30,000.	120,000.

DRAPED BUST TYPE
HERALDIC EAGLE REVERSE
1804-1807

DIAMETER—27.5mm
WEIGHT—6.74 Grams
COMPOSITION—.8924 Silver,
.1076 Copper
DESIGNER—Robert Scot
EDGE—Reeded

DATE	MINTAGE	G-4	VG-8	F-12	VF-20	EF-40	AU-50	MS-60	MS-65
1804	6,738	1000.	1600.	2600.	4200.	7000.	17,000.	24,500.	115,000.
1805	121,394	250.	300.	550.	1100.	2000.	3500.	4750.	60,000.
1806	206,124	250.	300.	550.	1100.	2000.	3500.	4750.	60,000.
1806/5	Inc. Above	275.	350.	600.	1200.	2200.	3500.	4750.	60,000.
1807	220,643	275.	350.	600.	1200.	2000.	4250.	6000.	60,000.

CAPPED BUST TYPE
1815-1838

VARIETY ONE -
LARGE SIZE 1815-1838

DIAMETER—27mm
WEIGHT—6.74 Grams
COMPOSITION—.8924 Silver,
.1076 Copper
DESIGNER—John Reich
EDGE—Reeded

DATE	MINTAGE	G-4	VG-8	F-12	VF-20	EF-40	AU-50	MS-60	MS-65
1815	89,235	65.00	80.00	110.	325.	650.	2100.	3100.	22,500.
1818	361,174	40.00	50.00	110.	325.	650.	1350.	1650.	20,000.
1818/15	Inc. Above	75.00	90.00	110.	325.	650.	2100.	3100.	22,500.
1819 Small 9	144,000	40.00	50.00	110.	275.	550.	1300.	1650.	20,000.
1819 Large 9	Inc. Above	40.00	50.00	110.	275.	550.	1300.	1650.	20,000.
1820 Small 0	127,444	40.00	50.00	110.	200.	550.	1500.	3000.	20,000.
1820 Large 0	Inc. Above	40.00	50.00	110.	200.	550.	1300.	1650.	20,000.
1821	216,851	40.00	50.00	110.	225.	550.	1300.	1650.	20,000.
1822	64,080	80.00	100.00	140.	350.	750.	1300.	1650.	20,000.
1822 25/50 C	Inc. Above	625.	875.	1300.	2800.	4500.	7500.	15,000.	25,000.
1823/22	17,800	2400.	6250.	9000.	12,000.	17,000.	—	PROOF	85,000.
1824/2	168,000	70.00	85.00	110.	200.	550.	1300.	1650.	20,000.
1825/22	Inc. Above	65.00	80.00	110.	275.	600.	1300.	1650.	20,000.
1825/23	Inc. Above	40.00	50.00	110.	275.	600.	1300.	1650.	20,000.
1825/24	Inc. Above	40.00	50.00	110.	275.	600.	1300.	1650.	20,000.
1827 Original	4,000			March 1980, Garrett Sale PROOF-65 $190,000.					
1827 Restrike	Inc. Above							PROOF	40,000.
1828	102,000	40.00	50.00	110.	425.	550.	1300.	1650.	20,000.
1828 25/50 C	Inc. Above	75.00	135.	225.	475.	600.	2100.	3200.	—

VARIETY TWO - REDUCED SIZE,
NO MOTTO ON REVERSE 1831-1838

DIAMETER—24.3mm
WEIGHT—6.74 Grams
COMPOSITION—.8924 Silver,
.1076 Copper
DESIGNER—William Kneass
EDGE—Reeded

DATE	MINTAGE	G-4	VG-8	F-12	VF-20	EF-40	AU-50	MS-60	MS-65
1831 Sm. Letters	398,000	25.00	35.00	50.00	125.	275.	750.	900.	18,000.
1831 Lg. Letters	Inc. Above	25.00	35.00	50.00	125.	275.	750.	900.	18,000.
1832	320,000	30.00	40.00	50.00	125.	275.	750.	900.	18,000.
1833	156,000	45.00	55.00	55.00	160.	300.	750.	900.	18,000.
1834	286,000	37.50	42.50	50.00	125.	275.	750.	900.	18,000.
1835	1,952,000	25.00	35.00	50.00	125.	275.	750.	900.	18,000.
1836	472,000	25.00	35.00	50.00	125.	275.	750.	900.	18,000.
1837	252,400	30.00	37.50	50.00	125.	275.	750.	900.	18,000.
1838	832,000	25.00	35.00	50.00	125.	275.	750.	900.	18,000.

LIBERTY SEATED TYPE
1838-1891

VARIETY ONE - NO MOTTO ABOVE EAGLE 1838-1853

DIAMETER—24.3mm
WEIGHT—6.68 Grams
COMPOSITION—.900 Silver,
.100 Copper
DESIGNER—Christian Gobrecht
EDGE—Reeded

DATE	MINTAGE	G-4	VG-8	F-12	VF-20	EF-40	MS-60
1838 No Drapery	Inc. Above	16.50	22.50	27.50	45.00	200.	1900.
1839 No Drapery	491,146	16.50	22.50	27.50	45.00	150.	1900.
1840 O No Drapery	425,200	16.50	22.50	27.50	45.00	150.	1900.
1840	188,127	30.00	45.00	80.00	170.	325.	2600.
1840 O	Inc. Above	30.00	45.00	80.00	125.	215.	1700.
1841	120,000	70.00	45.00	140.	185.	375.	1100.
1841 O	452,000	27.50	52.50	80.00	110.	215.	1000.
1842 Sm. Date	88,000				PROOF ONLY		35,000.
1842 Lg. Date	Inc. Above	100.	145.	200.	265.	375.	2650.
1842 O Sm. Date	769,000	425.	525.	750.	1100.	2100.	—
1842 O Lg. Date	Inc. Above	27.50	37.50	55.00	80.00	150.	—
1843	645,600	10.00	12.00	15.00	35.00	85.00	325.
1843 O	968,000	22.50	45.00	75.00	100.	185.	—
1844	421,200	10.00	12.00	15.00	35.00	115.	325.
1844 O	740,000	10.00	12.00	15.00	35.00	100.	1150.
1845	922,000	10.00	12.00	15.00	35.00	100.	325.
1846	510,000	10.00	12.00	15.00	35.00	95.00	325.
1847	734,000	10.00	12.00	15.00	35.00	95.00	375.
1847 O	368,000	32.50	52.50	80.00	165.	275.	750.
1848	146,000	45.00	75.00	125.	185.	350.	750.
1849	340,000	25.00	40.00	60.00	100.	165.	625.
1849 O	Inc. w/1850 O	450.	625.	950.	2100.	3850.	—
1850	190,800	37.50	55.00	85.00	100.	185.	975.
1850 O	412,000	27.50	55.00	80.00	110.	185.	1050.
1851	160,000	45.00	70.00	95.00	125.	235.	975.
1851 O	88,000	185.	240.	375.	575.	1250.	—
1852	177,060	45.00	70.00	95.00	125.	235.	900.
1852 O	96,000	240.	375.	475.	675.	1150.	—
1853 Recut Date	44,200	185.	300.	375.	500.	675.	4250.

VARIETY TWO - ARROWS AT DATE
RAYS AROUND EAGLE 1853

DIAMETER—24.3mm
WEIGHT—6.22 Grams
COMPOSITION—.900 Silver
 .100 Copper
DESIGNER—Christian Gobrecht
EDGE—Reeded

DATE	MINTAGE	G-4	VG-8	F-12	VF-20	EF-40	MS-60
1853	15,210,020	11.00	14.00	17.50	37.50	130.	1000.
1853/4	Inc. Above	55.00	110.	160.	375.	550.	2000.
1853 O	1,332,000	20.00	32.50	45.00	80.00	200.	3000.

VARIETY THREE - ARROWS AT DATE, NO RAYS 1854-1855

DATE	MINTAGE	G-4	VG-8	F-12	VF-20	EF-40	MS-60	Prf-65
1854	12,380,000	9.00	11.00	14.00	27.50	110.	450.	16,000.
1854 O	1,484,000	15.00	25.00	37.50	55.00	125.	2600.	—
1854 O Huge O	Inc. Above	160.	265.	375.	750.	1250.	—	—
1855	2,857,000	9.00	11.00	14.00	30.00	110.	450.	16,000.
1855 O	176,000	42.50	57.50	85.00	160.	375.	1900.	—
1855 S	396,400	30.00	45.00	75.00	130.	325.	1800.	—

VARIETY ONE RESUMED 1856-1866

DATE	MINTAGE	G-4	VG-8	F-12	VF-20	EF-40	MS-60	Prf-65
1856	7,264,000	9.00	11.00	14.00	22.50	55.00	375.	16,000.
1856 O	968,000	22.50	32.50	47.50	7.00	150.	850.	—
1856 S	286,000	37.50	57.50	80.00	165.	275.	—	—
1856 S/S	Inc. Above	110.	160.	425.	750.	1600.	—	—
1857	9,644,000	9.00	11.00	14.00	22.50	55.00	375.	16,000.
1857 O	1,180,000	9.00	11.00	14.00	22.50	60.00	925.	—
1857 S	82,000	52.50	80.00	180.	275.	475.	—	—
1858	7,368,000	9.00	11.00	14.00	22.50	55.00	375.	12,500.
1858 O	520,000	22.50	32.50	47.50	70.00	150.	900.	—
1858 S	121,000	32.50	37.50	150.	240.	300.	—	—
1859	1,344,000	9.00	11.00	14.00	22.50	55.00	375.	7500.
1859 O	260,000	37.50	57.50	85.00	125.	240.	925.	—
1959 S	80,000	52.50	90.00	160.	235.	450.	—	—
1860	805,400	9.00	11.00	14.00	22.50	55.00	925.	7500.
1860 O	388,000	27.50	37.50	55.00	80.00	175.	950.	—
1860 S	56,000	80.00	135.	240.	425.	650.	—	—
1861	4,854,600	9.00	11.00	14.00	22.50	55.00	375.	7500.
1861 S	96,000	27.50	32.50	65.00	85.00	240.	2700.	—
1862	932,550	9.00	22.50	15.00	67.50	135.	375.	7500.
1862 S	67,000	45.00	70.00	165.	250.	350.	—	—
1863	192,060	25.00	30.00	40.00	70.00	140.	800.	7500.
1864	94,070	55.00	70.00	100.	150.	375.	950.	7500.
1864 S	20,000	160.	215.	375.	525.	1900.	—	—
1865	59,300	55.00	70.00	100.	150.	275.	1300.	7500.
1865 S	41,000	65.00	90.00	150.	275.	500.	2100.	—
1866	UNIQUE		Not Issued For Circulation					

VARIETY FOUR - MOTTO ABOVE EAGLE 1866-1873

DIAMETER—24.3mm
WEIGHT—6.22 Grams
COMPOSITION—.900 Silver, .100 Copper
DESIGNER—Christian Gobrecht
EDGE—Reeded

DATE	MINTAGE	G-4	VG-8	F-12	VF-20	EF-40	MS-60	Prf-65
1866	17,525	190.	265.	325.	450.	725.	1350.	7000.
1866 S	28,000	135.	200.	325.	475.	775.	—	—
1867	20,625	125.	150.	215.	275.	475.	1250.	7000.
1867 S	48,000	65.00	90.00	175.	275.	425.	3150.	—
1868	30,000	100.	130.	200.	265.	375.	1150.	7000.
1868 S	96,000	27.50	37.50	75.00	130.	215.	2250.	—
1869	16,600	190.	240.	325.	425.	725.	1350.	7000.
1869 S	76,000	115.	160.	240.	350.	475.	—	—
1870	87,400	45.00	70.00	175.	250.	190.	950.	6800.
1870 CC	8,340	875.	1450.	2400.	3000.	4000.	—	—
1871	119,160	14.00	25.00	37.50	65.00	125.	950.	6800.
1871 CC	10,890	475.	675.	1050.	1600.	2500.	—	—
1871 S	30,900	160.	285.	475.	575.	900.	3000.	—
1872	182,950	13.00	15.00	32.50	60.00	125.	950.	6800.
1872 CC	22,850	225.	375.	525.	800.	2100.	—	—
1872 S	83,000	160.	285.	400.	500.	750.	4500.	—
1873 Closed 3	212,600	70.00	90.00	185.	230.	375.	—	6800.
1873 Open 3	Inc. Above	32.50	42.50	65.00	125.	215.	600.	—
1873 CC	4,000	New England April 1980 Auction $205,000.						

VARIETY FIVE - ARROWS AT DATE 1873-1874

DIAMETER—24.3mm
WEIGHT—6.25 Grams
COMPOSITION—.900 Silver, .100 Copper
DESIGNER—Christian Gobrecht
EDGE—Reeded

DATE	MINTAGE	G-4	VG-8	F-12	VF-20	EF-40	MS-60	Prf-65
1873	1,271,700	20.00	40.00	60.00	100.	180.	900.	9,000.
1873 CC	12,462	1200.	1600.	2300.	3400.	5250.	—	—
1873 S	156,000	27.50	70.00	100.	185.	265.	900.	—
1874	471,900	16.00	27.50	37.50	70.00	200.	900.	9,000.
1874 S	392,000	25.00	37.50	62.50	130.	265.	900.	—

VARIETY FOUR RESUMED 1875-1891

DATE	MINTAGE	G-4	VG-8	F-12	VF-20	EF-40	MS-60	Prf-65
1875	4,293,500	8.00	10.00	12.00	20.00	70.00	375.	4250.
1875 CC	140,000	45.00	60.00	125.	215.	375.	1500.	—
1875 S	680,000	17.50	27.50	42.50	70.00	110.	375.	—
1876	17,817,150	8.00	10.00	12.00	20.00	70.00	375.	4250.
1876 CC	4,994,000	8.00	10.00	12.00	20.00	85.00	375.	—

DATE	MINTAGE	G-4	VG-8	F-12	VF-20	EF-40	MS-60	Prf-65
1876 S	8,596,000	8.00	10.00	12.00	20.00	70.00	375.	—
1877	10,911,710	8.00	10.00	12.00	20.00	70.00	375.	3000.
1877 CC	4,192,000	12.00	17.50	27.50	52.50	110.	850.	—
1877 S	8,996,000	12.00	17.50	27.50	47.50	85.00	375.	—
1877 Over Horizontal S	Inc. Above	47.50	75.00	110.	215.	400.	1300.	—
1878	2,260,800	15.00	17.50	22.50	42.50	80.00	375.	3000.
1878 CC	996,000	25.00	40.00	60.00	80.00	140.	375.	—
1878 S	140,000	37.50	55.00	95.00	135.	240.	1400.	—
1879	14,700	85.00	105.	140.	215.	375.	600.	3000.
1880	14,955	85.00	105.	140.	215.	240.	600.	3000.
1881	12,975	115.	140.	170.	245.	425.	600.	3000.
1882	16,300	115.	140.	170.	245.	425.	600.	3000.
1883	15,439	115.	140.	170.	245.	375.	600.	3000.
1884	8,875	140.	200.	240.	315.	525.	650.	3000.
1885	14,530	115.	140.	175.	245.	400.	600.	3000.
1886	5,886	215.	265.	315.	375.	675.	725.	3000.
1887	10,710	115.	140.	170.	245.	375.	675.	3000.
1888	10,833	115.	140.	175.	245.	375.	600.	3000.
1888 S	1,216,000	15.00	17.50	25.00	40.00	75.00	375.	—
1889	12,711	115.	140.	170.	245.	375.	550.	3000.
1890	80,590	45.00	60.00	75.00	100.	200.	550.	3000.
1891	3,920,600	12.00	17.50	25.00	40.00	75.00	375.	3000.
1891 O	68,000	115.	140.	225.	375.	600.	—	—
1891 S	2,216,000	16.00	20.00	25.00	45.00	85.00	375.	—

BARBER TYPE
1892-1916

DIAMETER—24.3mm
WEIGHT—6.25 Grams
COMPOSITION—.900 Silver, .100 Copper
DESIGNER—Charles E. Barber
EDGE—Reeded
PURE SILVER CONTENT—.18084 Tr. Oz.

DATE	MINTAGE	G-4	VG-8	F-12	VF-20	EF-40	AU-50	MS-60	MS-65	Prf-65
1892	8,237,245	3.00	4.50	9.00	30.00	70.00	135.	220.	2000.	2400.
1892 O	2,640,000	4.50	8.00	14.00	35.00	72.50	145.	280.	2200.	—
1892 S	964,079	12.00	20.00	35.00	57.50	110.	185.	400.	7800.	—
1893	5,484,838	3.50	5.00	10.00	32.00	70.00	140.	220.	2000.	2400.
1893 O	3,396,000	3.50	7.00	12.50	37.50	72.50	145.	275.	3000.	—
1893 S	1,454,535	7.50	12.00	22.50	45.00	85.00	160.	400.	6800.	—
1894	3,432,972	3.00	6.00	11.00	32.50	70.00	140.	220.	2150.	2400.
1894 O	2,852,000	3.50	7.00	16.00	40.00	75.00	150.	325.	6400.	—
1894 S	2,648,821	3.25	6.50	15.00	37.50	75.00	150.	325.	6800.	—
1895	4,440,880	3.00	5.00	9.00	30.00	70.00	135.	220.	5000.	2400.
1895 O	2,816,000	4.00	6.00	15.00	38.00	75.00	150.	375.	3200.	—
1895 S	1,764,681	5.00	10.00	22.00	42.50	80.00	1150.	360.	6100.	—
1896	3,874,762	3.00	6.00	11.00	30.00	70.00	135.	225.	2750.	2400.
1896 O	1,484,000	3.50	9.00	17.50	47.50	100.	400.	800.	8700.	—
1896 S	188,039	225.	300.	450.	800.	1600.	2400.	3400.	25,000.	—
1897	8,140,731	2.00	3.50	8.00	28.00	65.00	135.	200.	2200.	2400.

DATE	MINTAGE	G-4	VG-8	F-12	VF-20	EF-40	AU-50	MS-60	MS-65	Prf-65
1897 O	1,414,800	5.00	8.00	19.00	50.00	95.00	235.	800.	5200.	—
1897 S	542,229	9.00	14.00	30.00	60.00	125.	275.	460.	6900.	—
1898	11,100,735	1.75	2.25	8.00	28.00	65.00	135.	200.	2100.	2400.
1898 O	1,868,000	4.00	8.00	19.00	38.50	75.00	150.	500.	8000.	—
1898 S	1,020,592	4.00	7.50	13.00	32.50	65.00	145.	360.	3800.	—
1899	12,624,846	1.75	2.25	8.00	28.00	65.00	135.	200.	2000.	2400.
1899 O	2,644,000	3.00	7.50	15.00	36.50	75.00	150.	380.	6400.	—
1899 S	708,000	6.00	13.00	27.50	45.00	85.00	185.	360.	3700.	—
1900	10,016,912	2.00	4.00	8.50	30.00	65.00	135.	200.	2000.	2400.
1900 O	3,416,000	4.50	9.00	20.00	42.50	82.50	160.	400.	4200.	—
1900 S	1,858,585	3.50	5.50	10.00	30.00	65.00	140.	325.	5700.	—
1901	8,892,813	2.25	4.00	10.00	30.00	67.50	140.	200.	2400.	2400.
1901 O	1,612,000	9.00	16.00	42.50	75.00	145.	235.	775.	7500.	—
1901 S	72,664	750.	1200.	1800.	2600.	4500.	6000.	10,000.	50,000.	—
1902	12,197,744	2.00	3.00	7.50	28.00	65.00	135.	200.	2000.	4250.
1902 O	4,748,000	3.00	6.00	12.00	35.00	72.50	145.	375.	5900.	—
1902 S	1,524,612	6.00	10.00	17.00	42.50	85.00	160.	375.	4500.	—
1903	9,670,064	2.00	3.50	8.00	30.00	65.00	135.	200.	2600.	2400.
1903 O	3,500,000	3.50	5.00	10.00	35.00	75.00	160.	285.	7600.	—
1903 S	1,036,000	6.00	10.00	20.00	45.00	90.00	195.	375.	3500.	—
1904	9,588,813	2.00	3.50	8.00	30.00	65.00	135.	200.	2500.	2400.
1904 O	2,456,000	4.00	6.50	16.00	42.50	100.	185.	700.	3300.	—
1905	4,968,250	2.25	3.75	9.00	30.00	65.00	135.	210.	2300.	2400.
1905 O	1,230,000	4.50	9.00	18.00	45.00	115.	175.	375.	6200.	—
1905 S	1,884,000	3.50	7.50	12.00	35.00	75.00	145.	300.	6800.	—
1906	3,656,435	3.00	5.00	9.50	32.50	70.00	140.	220.	2000.	2400.
1906 D	3,280,000	3.50	6.50	12.50	35.00	75.00	145.	220.	5500.	—
1906 O	2,056,000	4.50	8.00	13.50	37.50	78.00	155.	260.	2100.	—
1907	7,192,575	1.75	3.00	8.50	30.00	65.00	130.	200.	2000.	2400.
1907 D	2,484,000	3.75	7.00	13.00	35.00	75.00	145.	230.	4200.	—
1907 O	4,560,000	2.75	5.00	9.50	32.50	70.00	140.	260.	4100.	—
1907 S	1,360,000	3.00	6.50	12.50	35.00	75.00	145.	375.	5750.	—
1908	4,232,545	2.25	3.50	8.50	30.00	67.50	135.	210.	2000.	2400.
1908 D	5,788,000	2.00	3.25	8.00	28.00	65.00	130.	210.	2500.	—
1908 O	6,244,000	2.00	3.25	8.00	28.00	65.00	130.	210.	2000.	—
1908 S	784,000	4.00	7.50	15.00	40.00	85.00	185.	600.	8200.	—
1909	9,268,650	1.75	2.75	7.50	28.00	65.00	130.	200.	2000.	2400.
1909 D	5,114,000	1.75	2.75	7.50	28.00	65.00	130.	210.	2550.	—
1909 O	712,000	6.00	11.00	27.00	75.00	145.	210.	600.	13,000.	—
1909 S	1,348,000	2.00	3.50	8.00	32.50	70.00	140.	285.	2600.	—
1910	2,244,551	2.50	5.00	9.00	32.50	70.00	140.	200.	2000.	2400.
1910 D	1,500,000	4.00	7.50	10.00	38.50	80.00	145.	290.	3100.	—
1911	3,720,543	2.25	3.50	9.00	32.50	70.00	140.	200.	2000.	2400.
1911 D	933,600	3.00	10.00	20.00	42.50	90.00	160.	540.	7300.	—
1911 S	988,000	3.00	6.50	16.00	37.50	82.50	145.	300.	2100.	—
1912	4,400,700	2.00	3.00	7.50	30.00	67.50	135.	200.	2000.	2400.
1912 S	708,000	3.00	5.00	13.50	35.00	80.00	150.	360.	2550.	—
1913	484,613	5.50	11.00	35.00	110.	325.	700.	1200.	5600.	4500.
1913 D	1,450,800	3.00	6.00	11.00	40.00	85.00	150.	270.	2400.	—
1913 S	40,000	300.	400.	675.	1100.	1800.	3000.	4600.	11,000.	—
1914	6,244,610	1.75	2.75	7.00	28.00	65.00	130.	200.	2000.	4500.

DATE	MINTAGE	G-4	VG-8	F-12	VF-20	EF-40	AU-50	MS-60	MS-65	Prf-65
1914 D	3,046,000	2.00	3.00	7.50	28.00	67.50	135.	200.	2000.	—
1914 S	264,000	15.00	25.00	40.00	75.00	150.	290.	800.	4800.	—
1915	3,480,450	2.00	3.50	7.50	30.00	65.00	135.	200.	2000.	4500.
1915 D	3,694,000	2.00	3.00	8.00	29.00	65.00	130.	200.	2000.	—
1915 S	704,000	3.00	5.00	13.00	42.50	87.50	150.	260.	2400.	—
1916	1,788,000	2.00	3.00	8.00	30.00	67.50	135.	210.	2000.	—
1916 D	6,540,800	1.75	3.00	6.50	28.00	65.00	130.	200.	2000.	—

STANDING LIBERTY TYPE
1916-1930

VARIETY ONE
1916-1917

DIAMETER—24.3mm
WEIGHT—6.25 Grams
COMPOSITION—.900 Silver, .100 Copper
DESIGNER—Herman A. MacNeil
EDGE—Reeded
PURE SILVER CONTENT—.18084 Tr. Oz.

DATE	MINTAGE	G-4	VG-8	F-12	VF-20	EF-40	AU-50	MS-60	MS-65	FH-65
1916	52,000	950.	1150.	1600.	2000.	2750.	4000.	4600.	13,500.	22,000.
1917	8,792,000	10.00	12.00	15.00	24.00	55.00	110.	175.	900.	1100.
1917 D	1,509,200	16.00	20.00	25.00	50.00	100.	130.	200.	1050.	1400.
1917 S	1,952,000	15.00	18.00	22.50	45.00	90.00	140.	225.	1400.	2000.

*NOTE: For both varieties of this type, FH-65 denotes a MS-65 specimen with Liberty's Head
fully struck. Starting in 1925 the date was recessed to help prevent wear.*

VARIETY TWO
1917-1930

DIAMETER—24.3mm
WEIGHT—6.25 Grams
COMPOSITION—.900 Silver, .100 Copper
DESIGNER—Herman A. MacNeil
EDGE—Reeded
PURE SILVER CONTENT—.18084 Tr. Oz.

DATE	MINTAGE	G-4	VG-8	F-12	VF-20	EF-40	AU-50	MS-60	MS-65	FH-65
1917	13,880,000	8.50	12.00	17.50	27.50	46.00	75.00	120.	575.	1000.
1917 D	6,224,400	14.00	18.50	28.00	37.50	57.50	85.00	165.	1150.	2600.
1917 S	5,522,000	14.50	20.00	29.00	38.00	59.00	87.50	165.	1100.	2750.
1918	14,240,000	13.00	22.00	26.50	32.50	47.50	75.00	150.	575.	1000.
1918 D	7,380,000	16.50	22.00	32.50	47.50	80.00	130.	200.	1500.	4250.
1918 S	11,072,000	15.00	17.50	18.50	32.00	50.00	85.00	150.	1600.	17,000.
1918 S/17	Inc. Above	1400.	1600.	2000.	2750.	4500.	7500.	9000.	50,000.	80,000.
1919	11,324,000	26.50	32.50	37.50	45.00	65.00	95.00	150.	575.	1050.
1919 D	1,944,000	42.50	65.00	100.	135.	235.	340.	500.	2400.	20,000.
1918 S	1,836,000	42.50	57.50	95.00	130.	235.	325.	425.	3500.	18,500.
1920	27,860,000	11.00	14.00	16.50	22.00	45.00	80.00	125.	560.	1050.
1920 D	3,586,400	22.50	29.00	45.00	67.50	115.	185.	225.	1900.	5000.

DATE	MINTAGE	G-4	VG-8	F-12	VF-20	EF-40	AU-50	MS-60	MS-65	FH-65
1920 S	6,380,000	13.00	17.50	24.00	32.50	52.50	85.00	135.	2200.	20,000.
1921	1,916,000	52.50	80.00	120.	150.	215.	300.	425.	2150.	3000.
1923	9,716,000	13.00	15.00	17.50	22.00	45.00	80.00	130.	550.	1550.
1923 S	1,360,000	65.00	85.00	135.	160.	235.	350.	550.	1650.	3000.
1924	10,920,000	13.00	15.00	16.50	21.00	42.50	77.50	130.	550.	1025.
1924 D	3,112,000	20.00	30.00	42.50	65.00	95.00	135.	150.	550.	7250.
1924 S	2,860,000	13.00	16.50	26.00	35.00	57.50	85.00	150.	2000.	4900.

RECESSED DATE STYLE 1925-1930

DATE	MINTAGE	G-4	VG-8	F-12	VF-20	EF-40	AU-50	MS-60	MS-65	FH-65
1925	12,280,000	2.50	4.75	8.50	13.00	37.50	65.00	120.	550.	1025.
1926	11,316,000	2.50	4.75	8.50	13.00	37.50	65.50	120.	600.	1150.
1926 D	1,716,000	6.25	9.50	14.00	32.50	65.00	95.00	120.	675.	12,500.
1926 S	2,700,000	3.25	4.75	9.50	22.00	52.50	110.	175.	3400.	12,500.
1927	11,912,000	2.50	4.75	8.50	13.00	37.50	65.00	120.	550.	1025.
1927 D	976,400	7.00	11.00	17.50	37.00	70.00	110.	300.	550.	3000.
1927 S	396,000	9.00	12.00	40.00	120.	450.	950.	1500.	9500.	20,000.
1928	6,336,000	2.50	4.75	6.00	13.00	37.50	65.00	120.	600.	1050.
1928 D	1,627,600	4.50	5.50	9.50	15.00	42.50	85.00	135.	550.	4400.
1928 S	2,644,000	3.50	5.25	9.50	14.00	40.00	75.00	120.	550.	1025.
1929	11,140,000	2.50	4.75	6.00	13.00	37.50	65.00	110.	550.	1025.
1929 D	1,358,000	4.50	5.50	7.00	16.50	45.00	90.00	130.	550.	4200.
1929 S	1,764,000	4.00	5.25	6.50	16.50	45.00	90.00	110.	550.	1025.
1930	5,632,000	2.50	4.75	6.00	13.00	37.50	65.00	110.	550.	1025.
1930 S	1,556,000	4.00	5.25	6.50	15.00	42.50	75.00	130.	550.	1050.

WASHINGTON TYPE
1932 TO DATE

DIAMETER—24.3mm
WEIGHT - 1932-1964—6.25 Grams,
   1965 To Date 5.67 Grams
COMPOSITION - 1932-1964—.900 Silver,
   .100 Copper, 1965 To Date Copper Clad Issue,
   .750 Copper, .250 Nickel Outer Layers,
   Pure Copper Inner Core
DESIGNER—John Flanagan
EDGE—Reeded
PURE SILVER CONTENT - 1932-1964—.18084 Tr. Oz.

DATE	MINTAGE	G-4	VG-8	F-12	VF-20	EF-40	MS-60	MS-65	Prf-65
1932	5,404,000	3.25	3.50	5.00	7.00	10.00	27.50	180.	—
1932 D	436,800	35.00	40.00	47.50	70.00	160.	425.	5000.	—
1932 S	408,000	30.00	34.00	37.50	50.00	65.00	275.	3750.	—
1934	31,912,052	2.25	3.00	4.00	4.75	6.00	22.00	95.00	—
1934 D	3,527,200	3.50	4.00	6.00	7.25	10.00	100.	950.	—
1935	32,484,000	2.25	3.25	4.00	4.50	6.00	20.00	75.00	—
1935 D	5,780,000	2.50	4.25	6.00	7.50	10.00	115.	275.	—
1935 S	5,660,000	2.50	3.25	4.75	5.25	8.00	55.00	175.	—
1936	41,303,837	2.25	3.25	4.25	4.75	6.25	18.00	75.00	1000.
1936 D	5,374,000	3.00	3.75	4.25	15.00	32.00	32.00	950.	—
1936 S	3,828,000	3.00	3.25	4.25	7.25	10.00	58.00	100.	—

DATE	MINTAGE	G-4	VG-8	F-12	VF-20	EF-40	MS-60	MS-65	Prf-65
1937	19,701,542	2.25	3.25	4.25	6.00	7.75	24.00	75.00	260.
1937 D	7,189,600	3.00	3.25	4.25	7.25	9.50	40.00	105.	—
1937 S	1,652,000	3.75	4.25	4.75	12.50	21.00	100.	165.	—
1938	9,480,045	3.00	3.25	4.75	8.00	12.50	50.00	105.	155.
1938 S	2,832,000	3.00	3.25	4.75	8.00	11.00	52.00	125.	—
1939	33,548,795	2.25	3.25	4.00	4.50	5.75	15.00	47.50	155.
1939 D	7,092,000	2.75	3.25	4.00	4.75	8.00	30.00	70.00	—
1939 S	2,628,000	3.25	3.75	5.25	6.25	10.00	60.00	125.	—
1940	35,715,246	2.25	3.25	4.00	4.25	4.75	11.00	44.00	120.
1940 D	2,797,600	3.50	3.75	7.50	10.00	16.00	65.00	105.	—
1940 S	8,244,000	2.75	3.25	4.00	4.50	5.75	17.50	37.00	—
1941	79,047,287	—	—	—	—	3.50	8.00	24.00	120.
1941 D	16,714,800	—	—	—	—	3.50	19.00	35.00	—
1941 S	16,080,000	—	—	—	—	3.50	16.00	75.00	—
1942	102,117,123	—	—	—	—	3.50	7.00	24.00	115.
1942 D	17,487,200	—	—	—	—	3.50	10.00	30.00	—
1942 S	19,384,000	—	—	—	—	4.75	52.00	130.	—
1943	99,700,000	—	—	—	—	2.50	5.50	24.00	—
1943 D	16,095,600	—	—	—	—	3.50	15.00	30.00	—
1943 S	21,700,000	—	—	—	—	5.75	30.00	40.00	—
1944	104,956,000	—	—	—	—	3.50	5.00	17.00	—
1944 D	14,600,800	—	—	—	—	3.50	10.00	22.00	—
1944 S	12,560,000	—	—	—	—	3.50	9.50	27.00	—
1945	74,372,000	—	—	—	—	3.50	5.25	15.00	—
1945 D	12,341,600	—	—	—	—	3.50	8.00	23.00	—
1945 S	17,004,001	—	—	—	—	3.50	6.25	19.00	—
1946	53,436,000	—	—	—	—	2.50	5.00	16.00	—
1946 D	9,072,800	—	—	—	—	2.50	4.25	13.00	—
1946 S	4,204,000	—	—	—	—	2.50	4.25	20.00	—
1947	22,556,000	—	—	—	—	3.25	6.75	13.00	—
1947 D	15,338,400	—	—	—	—	3.25	5.75	15.00	—
1947 S	5,532,000	—	—	—	—	2.50	5.25	17.50	—
1948	35,196,000	—	—	—	—	2.50	4.25	10.00	—
1948 D	16,766,800	—	—	—	—	2.50	5.25	12.50	—
1948 S	15,960,000	—	—	—	—	3.50	5.25	13.50	—
1949	9,312,000	—	—	—	—	3.75	20.00	26.00	—
1949 D	10,068,400	—	—	—	—	4.25	9.00	21.00	—
1950	24,971,512	—	—	—	—	3.25	5.25	8.50	55.00
1950 D	21,075,600	—	—	—	—	3.00	4.75	8.50	—
1950 D D/S	Inc. Above	22.50	27.50	32.00	65.00	145.	270.	525.	—
1950 S	10,284,004	—	—	—	—	3.50	7.50	14.00	—
1950 S S/D	Inc. Above	22.50	27.50	32.00	65.00	175.	475.	650.	—
1951	43,505,602	—	—	—	—	2.25	5.00	6.25	40.00
1951 D	35,354,800	—	—	—	—	2.25	3.50	5.75	—
1951 S	9,048,000	—	—	—	—	4.50	13.00	19.00	—
1952	38,862,073	—	—	—	—	2.25	3.25	5.75	32.00
1952 D	49,795,200	—	—	—	—	2.25	3.50	6.25	—
1952 S	13,707,800	—	—	—	—	3.75	9.00	12.00	—
1953	18,664,920	—	—	—	—	2.25	3.50	5.50	27.00
1953 D	56,112,400	—	—	—	—	1.75	2.50	5.50	—
1953 S	14,016,000	—	—	—	—	2.50	4.25	6.75	—

DATE	MINTAGE	G-4	VG-8	F-12	VF-20	EF-40	MS-60	MS-65	Prf-65
1954	54,645,503	—	—	—	—	1.50	2.25	5.00	14.00
1954 D	42,305,500	—	—	—	—	1.50	2.25	4.75	—
1954 S	11,834,722	—	—	—	—	1.50	2.25	5.50	—
1955	18,558,381	—	—	—	—	1.50	2.25	6.25	11.00
1955 D	3,182,400	—	—	—	—	1.75	2.50	8.00	—
1956	44,813,384	—	—	—	—	1.50	2.25	4.25	7.00
1956 D	32,334,500	—	—	—	—	1.75	3.00	4.25	—
1957	47,779,952	—	—	—	—	1.00	3.00	6.75	4.50
1957 D	77,924,160	—	—	—	—	1.00	2.25	4.75	—
1958	7,235,652	—	—	—	—	1.00	2.75	6.75	8.00
1858 D	78,124,900	—	—	—	—	1.00	2.25	4.50	—
1959	25,533,291	—	—	—	—	—	2.25	4.25	4.00
1959 D	62,054,232	—	—	—	—	—	2.25	4.25	—
1960	30,855,602	—	—	—	—	—	2.25	5.25	4.00
1960 D	63,000,324	—	—	—	—	—	3.00	4.25	—
1961	40,064,244	—	—	—	—	—	2.25	4.25	3.50
1961 D	83,656,928	—	—	—	—	—	1.75	4.25	—
1962	39,374,019	—	—	—	—	—	1.75	4.25	3.50
1962 D	127,554,756	—	—	—	—	—	1.75	4.25	—
1963	77,391,645	—	—	—	—	—	1.75	4.00	3.50
1963 D	135,288,184	—	—	—	—	—	1.75	4.00	—
1964	564,341,347	—	—	—	—	—	1.75	4.00	3.50
1964 D	704,135,528	—	—	—	—	—	1.75	4.00	—

COPPER-NICKEL CLAD COINAGE

DATE	MINTAGE	MS-65	Prf-65
1965	1,819,717,540	.80	—
1966	821,101,500	.80	—
1967	1,524,031,848	.80	—
1968	220,731,500	.80	—
1968 D	101,534,000	1.00	—
1968 S	PROOF ONLY	—	.75
1969	176,212,000	.50	—
1969 D	114,372,000	1.25	—
1969 S	PROOF ONLY	—	.75
1970	136,420,000	.50	—
1970 D	417,341,364	.50	—
1970 S	PROOF ONLY	—	1.00
1971	109,284,000	.50	—
1971 D	258,634,428	.50	—
1971 S	PROOF ONLY	—	.75
1972	215,048,000	.50	—
1972 D	311,067,732	.50	—
1972 S	PROOF ONLY	—	.75
1973	346,924,000	.50	—
1973 D	232,977,400	.50	—
1973 S	PROOF ONLY	—	.75
1974	801,456,000	.50	—
1974 D	353,160,300	.50	—
1974 S	PROOF ONLY	—	.75
1977	468,566,000	.50	—

DATE	MINTAGE	MS-65	Prf-65
1977 D	258,898,212	.50	—
1977 S	PROOF ONLY	—	.75
1978	521,452,000	.50	—
1978 D	287,373,152	.50	—
1978 S	PROOF ONLY	—	.75
1979	515,708,000	.50	—
1979 D	489,789,780	.50	—
1979 S	PROOF ONLY	—	.75
1980 P	635,832,000	.50	—
1980 D	518,327,487	.50	—
1980 S	PROOF ONLY	—	.75
1981 P	601,716,000	.50	—
1981 D	575,722,833	.50	—
1981 S	PROOF ONLY	—	.75
1982 P	500,931,000	.50	—
1982 D	480,042,788	.50	—
1982 S	PROOF ONLY	—	.75
1983 P	673,535,000	.50	—
1983 D	617,806,446	.50	—
1983 S	PROOF ONLY	—	1.00
1984 P	676,545,000	.50	—
1984 D	546,483,064	.50	—
1984 S	PROOF ONLY	—	1.00
1985 P	775,818,962	.50	—
1985 D	519,962,888	.50	—
1985 S	PROOF ONLY	—	1.00
1986 P	551,199,333	.50	—
1986 D	504,298,660	.50	—
1986 S	PROOF ONLY	—	1.00
1987 P	582,499,481	.50	—
1987 D	655,594,696	.50	—
1987 S	PROOF ONLY	—	1.00
1988 P	562,052,000	.50	—
1988 D	596,810,688	.50	—
1988 S	PROOF ONLY	—	1.00
1989 P	512,868,000	.50	—
1989 D	896,535,597	.50	—
1989 S	PROOF ONLY	—	1.00
1990 P	613,792,000	.50	—
1990 D	927,638,181	.50	—
1990 S	PROOF ONLY	—	1.00
1991 P	570,968,000	.50	—
1991 D	630,966,693	.50	—
1991 S	PROOF ONLY	—	1.00
1992 P	—	.50	—
1992 D	—	.50	—
1992 S	PROOF ONLY	—	1.00
1993 P	—	.50	—
1993 D	—	.50	—
1993 S	PROOF ONLY	—	1.00

Half Dollars 1794 To Date

Half dollars have been coined almost every year since 1794. The half dollar types of the 18th and 19th centuries closely resemble the designs of the smaller silver coins in production during the same period.

The first half dollar, the Flowing Hair type, was minted in only 1794 and 1795. Most of its demand originates from the type collecting sector of the numismatic industry. Price movements have been very mixed since 1980. As a long term investment, though, you really can't go astray by purchasing these particular half dollars.

The Draped Bust half dollars with the small eagle on the reverse, coined in 1796 and 1797, are extremely rare, capable of bringing almost $10,000 in Good condition. With this half dollar, should you be able to afford it, you're virtually assured of an investment that will steadily rise in value year after year.

Draped Bust halves with the heraldic eagle reverse of 1801 to 1807 have been mildly progressive for a number of years now, and we'll probably see a sustainment of this improvement. Most notable is that Extremely Fine halves did poorly from 1980 to 1990, in relation to other grades, and there are huge gaps between some Extremely Fine and MS-60 Uncirculated values. These facts are evidence that Extremely Fine half dollars of this type are seriously undervalued coins at this time.

The Liberty Capped half dollar was a very important coin during its heyday of 1807 to 1836. Back then, there was a severe shortage of silver dollars and gold coins in circulation, leaving this half dollar as the largest denomination readily available for major transactions. Liberty Capped half dollars were also extensively utilized to maintain bank reserves and pay foreign debts. Since the coins were simply transferred in bags to consummate business proceedings rather than handled individually, many of them remain today in better than average condition. Unfortunately, few of these coins survive today in MS-65, as 19th century bankers were required to periodically count how many half dollars they held in storage. To do so required sliding them across the accounting table, often done in a careless manner, leaving most specimens with table scratches.

For investment purposes, the best opportunities for solid growth appear to be in the Fine to Extremely Fine grades. They've been in a dormant phase for several years now, coming on the heels of some pretty good appreciation in the 1980's. Being that we are presently in the midst of a slow down period, it is a safe assumption that these coins will fetch a much nicer price in a few short years from now.

The half dollar was reduced in size in 1836 with the introduction of the reeded edge Liberty Cap half. The previous type had a lettered edge. The first reeded edge half dollars are much more difficult to locate in upper grades because of lesser storage in bank vaults during their time of service, and yet the values of Extremely Fine and Uncirculated specimens approximate the value of earlier Liberty Capped halves with comparable mintages. To analyze the situation further, reeded edge examples of Capped halves were priced well above the lettered edge type throughout most of the previous three decades, and this ratio should be reinstated in the not too distant future. Therefore, you should buy the best grade you can afford in the reeded edge type.

The Liberty Seated half dollar came into existence in 1839 and ran its course until 1891. There were several variations of the basic theme along the way, adding up to a total of six distinct types of Liberty Seated halves.

For common date coins of the series, all slabbed Uncirculated specimens represent one of your best hopes for immediate advancements. In many instances, values have been slashed by more than half since the 1980's. If you've got an extra $5000 or more to spend, MS-65 Proof Liberty Seated halves offer excellent possibilities, having fallen nearly 40% from their 1989 high water mark. On the opposite side of the spectrum, individuals with less than $150 to spend should look for nice, problem-free Extremely Fine half dollars of this era. They have not yet attained the respect they deserve from the numismatic community. Investment dollars spent here should do quite well in the years ahead.

The Barber dollar bears the identical front and reverse design as the Barber quarter and was in production from 1892 to 1915, one year less than both small Barber coins. Barber halves offer a truly mixed bag for investors. Here is an overview of what you'll find: many MS-60 and MS-63 Uncirculated pieces are selling for about the same or less as they were ten years ago, while a few others have continued to climb in value ever since. Circulated specimens in higher grades have been rising in price, although not uniformly. Conversely, lower grade common date Barbers have nosedived as a response to the direction the bullion market has taken. The most shocking aspect of Barber half dollars is how poorly MS-65 Uncirculated and Proof coins have performed over the last four years. Almost any Barber half properly graded in these conditions signify a bargain at today's prices, though they are still expensive.

Another area with good potential can be found in the Extremely Fine and Almost Uncirculated grades. These coins enjoyed healthy advances in the late 1980's, but have fallen off badly in the 1990's. For the best return on your money, focus on the better date issues, such as the 1892-S or the 1897-S.

The artistically acclaimed Walking Liberty half dollar replaced the Barber half as our nation's fifty cent piece in 1916. "Walkers," as they are referred to by insiders, have traditionally been among the most well-liked United States coins, appealing to both collectors and investors. Because of their widespread popularity, Walkers should always enjoy a strong demand. As an added incentive to the investor, quality Walkers normally carry wholesale values relatively close to retail values, translating into smaller markdowns when you sell.

In terms of availability, the Walking Liberty half can be divided into two groups. The first group, comprised of halves dating 1916 through 1933, are less common, especially in upper grades. The second group, dating 1934 to the end of the series in 1947, saw annual production figures far in excess of the earlier issues, and are more readily available in higher grades. A collector contemplating purchasing a Walker for investment purposes would be wise to keep these facts in mind.

Walking Liberty half dollars in the best conditions are more volatile in price than nearly any other series of American coins. They have been a prime target of promoters and speculators for a long time now, which explains the roller coaster effect on values. An attractive, immensely popular coin with large supplies, it's a small wonder as to why the Walkers are so heavily promoted.

The majority of the speculator activity the last decade or so has been mainly confined to the MS-65 or better grades. In 1990-91, the market for Walkers, including common dates grading MS-65 and better, collapsed. To date, it has not yet recovered (recall from the Introduction the discussion concerning high grade "generic" pieces). To purchase a Walker matching this description at today's prices would have to be considered a bargain. Can we expect future price surges similar to those of the past? Probably so, but it's really difficult to say when it might happen with so much promoter involvement. One thing is certain: if you purchase even common date MS-65 Walking Liberty halves with long term objectives in mind, you're virtually guaranteed of enviable returns.

Of all the Walking Liberty half dollars, not even the key dates have escaped severe price plunges. The drops are evident from the lowest grades to the highest grades. In most instances, we see prices reduced from 25% to 50% off their 1983 highs. As an investor, though, the only halves to buy in less than Fine condition are the 1916, 1916-D, 1916-S, 1917-D (mint mark on obverse), 1917-S (mint mark on obverse), 1919, 1921, 1921-D, 1921-S, and the 1938-D. The rest of the low grade Walkers march to the tune of the metals market and shouldn't be counted on to appreciate solely on the basis of their numismatic integrity.

In all grades Extremely Fine to MS-63, Walkers dated before 1934 appear to be sound investments. They are very scarce in problem-free condition, but are not priced as such. Some of the issues of 1934 and beyond are desirable acquisitions in Extremely Fine and Almost Uncirculated, but on the whole, you need to look at Uncirculated specimens for the best potential. The generic Walkers fall within this range (most of the halves dated in the 1940's), and as mentioned above, right now is a great chance to land very high quality examples of these coins at garage sale prices!

For the first time in a long while, all pre-1934 Walkers properly graded at MS-65 Uncirculated should be considered, as prices have retreated dramatically from their 1989 record setting levels. With prices as low as they are, you can feel safe in supposing that they will rise sharply within the next few years. These increases could be very pronounced if promoters and speculators again become actively involved in the Walker market. The best possible action to take is to acquire these coins before the bandwagon pushes costs higher!

The Ben Franklin half dollar made its appearance in 1948 and continued its run until 1963. What we find in this series as a whole are coins that have never gained proper respect from collectors or investors. Long considered as nothing more than bullion coins, someday people will begin to acknowledge all Franklin halves as worthy collectibles. However, that day has not yet come, leaving foresighted investors with plenty of opportunities to acquire very nice coins at minimal costs.

Many Franklins in MS-65 Uncirculated condition increased 14 times their value from 1987 to 1990, but have dipped now to only about five times their 1987 prices. True, in 1990 the prices may have been artificially high, but in 1993 there is little downside risk to adding gem Franklins to your numismatic holdings. One can expect, if nothing else, some speculative attention to return to MS-65 Franklins, and those who act knowledgeably today, most certainly for pre-1959 production, should experience enviable gains.

Whatever uncirculated condition half you are able to buy, make the attempt to select well struck specimens having "Full Bell Lines" on the Liberty Bell reverse (abbreviated FBL). Most coin experts, but not all, believe this quality is every bit as important as the Full Split Bands in the Mercury dime series, and are happy to pay hefty premiums to obtain them. On the other hand, you won't have to spend too much extra for a FBL half in some instances. If buying a FBL Franklin half dollar, it would be generally safer to buy one with a lower premium attached to it.

The Ben Franklin half dollar in MS-65 Proof condition is also far more affordable than a few years ago. Any of these coins, properly graded, would be an excellent acquisition on your part. Some attention should be given to "cameo" proofs. These are proofs that were the very first strikes off new proof dies, and exhibit frosted surface features similar to current day proofs. Some numismatists contend cameo proofs are 30 times scarcer overall than ordinary proof Franklins, but are not priced as such.

For the very small budget investor who cannot afford the gem material, the Franklin half still holds out some hope. A collection of very inexpensive, well-worn specimens stands to benefit from an improvement in the metals market, it nothing else. As more collectors get interested in this obsolete series, we'll see more demand and hence more appreciation of these coins. Moreover, Franklins are not as plentiful as one might think, not even in lower grades, because of the huge melting losses over the years. No one has an inventory on the actual number of survivors, but we'll get a clearer picture of the situation when future buyers compete for the remaining supply of Franklins. There is one thing we do know: you will probably never be able to purchase Ben Franklin halves this cheaply again.

The Franklin half dollar series came to an abrupt end with the introduction of the Kennedy half dollar, issued with the intent to honor the fallen president. The first Kennedy halves appeared in circulation in 1964. Throughout its 28 year history, the speculator influence has been very minimal, leaving ground floor opportunities for investors with virtually no downside risk.

The 1964 pieces are the only Kennedy halves to contain 90% silver. Today, MS-65 Uncirculated 1964 Kennedys are selling for only slightly above their bullion value. Although no United States coin has ever been hoarded more than the 1964 issues, they are certainly poised for future price appreciation when collector interest and bullion prices are triggered. You shouldn't have any difficulty in obtaining MS-65 (or better) examples.

The rarest Kennedy half is the 1970-D, with a mintage of 2.15 million, very low by modern day standards. Priced at only $12 in MS-60 and $20 in MS-65, this coin is destined to multiply in value when Kennedys become widely collected. Just as the rarest coin in other series jumped in value when they became popular, we can rightfully expect a similar occurrence here.

The second scarcest Kennedy half is the 1970-S proof edition, having a production total of slightly over 2.6 million. This coin is priced well below its earlier highs and should be considered a sleeper with encouraging investment potential.

HALF DOLLARS
1794 TO DATE

FLOWING HAIR TYPE
1794-1795

DIAMETER—32.5mm
WEIGHT—13.48 Grams
COMPOSITION—.8924 Silver,
  .1076 Copper
DESIGNER—Robert Scot
EDGE—FIFTY CENTS
  OR HALF A DOLLAR
  With Decorations Between Words

DATE	MINTAGE	G-4	VG-8	F-12	VF-20	EF-40	MS-60
1794	23,464	1200.	1800.	2700.	4000.	7000.	—
1795	299,680	450.	550.	850.	1900.	3500.	14,000.
1795 Recut Date	Inc. Above	575.	650.	950.	2000.	3250.	—
1795 3-Leaves	Inc. Above	1800.	2400.	3250.	5750.	10,000.	—

DRAPED BUST TYPE
SMALL EAGLE REVERSE
1796-1797

DIAMETER—32.5mm
WEIGHT—13.48 Grams
COMPOSITION—.8924 Silver,
  .1076 Copper
DESIGNER—Robert Scot
EDGE—FIFTY CENTS
  OR HALF A DOLLAR
  With Decorations Between Words

DATE	MINTAGE	G-4	VG-8	F-12	VF-20	EF-40	MS-60
1796 15 Stars	3,918	10,000.	12,000.	16,500.	27,500.	40,000.	—
1796 16 Stars	Inc. Above	10,000.	12,000.	16,500.	27,500.	40,000.	—
1797	Inc. Above	10,000.	12,000.	16,500.	27,500.	40,000.	—

DRAPED BUST TYPE
HERALDIC EAGLE REVERSE
1801-1807

DIAMETER—32.5mm
WEIGHT—13.48 Grams
COMPOSITION—.8924 Silver,
  .1076 Copper
DESIGNER—Robert Scot
EDGE—FIFTY CENTS
  OR HALF A DOLLAR
  With Decorations Between Words

DATE	MINTAGE	G-4	VG-8	F-12	VF-20	EF-40	MS-60
1801	30,289	140.	350.	700.	1000.	1300.	9750.
1802	29,890	165.	375.	700.	1000.	1300.	9500.
1803 Small 3	188,234	100.	170.	275.	700.	1000.	5700.
1803 Large 3	Inc. Above	85.00	120.	200.	425.	850.	5700.
1805	211,722	75.00	110.	160.	350.	650.	5500.
1805/4	Inc. Above	150.	225.	450.	750.	1400.	5500.
1806 Knobbed 6, Large Stars	839,576	75.00	100.	160.	350.	650.	5200.
1806 Knobbed 6, Small Stars	Inc. Above	75.00	100.	160.	350.	650.	5200.
1806 Pointed 6, Stem Not Through Claw	Inc. Above	75.00	100.	160.	350.	650.	5200.
1806 Pointed 6, Stem Through Claw	Inc. Above	75.00	100.	160.	350.	650.	5200.
1806/5	Inc. Above	80.00	115.	200.	475.	800.	5200.
1806 Over Inverted 6	Inc. Above	95.00	130.	250.	650.	1200.	5200.
1807	301,076	80.00	100.	160.	425.	800.	5200.

CAPPED BUST TYPE 1807-1839

VARIETY ONE - LETTERED EDGE 1807-1836

DIAMETER—32.5mm
WEIGHT—13.48 Grams
COMPOSITION—.8924 Silver,
.1076 Copper
DESIGNER—John Reich
EDGE—1807-1814
FIFTY CENTS OR
HALF A DOLLAR
1814-1831, Stars Added Between
DOLLAR and FIFTY
1832-1836, Vertical Lines
Added Between Words

DATE	MINTAGE	G-4	VG-8	F-12	VF-20	EF-40	MS-60
1807 Sm. Stars	750,500	70.00	100.	160.	300.	500.	1250.
1807 Lg. Stars	Inc. Above	80.00	120.	180.	400.	600.	.2400.
1807 50/20C	Inc. Above	50.00	60.00	80.00	120.	325.	1200.
1808	1,368,600	35.00	40.00	52.50	70.00	150.	1750.
1808/7	Inc. Above	35.00	40.00	60.00	80.00	165.	2500.
1809	1,405,810	35.00	40.00	55.00	80.00	165.	2600.
1810	1,276,276	35.00	37.50	45.00	75.00	150.	1250.
1811 Small 8	1,203,644	32.50	37.50	45.00	75.00	150.	1900.
1811 Large 8	Inc. Above	32.50	37.50	45.00	90.00	170.	1900.
1811 Dt. 18.11	Inc. Above	32.50	37.50	57.50	100.	190.	1750.
1812	1,628,059	32.50	37.50	45.00	75.00	150.	1250.
1812/11	Inc. Above	37.50	42.50	55.00	120.	230.	900.
1813	1,241,903	32.50	37.50	45.00	75.00	150.	1150.
1814	1,039,075	35.00	40.00	47.50	75.00	150.	1750.
1814/13	Inc. Above	37.50	42.50	50.00	100.	210.	925.
1815/12	47,150	600.	900.	1300.	1700.	2200.	4500.
1817	1,215,567	30.00	32.50	40.00	70.00	140.	725.
1817/13	Inc. Above	85.00	140.	190.	340.	525.	1150.
1817/14	Inc. Above	5 KNOWN—EXTREMELY RARE					
1817 Dt. 181.7	Inc. Above	32.50	37.50	45.00	120.	200.	725.
1818	1,960,322	30.00	32.50	40.00	75.00	140.	725.

DATE	MINTAGE	G-4	VG-8	F-12	VF-20	EF-40	MS-60
1818/17 ....Inc. Above		30.00	32.50	40.00	75.00	140.	725.
1819 2,208,022		30.00	32.50	40.00	75.00	140.	725.
1819/18 Sm. 9 ....Inc. Above		30.00	32.50	40.00	75.00	140.	725.
1819/18 Lg. 9.......................................Inc. Above		30.00	32.50	40.00	75.00	140.	725.
1820 Sm. Date 751,122		35.00	47.50	55.00	140.	215.	725.
1820 Lg. Date ....Inc. Above		35.00	47.50	55.00	140.	215.	725.
1820/19 ....Inc. Above		35.00	45.00	52.50	135.	230.	725.
1821 1,305,797		32.50	35.00	40.00	75.00	140.	725.
1822 1,559,573		30.00	35.00	40.00	70.00	140.	725.
1822/1 ....Inc. Above		45.00	55.00	75.00	190.	325.	1150.
1823 1,694,200		30.00	32.50	40.00	70.00	140.	725.
1823 Broken 3 ....Inc. Above		35.00	50.00	75.00	120.	225.	725.
1823 Patched 3 ....Inc. Above		35.00	50.00	70.00	100.	200.	725.
1823 Ugly 3 ....Inc. Above		30.00	35.00	40.00	100.	190.	725.
1824 3,504,954		30.00	32.50	40.00	52.50	100.	725.
1824/21 ....Inc. Above		32.50	37.50	42.50	100.	190.	725.
1824/Various Dates ....Inc. Above		30.00	32.50	40.00	70.00	150.	725.
1825 2,943,166		30.00	32.50	40.00	52.50	100.	725.
1826 4,004,180		30.00	32.50	40.00	52.50	100.	725.
1827 Curled 2......................................5,493,400		32.50	35.00	42.50	90.00	155.	725.
1827 Square 2.....................................Inc. Above		30.00	32.50	40.00	52.50	100.	725.
1827/6 ....Inc. Above		32.50	35.00	40.00	95.00	150.	1150.
1828 Curled Base 2, No Knob 3,075,200		29.00	32.50	37.50	52.50	100.	725.
1828 Curled Base 2, Knobbed 2..............Inc. Above		35.00	45.00	60.00	90.00	155.	775.
1828 Sm. 8's, Square Base 2, Lg. Letters ...Inc. Above		29.00	32.50	37.50	45.00	95.00	725.
1828 Sm. 8's, Square Base 2, Sm. Letters..Inc. Above		29.00	32.50	37.50	130.	260.	775.
1828 Lg. 8's Square Base 2......................Inc. Above		29.00	32.50	37.50	45.00	95.00	725.
1829 3,712,156		29.00	32.50	40.00	45.00	95.00	725.
1829/7 ....Inc. Above		30.00	32.50	40.00	90.00	170.	825.
1830 Sm. O in Date 4,764,800		29.00	32.50	37.50	45.00	90.00	725.
1830 Lg. O in Date................................Inc. Above		29.00	32.50	37.50	45.00	90.00	725.
1831 5,873,660		29.00	32.50	37.50	45.00	90.00	725.
1832 Sm. Letters...................................4,797,000		29.00	32.50	50.00	45.00	90.00	725.
1832 Lg. Letters ....Inc. Above		29.00	32.50	37.50	70.00	200.	1300.
1833 5,206,000		29.00	32.50	37.50	45.00	90.00	725.
1834 Sm. Date, Lg. Stars, Sm. Letters........6,412,004		29.00	32.50	37.50	45.00	90.00	725.
1834 Sm. Date, Sm. Stars, Sm. Letters.......Inc. Above		29.00	32.50	37.50	45.00	90.00	725.
1834 Lg. Date, Sm. Letters.....................Inc. Above		29.00	32.50	37.50	45.00	90.00	725.
1834 Lg. Date, Lg. Letters ....Inc. Above		29.00	32.50	37.50	45.00	90.00	725.
1835 5,352,006		29.00	32.50	37.50	45.00	90.00	725.
1836 6,545,000		29.00	32.50	37.50	45.00	90.00	725.
1836 50/00..Inc. Above		37.50	45.00	60.00	165.	230.	1200.

VARIETY TWO - REEDED EDGE
REVERSE 50 CENTS 1836-1837

DIAMETER—30mm
WEIGHT—13.36 Grams
COMPOSITION—.900 Silver,
    .100 Copper
DESIGNER—Christian Gobrecht
EDGE—Reeded

DATE	MINTAGE	G-4	VG-8	F-12	VF-20	EF-40	MS-60
1836	1,200	265.	375.	700.	1050.	1850.	5000.
1837	3,629,820	35.00	42.50	50.00	80.00	130.	1000.

VARIETY THREE - REEDED EDGE
REVERSE HALF DOLLAR 1838-1839

DIAMETER—30mm
WEIGHT—13.36 Grams
COMPOSITION—
    .900 Silver, .100 Copper
DESIGNER—Christian Gobrecht
EDGE—Reeded

DATE	MINTAGE	G-4	VG-8	F-12	VF-20	EF-40	MS-60
1838	3,546,000	35.00	42.50	50.00	80.00	130.	1250.
1838 O	20				PROOF ONLY		50,000.
1839	3,334,560	35.00	42.50	50.00	80.00	130.	900.
1839 O	178,976	80.00	120.	180.	350.	600.	3400.

LIBERTY SEATED TYPE
1839-1891

**VARIETY ONE -NO MOTTO
ABOVE EAGLE 1839-1853**

DIAMETER—30.6mm
WEIGHT—13.36 Grams
COMPOSITION—.900 Silver,
  .100 Copper
DESIGNER—Christian Gobrecht
EDGE—Reeded

DATE	MINTAGE	G-4	VG-8	F-12	VF-20	EF-40	MS-60
1839 No Drapery	Inc. Above	37.50	50.00	65.00	220.	500.	2500.
1839 Drapery	Inc. Above	22.00	27.50	32.50	65.00	110.	475.
1840 Sm. Letters	1,435,008	18.00	20.00	25.00	60.00	75.00	600.
1840 Med. Letters	Inc. Above	65.00	85.00	120.	265.	350.	2000.
1840 O	855,100	18.00	22.00	27.50	65.00	80.00	600.
1841	310,000	47.50	57.50	72.50	130.	265.	1350.
1841 O	401,000	25.00	30.00	38.00	70.00	110.	900.
1842 Sm. Date	2,012,764	28.00	32.50	40.00	80.00	120.	1350.
1842 Lg. Date	Inc. Above	17.00	20.00	24.00	47.50	72.50	1300.
1842 O Sm. Date	957,000	575.	750.	1350.	2600.	5200.	—
1842 O Lg. Date	Inc. Above	18.00	22.00	27.50	52.50	80.00	525.
1843	3,884,000	17.00	20.00	24.00	45.00	72.50	425.
1843 O	2,268,000	17.00	20.00	24.00	45.00	72.50	575.
1844	1,766,000	17.00	20.00	24.00	45.00	72.50	425.
1844 O	2,005,000	17.00	20.00	24.00	45.00	72.50	550.
1845	589,000	27.50	32.50	40.00	95.00	120.	925.
1845 O	2,094,000	17.00	20.00	24.00	45.00	72.50	575.
1845 O No Drapery	Inc. Above	40.00	60.00	80.00	120.	170.	775.
1846 Medium Date	2,210,000	16.00	19.00	22.50	42.50	67.50	525.
1846 Tall Date	Inc. Above	17.50	21.00	26.00	70.00	75.00	675.
1846/Horizontal 6	Inc. Above	50.00	60.00	75.00	235.	240.	2600.
1846 O Medium Date	2,304,000	16.00	19.00	22.50	37.50	67.50	575.
1846 O Tall Date	Inc. Above	50.00	65.00	85.00	200.	240.	3750.
1847/46	1,156,000	1400.	1800.	2600.	3400.	4750.	—
1847	Inc. Above	16.00	19.00	22.50	37.50	67.50	500.
1847 O	2,584,000	16.00	19.00	22.50	37.50	67.50	660.
1848	580,000	27.50	32.50	40.00	80.00	120.	1450.
1848 O	3,180,000	16.00	19.00	22.50	37.50	67.50	775.
1849	1,252,000	16.00	19.00	22.50	37.50	67.50	1300.
1849 O	2,310,000	16.00	19.00	22.50	37.50	67.50	675.
1850	227,000	72.50	80.00	135.	235.	350.	1550.
1850 O	2,456,000	16.00	19.00	22.50	42.50	67.50	675.
1851	200,750	85.00	110.	140.	300.	400.	1900.
1851 O	402,000	35.00	47.50	65.00	95.00	165.	625.
1852	77,130	120.	140.	200.	420.	600.	1500.
1852 O	144,000	72.50	85.00	120.	225.	350.	1900.
1853 O	Unknown		Nov. 1979 Garrett Sale VF 40,000.				

VARIETY TWO - ARROW AT DATE
RAYS AROUND EAGLE 1853

DIAMETER—30.6mm
WEIGHT—12.44 Grams
COMPOSITION—.900 Silver,
.100 Copper
DESIGNER—Christian Gobrecht
EDGE—Reeded

DATE	MINTAGE	G-4	VG-8	F-12	VF-20	EF-40	MS-60
1853	3,532,708	17.50	24.00	32.50	85.00	265.	2250.
1853 O	1,328,000	18.50	24.00	32.50	100.	280.	2250.

VARIETY THREE - ARROWS AT DATE
NO RAYS 1854-1855

DIAMETER—30.6mm
WEIGHT—12.44 Grams
COMPOSITION—.900 Silver,
.100 Copper
DESIGNER—Christian Gobrecht
EDGE—Reeded

DATE	MINTAGE	G-4	VG-8	F-12	VF-20	EF-40	MS-60	Prf-65
1854	2,982,000	16.00	19.00	22.50	50.00	120.	700.	—
1854 O	5,240,000	16.00	19.00	22.50	50.00	120.	475.	—
1855	759,500	19.00	22.00	28.00	60.00	165.	1250.	24,000.
1855 O	3,688,000	16.00	19.00	22.50	50.00	120.	675.	—
1855 S	129,950	275.	400.	500.	950.	2200.	—	—

VARIETY ONE RESUMED 1856-1866

DATE	MINTAGE	G-4	VG-8	F-12	VF-20	EF-40	MS-60	Prf-65
1856	938,000	17.00	20.00	24.00	45.00	72.50	425.	14,000.
1856 O	2,658,000	16.00	19.00	22.50	36.00	67.50	475.	—
1856 S	211,000	25.00	30.00	45.00	105.	200.	1500.	—
1857	1,988,000	16.00	19.00	22.50	36.00	67.50	425.	14,000.
1857 O	818,000	17.50	21.00	26.00	57.50	75.00	875.	—
1857 S	158,000	45.00	70.00	110.	180.	285.	1400.	—
1858	4,226,000	16.00	19.00	22.50	36.00	67.50	425.	14,000.
1858 O	7,294,000	16.00	19.00	22.50	36.00	67.50	475.	—
1858 S	476,000	19.00	22.00	28.00	65.00	90.00	975.	—
1859	748,000	17.50	21.00	26.00	47.50	75.00	675.	8000.
1859 O	2,834,000	16.00	19.00	22.50	36.00	67.50	475.	—
1859 S	566,000	18.00	22.00	27.00	67.50	80.00	775.	—
1860	303,700	19.00	22.00	28.00	75.00	100.	1000.	8000.
1860 O	1,290,000	16.00	19.00	22.50	36.00	67.50	475.	—
1860 S	472,000	19.00	22.00	27.50	80.00	90.00	875.	—

DATE	MINTAGE	G-4	VG-8	F-12	VF-20	EF-40	MS-60	Prf-65
1861	2,888,400	16.00	19.00	22.50	36.00	67.50	425.	8000.
1861 O	2,532,633	16.00	19.00	22.50	36.00	67.50	475.	—
1861 S	939,500	16.00	19.00	22.50	36.00	67.50	1000.	—
1862	253,550	22.00	26.00	32.00	52.50	105.	775.	8000.
1862 S	1,352,000	16.00	19.00	22.50	36.00	67.50	475.	—
1863	503,660	19.00	22.00	27.50	45.00	95.00	775.	8000.
1863 S	916,000	16.00	19.00	22.50	36.00	67.50	425.	—
1864	379,570	19.00	22.00	28.00	45.00	95.00	775.	8000.
1864 S	658,000	17.50	21.00	26.00	39.00	75.00	475.	—
1865	511,900	17.50	21.00	26.00	39.00	75.00	775.	8000.
1865 S	675,000	17.00	20.00	24.00	38.00	72.50	475.	—
1866	Unique		Not Issued For Circulation					
1866 S	1,054,000	70.00	85.00	150.00	235.00	340.	5000.	—

VARIETY FOUR - MOTTO ABOVE EAGLE 1866-1873

DIAMETER—30.6mm
WEIGHT—12.44 Grams
COMPOSITION—.900 Silver,
  .100 Copper
DESIGNER—Christian Gobrecht:
EDGE—Reeded

DATE	MINTAGE	G-4	VG-8	F-12	VF-20	EF-40	MS-60	Prf-65
1866	745,625	15.00	17.50	21.00	32.00	62.50	800.	3750.
1866 S	Inc. Above	15.00	17.50	21.00	32.00	62.50	800.	—
1867	449,925	18.50	21.00	26.00	37.00	80.00	1000.	3750.
1867 S	1,196,000	15.00	17.50	21.00	32.00	62.50	800.	—
1868	418,200	19.00	22.00	26.00	38.00	85.00	1000.	3750.
1868 S	1,160,000	15.00	17.50	21.00	32.00	62.50	800.	—
1869	795,900	15.00	17.50	21.00	32.00	62.50	800.	3750.
1869 S	656,000	17.00	20.00	22.50	34.00	75.00	825.	—
1870	634,900	17.00	20.00	22.50	34.00	75.00	825.	3750.
1870 CC	54,617	450.	625.	875.	1500.	2500.	—	—
1870 S	1,004,000	15.00	17.50	21.00	32.00	62.50	800.	—
1871	1,204,560	15.00	17.50	21.00	32.00	62.50	800.	3750.
1871 CC	153,950	120.	140.	160.	275.	550.	4000.	—
1871 S	2,178,000	15.00	17.50	21.00	32.00	62.50	800.	—
1872	881,550	15.00	17.50	21.00	32.00	62.50	800.	3750.
1872 CC	272,000	70.00	85.00	100.	165.	350.	2500.	—
1872 S	580,000	18.50	21.00	26.00	37.00	80.00	900.	—
1873 Closed 3	801,800	15.00	17.50	21.00	32.00	62.50	800.	3750.
1873 Open 3	Inc. Above	725.	900.	1200.	1800.	4200.	—	—
1873 CC	122,500	100.	120.	150.	235.	450.	3000.	—
1873 S	5,000		None Known to Exist					

VARIETY FIVE - ARROWS
AT DATE 1873-1874

DIAMETER—30.6mm
WEIGHT—12.50 Grams
COMPOSITION—.900 Silver,
 .100 Copper
DESIGNER—Christian Gobrecht
EDGE—Reeded

DATE	MINTAGE	G-4	VG-8	F-12	VF-20	EF-40	MS-60	Prf-65
1873	1,815,700	23.00	28.00	36.00	85.00	225.	1250.	15,000.
1873 CC	214,560	45.00	55.00	72.00	235.	425.	2500.	—
1873 S	233,000	28.00	34.00	45.00	120.	300.	1900.	—
1874	2,360,300	23.00	25.00	36.00	85.00	225.	1250.	15,000.
1874 CC	59,000	140.	200.	340.	500.	900.	4400.	—
1874 S	394,000	26.00	31.00	39.00	110.	265.	2000.	—

VARIETY FOUR RESUMED 1875-1891

DATE	MINTAGE	G-4	VG-8	F-12	VF-20	EF-40	MS-60	Prf-65
1875	6,027,500	15.00	17.50	21.00	38.00	62.50	825.	3750.
1875 CC	1,008,000	17.00	20.00	22.50	55.00	67.50	875.	—
1875 S	3,200,000	15.00	17.50	21.00	38.00	62.50	350.	—
1876	8,419,150	15.00	17.50	21.00	38.00	62.50	335.	3750.
1876 CC	1,956,000	17.00	20.00	22.50	42.50	67.50	875.	—
1876 S	4,528,000	15.00	17.50	21.00	38.00	62.50	335.	—
1877	8,304,510	15.00	17.50	21.00	38.00	62.50	335.	3750.
1877 CC	1,420,000	17.00	20.00	22.50	42.50	67.50	825.	—
1877 S	5,356,000	15.00	17.50	21.00	38.00	62.50	335.	—
1878	1,378,400	15.00	17.50	21.00	42.50	62.50	335.	3750.
1878 CC	62,000	235.	275.	375.	675.	1200.	3150.	—
1878 S	12,000	4000.	5250.	7250.	12,000.	18,000.	24,000.	—
1879	5,900	280.	300.	325.	400.	525.	1650.	10,500.
1880	9,755	225.	250.	275.	350.	450.	1550.	10,500.
1881	10,975	225.	240.	270.	325.	425.	1450.	10,500.
1882	5,500	275.	300.	325.	400.	525.	1650.	10,500.
1883	9,039	225.	240.	270.	350.	450.	1650.	10,500.
1884	5,275	280.	300.	330.	425.	550.	1750.	10,500.
1885	6,130	300.	320.	350.	450.	550.	1750.	10,500.
1886	5,886	300.	320.	350.	450.	550.	1750.	10,500.
1887	5,710	300.	320.	350.	450.	550.	1750.	10,500.
1888	12,833	200.	225.	250.	320.	400.	1200.	10,500.
1889	12,711	200.	225.	250.	320.	400.	1200.	10,500.
1890	12,590	200.	225.	250.	320.	400.	1200.	10,500.
1891	200,600	36.00	42.50	60.00	100.	200.	1200.	10,500.

BARBER TYPE
1892-1915

DIAMETER—30.6mm
WEIGHT—12.50 Grams
COMPOSITION—.900 Silver,
 .100 Copper
DESIGNER—Charles E. Barber
EDGE—Reeded
PURE SILVER CONTENT—.36169 Tr. Oz.

DATE	MINTAGE	G-4	VG-8	F-12	VF-20	EF-40	AU-50	MS-60	MS-65	Prf-65
1892	935,245	9.00	15.00	30.00	55.00	175.	300.	425.	3400.	3000.
1892 O	390,000	70.00	125.	200.	300.	450.	625.	950.	6000.	—
1892 S	1,020,028	65.00	120.	185.	275.	375.	550.	800.	6000.	—
1893	1,826,792	9.00	16.00	32.50	65.00	195.	320.	480.	3600.	3000.
1893 O	1,389,000	13.00	22.50	42.50	90.00	250.	425.	625.	11,000.	—
1893 S	740,000	42.50	75.00	120.	250.	350.	525.	1000.	11,000.	—
1894	1,148,972	9.00	17.50	38.00	85.00	215.	350.	550.	3600.	3000.
1894 O	2,138,000	8.00	13.00	35.00	85.00	235.	375.	475.	8000.	—
1894 S	4,048,690	7.00	11.00	22.50	55.00	175.	300.	475.	10,000.	—
1895	1,835,218	7.00	11.00	25.00	55.00	185.	310.	480.	4500.	3000.
1895 O	1,766,000	8.00	16.00	36.00	75.00	200.	315.	550.	8500.	—
1895 S	1,108,086	12.00	20.00	45.00	85.00	250.	375.	500.	12,000.	—
1896	950,762	8.00	12.00	35.00	68.00	225.	350.	500.	8500.	3000.
1896 O	924,000	9.00	15.00	42.50	95.00	300.	450.	1000.	13,000.	—
1896 S	1,140,948	40.00	60.00	95.00	175.	350.	500.	1100.	12,000.	—
1897	2,480,731	7.00	10.00	22.50	60.00	165.	275.	425.	3400.	3000.
1897 O	632,000	32.50	47.50	90.00	160.	375.	675.	1400.	7200.	—
1897 S	933,900	60.00	85.00	135.	235.	400.	625.	1200.	9500.	—
1898	2,956,735	6.00	9.00	22.50	58.00	160.	250.	425.	3400.	3000.
1898 O	874,000	9.00	16.00	47.50	125.	350.	500.	740.	7700.	—
1898 S	2,358,550	8.00	11.00	27.50	60.00	170.	265.	610.	10,500.	—
1899	5,538,846	6.00	8.00	22.50	58.00	160.	250.	425.	3400.	3000.
1899 O	1,724,000	7.00	10.00	26.00	65.00	200.	265.	575.	7400.	—
1899 S	1,686,411	8.00	11.00	27.50	60.00	165.	265.	550.	7000.	—
1900	4,762,912	6.00	8.00	20.00	58.00	160.	265.	425.	3400.	3000.
1900 O	2,744,000	7.00	10.00	24.00	62.00	175.	275.	700.	15,000.	—
1900 S	2,560,322	7.00	10.00	25.00	62.00	160.	265.	525.	10,500.	—
1901	4,268,813	6.00	8.00	20.00	54.00	160.	265.	425.	4400.	3000.
1901 O	1,124,000	8.00	11.00	32.50	95.00	275.	365.	1200.	30,000.	—
1901 S	847,044	12.00	22.00	48.00	170.	400.	625.	1300.	13,000.	—
1902	4,922,777	6.00	8.00	20.00	50.00	160.	265.	425.	3400.	3000.
1902 O	2,526,000	7.00	10.00	25.00	60.00	165.	750.	675.	11,500.	—
1902 S	1,460,670	8.00	11.00	30.00	85.00	200.	290.	540.	5250.	—

DATE	MINTAGE	G-4	VG-8	F-12	VF-20	EF-40	AU-50	MS-60	MS-65	Prf-65
1903	2,278,755	6.00	9.00	25.00	58.00	175.	280.	425.	7700.	3000.
1903 O	2,100,000	7.00	10.00	25.00	65.00	190.	290.	575.	9200.	—
1903 S	1,920,772	7.00	10.00	25.00	65.00	175.	275.	540.	9200.	—
1904	2,992,670	6.00	8.00	23.00	58.00	160.	265.	425.	4700.	3000.
1904 O	1,117,600	7.00	14.00	37.50	95.00	275.	375.	1200.	11,500.	—
1904 S	553,038	8.00	15.00	47.50	95.00	325.	450.	1500.	12,750.	—
1905	662,727	8.00	14.00	42.50	90.00	275.	400.	540.	6100.	3000.
1905 O	505,000	8.00	16.00	47.50	95.00	300.	425.	700.	6800.	—
1905 S	2,494,000	7.00	9.00	23.00	55.00	160.	265.	500.	10,700.	—
1906	2,638,675	5.00	8.00	19.00	50.00	160.	260.	425.	3400.	3000.
1906 D	4,028,000	6.00	8.00	20.00	52.00	160.	265.	425.	4100.	—
1906 O	2,446,000	6.00	9.00	23.00	57.00	160.	265.	540.	7000.	—
1906 S	1,740,154	7.00	10.00	24.00	60.00	175.	285.	525.	7100.	—
1907	2,598,575	5.00	8.00	19.00	50.00	155.	265.	425.	3400.	3000.
1907 D	3,856,000	6.00	8.00	19.00	50.00	155.	265.	425.	3400.	—
1907 O	3,946,000	7.00	8.00	20.00	52.00	155.	265.	450.	3400.	—
1907 S	1,250,000	6.00	10.00	25.00	60.00	175.	275.	550.	12,500.	—
1908	1,354,545	5.00	8.00	24.00	60.00	200.	290.	425.	3400.	3000.
1908 D	3,280,000	5.00	7.00	19.00	50.00	155.	255.	425.	3400.	—
1908 O	5,360,000	6.00	7.00	19.00	50.00	155.	255.	425.	3400.	—
1908 S	1,644,828	5.00	9.00	22.00	58.00	175.	265.	600.	7800.	—
1909	2,368,650	6.00	8.00	20.00	50.00	155.	255.	425.	3400.	3000.
1909 O	925,400	6.00	9.00	23.00	65.00	225.	290.	750.	6400.	—
1909 S	1,764,000	7.00	8.00	20.00	55.00	165.	255.	525.	4000.	—
1910	418,551	5.00	11.00	40.00	85.00	285.	425.	600.	3400.	3000.
1910 S	1,948,000	5.00	9.00	20.00	55.00	155.	265.	520.	4400.	—
1911	1,406,543	6.00	9.00	20.00	55.00	165.	265.	425.	3400.	3000.
1911 D	695,080	5.00	9.00	22.00	65.00	200.	290.	525.	3400.	—
1911 S	1,272,000	5.00	9.00	20.00	55.00	165.	265.	525.	8600.	—
1912	1,550,700	5.00	8.00	19.00	50.00	155.	265.	425.	3700.	3000.
1912 D	2,300,800	5.00	8.00	20.00	50.00	155.	255.	425.	3400.	—
1912 S	1,370,000	5.00	8.00	20.00	53.00	155.	265.	500.	5200.	—
1913	188,627	14.00	20.00	65.00	135.	350.	500.	875.	3600.	5500.
1913 D	534,000	7.00	11.00	27.50	65.00	215.	300.	500.	7300.	—
1913 S	604,000	7.00	10.00	26.00	62.00	200.	280.	540.	4000.	—
1914	124,610	22.50	32.50	85.00	210.	400.	550.	925.	11,500.	5700.
1914 S	992,000	6.00	9.00	20.00	60.00	175.	275.	500.	3800.	—
1915	138,450	16.00	25.00	55.00	170.	375.	525.	1000.	5000.	5800.
1915 D	1,170,400	5.00	8.00	19.00	50.00	155.	255.	425.	3400.	—
1915 S	1,604,000	5.00	8.00	19.00	50.00	155.	255.	450.	3400.	—

WALKING LIBERTY TYPE 1916-1947

DIAMETER—30.6mm
WEIGHT—12.50 Grams
COMPOSITION—.900 Silver,
  .100 Copper
DESIGNER—Adolph A. Weinman
EDGE—Reeded
PURE SILVER CONTENT—.36169 Tr. Oz.

MINT MARK ON OBVERSE

DATE	MINTAGE	G-4	VG-8	F-12	VF-20	EF-40	AU-50	MS-60	MS-65	Prf-65
1916 608,000		15.00	20.00	50.00	110.	195.	315.	450.	1550.	—
1916 D 1,014,400		8.00	13.00	25.00	60.00	145.	225.	375.	1800.	—
1916 S 508,000		24.00	32.50	120.	225.	350.	550.	800.	4500.	—
1917 D 765,400		9.00	12.00	28.00	75.00	155.	275.	500.	5600.	—
1917 S 952,000		10.00	16.00	32.50	150.	350.	550.	1100.	10,000.	—

MINT MARK ON REVERSE

DATE	MINTAGE	G-4	VG-8	F-12	VF-20	EF-40	AU-50	MS-60	MS-65	Prf-65
1917 12,292,000		5.50	6.00	9.00	20.00	32.50	65.00	120.	900.	—
1917 D 1,940,000		5.75	9.00	20.00	52.50	150.	300.	650.	15,000.	—
1917 S 5,554,000		5.50	6.00	17.00	26.00	52.50	120.	265.	9000.	—
1918 6,634,000		5.50	6.00	9.00	47.50	145.	250.	375.	3750.	—
1918 D 3,853,040		5.50	6.50	9.00	52.50	170.	280.	750.	16,500.	—
1918 S 10,282,000		5.50	6.00	9.00	30.00	52.50	120.	265.	11,500.	—
1919 962,000		11.00	15.00	29.00	110.	375.	600.	1000.	5500.	—
1919 D 1,165,000		9.50	11.00	31.00	140.	415.	875.	2200.	38,000.	—
1919 S 1,552,000		8.50	10.00	26.00	95.00	380.	775.	2000.	9000.	—
1920 6,372,000		5.50	6.00	9.00	22.50	55.00	115.	260.	6000.	—
1920 D 1,551,000		6.50	8.00	23.00	110.	255.	500.	1000.	8000.	—
1920 S 4,624,000		5.50	6.00	9.00	42.50	125.	350.	850.	7200.	—
1921 246,000		55.00	85.00	180.	450.	1000.	1500.	2250.	11,000.	—
1921 D 208,000		85.00	120.	250.	550.	1100.	1600.	2400.	7800.	—
1921 S 548,000		13.00	18.00	39.00	240.	1100.	2750.	6750.	32,000.	—
1923 S 2,178,000		5.50	6.50	9.00	37.50	160.	400.	925.	10,000.	—
1927 S 2,392,000		5.50	6.50	9.00	27.50	90.00	250.	750.	7500.	—
1928 S 1,940,000		5.50	6.50	9.00	30.00	100.	285.	850.	5800.	—
1929 D 1,001,200		6.50	8.50	9.00	22.50	75.00	160.	375.	1800.	—
1929 S 1,902,000		5.50	6.00	9.00	22.50	70.00	180.	375.	2100.	—
1933 S 1,786,000		6.50	8.50	9.00	21.00	52.50	160.	350.	1900.	—
1934 6,964,000		5.00	5.50	6.00	11.00	21.00	42.50	125.	325.	—
1934 D 2,361,400		5.00	5.50	6.00	18.00	21.00	47.50	240.	1100.	—
1934 S 3,652,000		5.00	5.50	6.00	15.00	32.50	110.	450.	1900.	—
1935 9,162,000		5.00	5.50	6.00	11.00	20.00	35.00	70.00	225.	—
1935 D 3,003,800		5.00	5.50	6.00	16.00	47.50	110.	235.	1100.	—
1935 S 3,854,000		5.00	5.50	6.00	15.00	40.00	110.	300.	1250.	—
1936 12,617,901		4.50	5.00	5.50	11.00	20.00	32.50	65.00	150.	2600.
1936 D 4,252,400		4.50	5.00	5.50	15.00	33.00	65.00	165.	275.	—

DATE	MINTAGE	G-4	VG-8	F-12	VF-20	EF-40	AU-50	MS-60	MS-65	Prf-65
1936 S	3,884,000	4.50	5.00	5.50	13.00	36.00	70.00	200.	525.	—
1937	9,527,728	4.50	5.00	5.50	11.00	20.00	34.00	65.00	160.	950.
1937 D	1,676,000	4.50	5.00	5.50	17.50	50.00	130.	315.	600.	—
1937 S	2,090,000	4.50	5.00	5.50	11.00	37.50	90.00	250.	425.	—
1938	4,118,152	4.50	5.00	5.50	11.00	21.00	50.00	150.	225.	725.
1938 D	491,600	18.00	22.00	27.50	35.00	100.	290.	850.	1150.	—
1939	6,820,808	4.50	5.00	5.50	11.00	20.00	32.50	120.	120.	650.
1939 D	4,267,800	4.50	5.00	5.50	13.00	21.00	37.50	115.	120.	—
1939 S	2,552,000	4.50	5.00	5.50	12.50	22.50	57.50	170.	225.	—
1940	9,167,279	4.50	5.00	5.50	7.00	20.00	30.00	45.00	115.	575.
1940 S	4,550,000	4.50	5.00	5.50	12.00	22.00	35.00	45.00	400.	—
1941	24,207,412	4.50	5.00	5.50	6.00	12.50	17.50	37.00	105.	575.
1941 D	11,248,400	4.50	5.00	5.50	6.00	18.00	36.00	45.00	115.	—
1941 S	8,098,000	4.50	5.00	5.50	6.00	22.00	62.00	95.00	1300.	—
1942	47,839,120	4.50	5.00	5.50	6.00	12.50	20.00	37.00	120.	575.
1942 D	10,973,800	4.50	5.00	5.50	6.00	16.00	32.50	45.00	230.	—
1942 S	12,706,000	4.50	5.00	5.50	6.00	17.00	50.00	60.00	700.	—
1943	53,190,000	4.50	5.00	5.50	6.00	12.50	19.00	37.00	115.	—
1943 D	11,346,000	4.50	5.00	5.50	6.00	18.00	34.00	45.00	135.	—
1943 S	13,450,000	4.50	5.00	5.50	6.00	20.00	42.50	60.00	500.	—
1944	28,206,000	4.50	5.00	5.50	6.00	12.50	20.00	37.00	115.	—
1944 D	9,769,000	4.50	5.00	5.50	6.00	12.50	32.50	40.00	115.	—
1944 S	8,904,000	4.50	5.00	5.50	6.00	12.50	42.50	45.00	900.	—
1945	31,502,000	4.50	5.00	5.50	6.00	12.50	19.00	45.00	115.	—
1945 D	9,966,800	4.50	5.00	5.50	6.00	13.00	18.00	40.00	120.	—
1945 S	10,156,000	4.50	5.00	5.50	6.00	13.00	27.00	45.00	200.	—
1946	12,118,000	4.50	5.00	5.50	6.00	13.00	22.50	40.00	115.	—
1946 D	2,151,000	4.75	5.50	6.00	7.00	15.00	42.50	40.00	115.	—
1946 S	3,724,000	4.50	5.00	5.50	6.00	14.00	32.00	40.00	115.	—
1947	4,094,000	4.50	5.00	5.50	6.00	12.50	32.00	40.00	130.	—
1947 D	3,900,600	4.50	5.00	5.50	6.00	12.50	20.00	40.00	115.	—

FRANKLIN TYPE
1948-1963

DIAMETER—30.6mm
WEIGHT—12.50 Grams
COMPOSITION—.900 Silver,
  .100 Copper
DESIGNER—John R. Sinnock
EDGE—Reeded
PURE SILVER CONTENT—.36169 Tr. Oz.

DATE	MINTAGE	EF-40	AU-50	MS-60	MS-65	Prf-65
1948	3,006,814	—	10.00	18.00	85.00	—
1948 D	4,028,600	—	9.50	12.00	160.	—
1949	5,614,000	11.00	15.00	40.00	95.00	—
1949 D	4,120,600	12.00	20.00	52.00	1400.	—
1949 S	3,744,000	25.00	52.00	80.00	150.	—
1950	7,793,509	—	12.50	40.00	100.	450.
1950 D	8,031,600	—	10.00	26.00	385.	—
1951	16,859,602	—	10.00	15.00	75.00	260.
1951 D	9,475,200	—	12.50	42.00	200.	—
1951 S	13,696,000	—	20.00	32.50	60.00	—
1952	21,274,073	—	10.00	12.50	60.00	140.
1952 D	25,395,600	—	10.00	10.00	175.	—
1952 S	5,526,000	—	17.50	40.00	60.00	—
1953	2,796,920	—	14.00	26.00	130.	100.
1953 D	20,900,400	—	8.00	9.00	170.	—
1953 S	4,148,000	—	10.00	24.00	40.00	—
1954	13,421,503	—	6.00	8.00	65.00	60.00
1954 D	25,445,580	—	5.25	6.00	125.	—
1954 S	4,993,400	—	7.00	8.00	35.00	—
1955	2,876,381	—	8.00	9.00	45.00	55.00
1956	4,701,384	—	5.75	7.00	35.00	20.00
1957	6,361,952	—	7.00	9.00	35.00	17.50
1957 D	19,966,850	—	5.25	6.00	35.00	—
1958	4,917,652	—	4.75	5.50	35.00	20.00
1958 D	23,962,412	—	3.75	4.25	35.00	—
1959	7,349,291	—	5.00	6.00	130.	17.50
1959 D	13,053,750	—	4.75	6.00	175.	—
1960	7,715,602	—	4.25	5.00	185.	16.00
1960 D	18,215,812	—	3.75	5.00	750.	—
1961	11,318,244	—	3.75	5.00	320.	15.00
1961 D	20,276,442	—	3.75	5.00	450.	—
1962	12,932,019	—	3.75	4.50	250.	15.00
1962 D	35,473,281	—	3.25	4.25	500.	—
1963	25,239,645	—	2.75	3.00	85.00	15.00
1963 D	67,069,292	—	2.50	2.75	80.00	—

KENNEDY TYPE
1964 TO DATE

DIAMETER—30.6mm
WEIGHT—1964, 12.50 Grams,
  1965-1970, 11.50 Grams,
  1971 To Date, 11.34 Grams
COMPOSITION—1964: .900 Silver,
  .100 Copper,
  1965-1970 Silver Clad
  overall composition
  .400 Silver .600 Copper,
  1971 To Date: Copper Clad Issue
  .750 Copper, .250 Nickel Outer Layers,
  Pure Copper Inner Core
DESIGNERS—Gilroy Roberts and
  Frank Gasparro
EDGE—Reeded
PURE SILVER CONTENT—1964:
  .36169 Tr. Oz.,
  1965-1970: .14792 Tr. Oz.

SILVER COINAGE 1964

DATE	MINTAGE	MS-60	MS-65	Prf-65
1964	277,254,766	2.50	3.75	13.00
1964 D	156,205,446	2.50	3.75	

SILVER CLAD COINAGE 1965-1970

DATE	MINTAGE	MS-60	MS-65	Prf-65
1965	65,879,366	1.25	2.75	—
1966	108,984,932	1.25	2.75	—
1967	295,046,978	1.10	2.50	—
1968 D	246,951,930	1.10	2.50	—
1968 S	3,041,506	PROOF ONLY		7.00
1969 D	129,881,800	1.10	2.25	—
1969 S	2,934,631	PROOF ONLY		5.50
1970 D	2,150,000	12.00	17.00	—
1970 S	2,632,810	PROOF ONLY		8.00

COPPER-NICKEL CLAD COINAGE

DATE	MINTAGE	MS-65	Prf-65
1971	155,164,000	1.00	—
1971 D	302,097,424	1.00	—
1971 S	PROOF ONLY	—	2.00
1972	153,180,000	.75	—
1972 D	141,890,000	.75	—
1972 S	PROOF ONLY	—	2.00
1973	64,964,000	.75	—
1973 D	83,171,400	.75	—
1973 S	PROOF ONLY	—	2.50
1974	201,596,000	.75	—
1974 D	79,066,300	.75	—
1974 S	PROOF ONLY	—	2.75
1977	43,598,000	.75	—
1977 D	31,449,106	.75	—
1977 S	PROOF ONLY	—	1.50
1978	14,350,000	.75	—
1978 D	13,765,799	.75	—
1978 S	PROOF ONLY	—	3.00
1979	68,312,000	.75	—
1979 D	15,815,422	.75	—
1979 S	PROOF ONLY	—	2.00
1980 P	44,134,000	.75	—

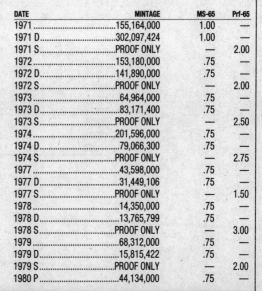

DATE	MINTAGE	MS-65	Prf-65
1980 D	33,456,449	.75	—
1980 S	PROOF ONLY	—	1.50
1981 P	29,544,000	.75	—
1981 D	27,839,533	.75	—
1981 S	PROOF ONLY	—	1.75
1982 P	10,819,000	2.25	—
1982 D	13,140,102	2.25	—
1982 S	PROOF ONLY	—	6.50
1983 P	34,139,000	3.00	—
1983 D	32,472,244	3.50	—
1983 S	PROOF ONLY	—	6.00
1984 P	26,029,000	3.25	—
1984 D	26,262,158	2.75	—
1984 S	PROOF ONLY	—	7.00
1985 P	18,706,962	2.25	—
1985 D	19,814,034	2.25	—
1985 S	PROOF ONLY	—	5.50
1986 P	13,107,633	3.00	—
1986 D	15,336,145	2.50	—
1986 S	PROOF ONLY	—	12.50
1987 P	2,890,758	3.00	—
1987 D	2,890,758	2.50	—
1987 S	PROOF ONLY	—	6.00
1988 P	13,626,000	2.50	—
1988 D	12,000,096	2.50	—
1988 S	PROOF ONLY	—	7.50
1989 P	24,542,000	2.50	—
1989 D	23,000,216	2.50	—
1989 S	PROOF ONLY	—	5.00
1990 P	22,278,000	1.50	—
1990 D	20,096,242	1.50	—
1990 S	PROOF ONLY	—	5.00
1991 P	14,874,000	1.50	—
1991 D	15,054,678	1.50	—
1991 S	PROOF ONLY	—	5.00
1992 P	—	1.00	—
1992 D	—	1.00	—
1992 S	PROOF ONLY	—	5.00
1993 P	—	1.00	—
1993 D	—	1.00	—
1993 S	PROOF ONLY	—	7.50

Silver Dollars 1794 To Date

Silver dollars were a part of the American coinage system from 1794 to 1981, with several lengthy breaks interspersed. The dollar unit has always been the foundation upon which the face values of all other United States coins are based. In all, there are eleven different types of silver dollars to collect; some don't cost very much, while others are very expensive. Nevertheless, solid investment opportunities abound in all types of silver dollars for the buyer who knows how to analyze market trends.

The Flowing Hair silver dollar saw production in 1794 and 1795. The 1794 is a consistent gainer suitable for big-time investors. Only twice over the last 40 years has there been a let-down in performance; once in the late 1960's and again in the late 1980's and early 1990's. Watch for the 1794 dollar to take off again shortly toward many years of sustained growth.

Both varieties of the 1795 Flowing Hair dollar are currently valued well below their 1983 highs, and probably will not fall much further. Although not nearly as expensive as the 1794, you'll still require over $700 to purchase a specimen in Good condition. That's a considerable sum of money to spend, but for a collectible of this caliber, it's really a bargain.

The Draped Bust silver dollar with the small eagle reverse had a short lifespan also, running from 1795 to 1798. There are many interesting varieties to study as these were the days when dies were engraved by hand. These silver dollars have followed almost identically the value trends of the 1795 Flowing Hair dollars, translating into more good buys for the investor or collector. This series contains a number of issues that are more easily affordable to the buying public than the previous silver dollars, although they're by no means inexpensive.

The large eagle reverse type of the Draped Bust motif was struck from 1798 to 1804. At the conclusion of this series, the dollar denomination entered into a period of hibernation which eventually stretched to 32 years. The latest value trends of these silver dollars cannot be categorically lumped into one overall summary; the price movements are varied from date to date and from condition to condition. However, judging from the 40 year track record of these coins, you should be guaranteed of future appreciation no matter which one you decide upon.

The Gobrecht dollars of 1836-1839 are technically defined as pattern coins because they were designed in preparation for the origination of a new dollar type Congress hoped would circulate more actively than its predecessors. The principal action making this possible was a reduction of the silver standard in 1837.

Gobrecht dollars in circulated grades have declined slightly in the 1990's, while uncirculated specimens have edged upward. Although still at bargain prices, Gobrecht dollars are still well beyond the reach of the average coin buyer.

The Liberty Seated silver dollar was patterned after the Gobrecht dollar, although the coin's reverse was completely overhauled before its release in 1840. The Liberty Seated dollar saw heavy circulation until its demise in 1873.

Liberty Seated dollars are indeed rare coins. Only a small fraction of the original 6½ million total survive this day. In spite of this restricted supply, Liberty Seated dollars are priced much lower than comparable rarities. A lack of collector passion has prevented examples of this series from being virtually unavailable and priced at levels far above those realized today.

If you're looking for a coin having practically no adverse potential, then Liberty Seated dollars are a good choice despite their noteworthy appreciation of late in MS-60. As an investment device, Liberty Seated dollars have displayed consistent, if not spectacular growth. On the occasions when there has been a softening in the Seated dollar market, prices merely remain stable, unlike most other series. We can expect similar occurances in the forseeable future. If you are an investor with a great deal of money at your disposal, you may want to entertain thoughts about the MS-65 and Proof Seated dollars. Of course there looms the possibility of a short term fallout since prices are already so much higher than they were a few years ago. As a far sighted investment, however, they have very promising potential, as genuine specimens of these grades border on being non-existent.

When choosing Liberty Seated dollars, make the extra effort to locate examples free of rough gouges and nicks or damaged otherwise. During their day, Seated dollars were extensively used and abused, which explains why so many of the surviving number are slightly impaired. This could require persistence on your part, since most dealers are apt to have at best only a small inventory of Seated dollars to choose from. Once you find the problem-free specimen you've been searching for, don't feel uneasy about paying a premium well over the list price; it's an investment you'll someday be happy you made.

The issuance of regular silver dollars came to a standstill in 1873 with the release of the slightly larger Trade dollar. The plan for the Trade dollar was to make commerce easier for United States businessmen operating in the Far East. For years, American coins were snubbed by Oriental merchants in favor of the Mexican peso, which contained more silver than our silver dollar. In order to compete in the region, Americans were forced to negotiate for pesos to trade with. Not coincidentally, Mexican dealers assessed extra charges to the Americans during the currency swaps. The heavier Trade dollar was supposed to eliminate the advantages the peso held over the dollar.

On the homefront, Trade dollars were approved by Congress as legal tender in transactions up to five dollars. When the price of silver dropped a few years after the Trade dollar was introduced, the government revoked its domestic legal tender status, making it in effect the only United States coin ever to be demonetized. Because there were so many Trade dollars circulating about, widespread confusion resulted. To compound matters, the mints kept releasing new Trade dollars upon an already confused nation. Confronted with an angry population, the government acted to suspend the production of Trade dollars for any reason other than proof sets in 1878. Proof examples were struck each year thereafter until 1885. The 1884 and 1885 proofs are among the rarest and most prized of all United States coins.

The quantity of Trade dollars existing today is deceivingly small for the total number minted. Remember, millions of these coins went overseas, but many never returned to the United States. Additionally, after Congress repealed the act authorizing the Trade dollar, over 7.7 million Trade dollars were redeemed in a government sponsored program.

For an investor planning to resell a newly purchased Trade dollar in five years or so at a respectable profit, the best hope lies in the MS-65 Uncirculated grade, which has lost a lot of ground since 1989. In fact, all other grades have partaken in a cooling off period in recent years, and now stand poised for positive growth. For long range planners, there is every reason to expect appreciation records similar to those in the past experienced by Trade dollars.

The restoration of the regular silver dollar was provided for by the passage of the Bland-Allison Act of 1878. The new type of dollar, called the Morgan dollar, was named after its designer, George T. Morgan. The powerful silver mining lobby, concerned over the decreasing value of their commodity, pressured Congress into approving the Bland-Allison Act. As part of the new law, the Treasury Department was required to purchase huge amounts of silver and convert it into dollar coins, in the hope of maintaining the price of silver at high levels. Under this plan, quantities of silver dollars became so large that they far exceeded the need, resulting in millions of unused dollars piling up in bank and Treasury vaults.

The Bland-Allison Act was modified by the Sherman Silver Purchase Act of 1890. The Act mandated a government purchase of 4.5 million ounces of silver each month, to be paid for with Treasury bonds redeemable either in gold or silver. Unexpectedly, most bond holders redeemed their notes in gold, depleting the Treasury's gold reserve and throwing the entire country into a severe financial panic in 1893. The financial panic led to the repeal of the Sherman Act, whichgreatly slowed the production of silver dollars throughout most of the 1890's. Coinage of the silver dollar was suspended after 1904 when the bullion supply allotted for the dollar pieces became exhausted.

Under the guidelines of the Pittman Act of 1918, over 270 million silver dollars were melted down for export and recoinage into smaller coins. The big melt-down explains why some of the Morgan dollars with reported mintages of over a million pieces are so scarce today. Some of the silver derived from the Pinman Act was used in the production of the 1921 dollars, the final year of the Morgan dollar.

Many dates of the Morgan dollars are not exceptionally rare, not even in MS-60 Uncirculated. As you'll recall, great numbers of the dollars never reached circulation. However, top grade Morgan dollars in MS-65 or better Uncirculated condition are much tougher to come by. The size and weight of silver dollars, when stored and handled in bags of 1000, left relatively few unscratched. Moreover, in the rush to produce the required quotas, Morgans were often struck in less than top quality form and luster. Morgan dollars having only a few blemishes with sharply detailed features on a bright reflective surface are indeed rare coins.

As investment coins, there is no doubt Morgan dollars have been a major force in the numismatic market. The total number of investor dollars spent on Morgans over the last ten years probably surpasses any other style of coin or denomination. For many, buying Morgan dollars before they became such a force resulted in stunning profits. The situation is not quite as simple today, but by carefully interpreting market trends and other external indicators, you can still choose Morgan dollars with excellent potential.

Morgan dollars in upper grades can be extremely volatile. The momentous price shifts of the 1980's have been caused by unparalleled promoter and speculator involvement. Morgan dollars are ideal objectives for promoters because of the relatively large quantity of uncirculated specimens available and the silver content of each coin. Their size and beauty makes it easier to push Morgan dollars as well. The recommendations that follow for investing in Morgan dollars will be expressed in generalities only, for in this segment of the coin market, what is true today may very well be completely untrue in a short while.

Presently, MS-65 Uncirculated specimens have tumbled to small fractions of their previous highs. Prices have been consistently soft for some time, suggesting that Morgans no longer enjoy a disproportionate share of the coin commodity headlines, as they once did. This fall from grace pertains to better dates as well as common date issues. The best time to buy is following a price collapse, meaning that now is the prime time to purchase these gems.

If you wanted to purchase only one Morgan dollar, consider the 1893-S. It is the rarest of the business strike Morgans and the critical key date of the set. If a price tag of $2000 for a Very Fine example frightens you, then remember this: the 1893-S has been, now is, and always will be a prized acquisition for numismatists and investors alike. Downside risk is something owners of this rarity need not worry about.

In short, the Morgan dollar is an interesting, historically significant series, which is sure to continue to attract investment capital. As an investor you will be able to profit best by staying informed of the latest price movements, and not by following the psychology of the masses. Think for yourself and use every method available to analyze the market, and you should do very, very well with Morgan dollars.

The Peace dollar type was commenced in 1921, the same year the Morgan dollar was put to rest. The new dollar was belatedly issued to celebrate the end of the Great War (later renamed World War I) and dedicated to the ideal of a just and lasting peace worldwide. Production of the Peace dollar continued until 1928, when it was suspended because of lack of demand. More Peace dollars were struck in 1934 to help eliminate war-debt accounts, but a law passed later in the year stated that paper Silver Certificates should be backed by "one dollar in silver" rather than "one silver dollar," as in the past. The Silver Act of 1934, as the new law was called, ended any further need for silver dollars. After the 1935 silver dollars were released, the Peace dollar series drew to a close.

As investment pieces, the Peace dollars have been exploited by promoters and speculators almost as much as Morgan dollars. Similar to the strategy for Morgans, buy the least expensive of the properly graded MS-65 Uncirculated dollars. Other than patience, there is no guaranteed formula for successfully investing in Morgan or Peace dollars, but if you start with these basic philosophies, you ought to make a high percentage of wise decisions.

Many dealers have stated in numismatic publications they believe hobbyists are again becoming more involved in the Morgan and Peace dollar arena. And so, now that the stampede of speculators has departed the collector has reasserted himself as a prominent part of the dollar market. With this in mind, your efforts will not be fruitless by focusing on key and semi-key dates grading Very Fine or better. Some to consider, among others, are the 1889-CC, 1894, 1928, and of course, the aforementioned 1893-S.

Silver dollar production was resumed in 1971 with the Eisenhower, or "Ike" dollar. "Metallic" dollar is a more accurate description of an Eisenhower coin since all Eisenhower dollars struck for circulation were composed of the familiar copper-nickel combination used beginning in 1965.

The last Eisenhower dollar was released in 1978, making it one of the shortest series of American coins. For such a brief time span, however, the Ike dollar series has plenty of varieties to study and collect. In all, there are 32 distinct coins compressed into only eight years of production! Many of the varieties came about because of composition changes.

One of the varieties you'll run into when you read about Ikes is the "Blue Box" Ikes. This refers to 40% silver Uncirculated Ikes sold directly by the Mint to collectors, and packaged in blue boxes. The dates for the Blue Box Ikes are 1971-S, 1972-S, 1973-S, 1974-S, and 1776-1976-S. In a similar fashion, "Brown Box" Ikes are Proof coins mailed in brown boxes, also containing 40% silver. Brown Box Ikes are dated 1971-S, 1972-S, 1973-S, 1974-S, and 1976-S. All other Eisenhower dollars were minted in the copper-nickel composition.

All Ike dollars made in 1975 and 1976 carry the dual date 1776-1976, in observance of our bicentennial celebration, meaning of course, there are no dollars dated 1975. Dollars struck in 1975 can easily be distinguished from those produced in 1976, despite the fact they bear the identical dual date. Numismatists therefore classify 1776-1976 dollars as Type I and Type II. The Type I dollars have the design in low relief and bold flat lettering on the reverse. The Type II coins have a sharp design and the lettering on the reverse is thinner and more contoured. Taking into account the two designs, the metallic diversity, and mint marks, there are eight different varieties alone of the 1776-1976 dollars to collect.

Eisenhower dollars are good long term investments, particularly if purchased at today's prices. Their values have plunged recently, most notably the MS-65 Uncirculated and Proof Ikes, now selling for only about one-third their 1989 record highs. Overall, the cost of assembling a complete set of quality Ikes is extremely low.

As you go about assembling your collection of Ikes, work your hardest to locate MS-67 specimens. The bidding for these pieces is not fierce, so you ought to be able to purchase them at reasonable prices. Be prepared to do some searching, as many notable dealers say locating true MS-67 Eisenhower dollars is more difficult than finding MS-67 Morgan dollars, especially with the regular clad Ikes. It could be a real challenge!

The ill-fated Susan B. Anthony dollar was minted only from 1979 to 1981. After what seemed like a good idea, the government halted production following objections from many groups representing various special interests. It seems as if the Anthony dollar satisfied hardly anyone.

Not only were the Anthony dollars not accepted as a medium for exchange, most have little potential as investment items. Hundreds of millions sit idle in Treasury vaults, never released for circulation. The day these common coins become attractive investments will probably be a day well beyond our lifetime. But let's use our imagination for a moment. It is entirely possible our government could act on an edict to destroy all Anthony dollars currently in storage, which in effect would transform all privately held Anthonys into scarce coins. Those MS-67 Anthonys purchased in 1993 for next to nothing, all of a sudden will become highly prized collectibles. Who is to say that a scenario like this couldn't unfold?

SILVER DOLLARS
1794 TO DATE

FLOWING HAIR TYPE
1794-1795

DIAMETER—39-40mm
WEIGHT—26.96 Grams
COMPOSITION—.8924 Silver,
    .1076 Copper
DESIGNER—Robert Scot
EDGE—HUNDRED CENTS ONE DOLLAR OR UNIT With Decorations Between Words

DATE	MINTAGE	G-4	VG-8	F-12	VF-20	EF-40	MS-60
1794	1,758	10,000.	14,000.	19,000.	30,000.	45,000.	—
1795 2 Leaves	203,033	800.	950.	1500.	2250.	4000.	42,000.
1795 3 Leaves	Inc. Above	800.	950.	1500.	2250.	4000.	42,000.

DRAPED BUST TYPE
SMALL EAGLE REVERSE
1795-1798

DIAMETER—39-40mm
WEIGHT—26.96 Grams
COMPOSITION—.8924 Silver, .1076 Copper
DESIGNER—Robert Scot
EDGE—HUNDRED CENTS ONE DOLLAR OR UNIT With Decorations Between Words

DATE	MINTAGE	G-4	VG-8	F-12	VF-20	EF-40	MS-60
1795	Inc. Above	625.	850.	1150.	1800.	3800.	17,500.
1796 Sm. Date, Sm. Letters	72,920	575.	750.	1050.	1800.	3500.	16,000.
1796 Sm. Date, Lg. Letters	Inc. Above	575.	750.	1050.	1800.	3500.	16,000.
1796 Lg. Date, Sm. Letters	Inc. Above	575.	750.	1050.	1800.	3500.	16,000.
1797 9 Stars Left, 7 Stars, Sm. Letters	7,776	1600.	1900.	2700.	4400.	8500.	24,000.

DATE	MINTAGE	G-4	VG-8	F-12	VF-20	EF-40	MS-60
1797 9 Stars Left, 7 Stars Right, Lg. Letters ...Inc. Above		600.	750.	1025.	1800.	3500.	16,000.
1797 10 Stars Left, 6 Stars Right.............Inc. Above		600.	750.	1025.	1800.	3500.	16,000.
1798 13 Stars............................327,536		950.	1200.	1500.	2500.	4800.	19,000.
1798 15 Stars..............................Inc. Above		1150.	1700.	2200.	3250.	7000.	19,000.

DRAPED BUST TYPE
HERALDIC EAGLE
REVERSE
1798-1804

DIAMETER—39-40mm
WEIGHT—26.96 Grams
COMPOSITION—
 .8924 Silver, .1076 Copper
DESIGNER—Robert Scot
EDGE—HUNDRED CENTS ONE DOLLAR
 OR UNIT With Decorations Between Words

DATE	MINTAGE	G-4	VG-8	F-12	VF-20	EF-40	MS-60
1798 Knob 9.........................Inc. Above		350.	400.	475.	850.	1700.	10,000.
1798 10 Arrows.....................Inc. Above		350.	400.	475.	700.	1350.	10,000.
1798 Close Date ....Inc. Above		350.	400.	475.	700.	1350.	10,000.
1798 Wide Date, 13 Arrows .....Inc. Above		350.	400.	475.	700.	1350.	10,000.
1799/98 13 Star Rev. 423,515		350.	400.	475.	700.	1350.	16,000.
1799/98 15 Star Rev. ....Inc. Above		450.	550.	1000.	1200.	2100.	16,000.
1799 Irregular Date, 13 Star Reverse.......Inc. Above		350.	400.	475.	700.	1350.	10,000.
1799 Irregular Date, 15 Star Reverse.......Inc. Above		350.	400.	475.	700.	1350.	10,000.
1799 Normal Date ....Inc. Above		350.	400.	475.	700.	1350.	10,000.
1799 Stars-8 Left, 5 Right ......Inc. Above		450.	550.	900.	1200.	2100.	10,000.
1800 229,920		350.	400.	475.	700.	1350.	10,000.
1800 Very Wide Date, Low 8.....Inc. Above		350.	400.	475.	700.	1350.	10,000.
1800 Dotted Date ....Inc. Above		350.	400.	475.	700.	1350.	10,000.
1800 12 Arrows.....................Inc. Above		350.	400.	475.	700.	1350.	10,000.
1800 10 Arrows.....................Inc. Above		350.	400.	475.	700.	1350.	10,000.
1800 AMERICAI ....Inc. Above		350.	400.	475.	850.	1650.	10,000.
1801 54,454		350.	400.	475.	850.	1850.	10,000.
1801 Restrike.......................Unknown			PROOF ONLY—EXTREMELY RARE				
1802/1 Narrow Date 41,650		425.	500.	825.	950.	2000.	10,000.
1802/1 Wide Date...................Inc. Above		425.	500.	700.	900.	1600.	10,000.
1802 Narrow Date ....Inc. Above		450.	525.	700.	900.	1600.	10,000.
1802 Wide Date.....................Inc. Above		450.	525.	700.	900.	1600.	10,000.
1802 Restrike.......................Unknown			PROOF ONLY—EXTREMELY RARE				
1803 Large 3........................85,634		350.	400.	600.	900.	1600.	10,000.
1803 Small 3 ....Inc. Above		350.	450.	700.	1100.	1800.	10,000.
1803 Restrike.......................Unknown			PROOF ONLY—EXTREMELY RARE				
1804 (3 Varieties) ....15 Known			Auction '89 Sale $990,000.				

GOBRECHT TYPE (PATTERNS)
1836-1839

THESE PATTERN
COINS DESIGNED BY
CHRISTIAN GOBRECHT
LED TO THE INTRODUCTION
OF THE U.S. LIBERTY
SEATED COINAGE
ALTHOUGH
THESE PATTERNS
WERE NEVER INTENDED
TO CIRCULATE, SEVERAL
EXISTING SPECIMENS
SHOW CONSIDERABLE WEAR.

DATE	MINTAGE	VF-20	EF-40	Prf-65
1836 No Stars Obv.	Est. 1000	3800.	4500.	7000.
1838 No Stars Rev.	Est. 25	3000.	3400.	11,500.
1839 No Stars Rev.	Est. 300	4750.	6000.	8000.

LIBERTY SEATED TYPE
1840-1873
VARIETY ONE - NO MOTTO ABOVE EAGLE
1840-1866

DIAMETER—38.1mm
WEIGHT—26.73 Grams
COMPOSITION—.900 Silver,
   .100 Copper
DESIGNER—Christian Gobrecht
EDGE—Reeded

DATE	MINTAGE	G-4	VG-8	F-12	VF-20	EF-40	MS-60	MS-65	Prf-65
1840	61,005	170.	225.	265.	340.	525.	1500.	—	—
1841	173,000	120.	190.	250.	300.	400.	1250.	25,000.	—
1842	184,618	100.	170.	250.	300.	400.	1100.	25,000.	—
1843	165,100	100.	170.	250.	300.	400.	1350.	25,000.	—
1844	20,000	200.	260.	310.	420.	600.	2000.	—	—
1845	24,500	190.	250.	290.	380.	575.	3000.	—	—
1846	110,600	100.	170.	250.	300.	400.	900.	25,000.	—
1846 O	59,000	225.	250.	300.	425.	600.	4000.	—	—
1847	140,750	100.	170.	250.	300.	400.	900.	25,000.	—
1848	15,000	250.	325.	475.	625.	800.	2000.	25,000.	—
1849	62,600	150.	190.	250.	300.	400.	1800.	25,000.	—
1850	7,500	300.	400.	575.	775.	950.	3500.	—	—
1850 O	40,000	275.	375.	600.	900.	1200.	3500.	—	—
1851	1,300				RARE				
1852	1,100				RARE				

DATE	MINTAGE	G-4	VG-8	F-12	VF-20	EF-40	MS-60	MS-65	Prf-65
1853	46,110	165.	225.	275.	375.	500.	1200.	—	—
1854	33,140	525.	725.	1000.	1400.	2000.	5700.	—	—
1855	26,000	475.	650.	900.	1200.	1750.	5200.	—	35,000.
1856	63,500	175.	200.	270.	380.	550.	1850.	—	35,000.
1857	94,000	160.	190.	250.	360.	525.	2400.	—	35,000.
1858	Est. 80			PROOF ONLY					42,500.
1859	256,500	275.	350.	475.	625.	775.	2000.	25,000.	15,000.
1859 O	360,000	85.00	125.	175.	200.	320.	900.	25,000.	—
1859 S	20,000	250.	300.	375.	575.	900.	—	—	—
1860	218,930	300.	375.	575.	675.	900.	2100.	25,000.	15,000.
1860 O	515,000	85.00	125.	175.	200.	320.	900.	25,000.	—
1861	78,500	325.	390.	525.	675.	850.	2100.	25,000.	15,000.
1862	12,090	300.	375.	500.	650.	800.	2300.	25,000.	15,000.
1863	27,660	150.	190.	250.	350.	450.	1900.	25,000.	15,000.
1864	31,170	170.	225.	280.	375.	450.	1700.	25,000.	15,000.
1865	47,000	150.	210.	260.	350.	425.	1600.	25,000.	15,000.
1866	2 Known			Not Issued For Circulation					

***VARIETY TWO -
MOTTO ABOVE EAGLE
1866-1873***

DIAMETER—38.1mm
WEIGHT—26.73 Grams
COMPOSITION—.900 Silver,
 .100 Copper
DESIGNER—Christian Gobrecht
EDGE—Reeded

DATE	MINTAGE	G-4	VG-8	F-12	VF-20	EF-40	MS-60	MS-65	Prf-65
1866	49,625	150.	220.	250.	350.	475.	2300.	28,000.	15,000.
1867	47,525	150.	220.	250.	350.	475.	2300.	28,000.	15,000.
1868	162,700	135.	175.	225.	300.	400.	2200.	28,000.	15,000.
1869	424,300	110.	150.	120.	275.	385.	2200.	28,000.	15,000.
1870	416,000	100.	140.	195.	260.	350.	2200.	28,000.	15,000.
1870 CC	12,462	285.	375.	475.	600.	750.	2600.	—	—
1870 S	Unknown			A.N.A. Auction 1978 VF $39,000.					
1871	1,074,760	85.00	125.	160.	200.	320.	900.	28,000.	15,000.
1871 CC	1,376	1200.	1650.	2000.	2900.	4200.	7800.	—	—
1872	1,106,450	85.00	125.	160.	200.	320.	900.	28,000.	15,000.
1872 CC	3,150	850.	1200.	1500.	2000.	2850.	4700.	—	—
1872 S	9,000	250.	325.	475.	750.	1000.	3400.	—	—
1873	293,600	100.	140.	190.	275.	375.	2300.	28,000.	15,000.
1873 CC	2,300	2300.	3000.	3800.	5000.	7500.	16,000.	—	—
1873 S	700			None Known To Exist					

TRADE DOLLARS
1873-1885

DIAMETER—38.1mm
WEIGHT—27.22 Grams
COMPOSITION—.900 Silver,
  .100 Copper
DESIGNER—William Barber
EDGE—Reeded

DATE	MINTAGE	G-4	VG-8	F-12	VF-20	EF-40	MS-60	MS-65	Prf-65
1873	397,500	80.00	90.00	110.	160.	240.	1100.	20,000.	20,000.
1873 CC	124,500	145.	170.	200.	250.	400.	1600.	20,000.	—
1873 S	703,000	90.00	105.	125.	170.	275.	1300.	14,000.	—
1874	987,800	100.	120.	150.	200.	300.	725.	10,000.	20,000.
1874 CC	1,373,200	75.00	85.00	100.	120.	220.	1000.	18,000.	—
1874 S	2,549,000	70.00	75.00	90.00	110.	200.	675.	10,000.	—
1875	218,900	220.	250.	325.	575.	850.	1800.	20,000.	20,000.
1875 CC	1,573,700	70.00	75.00	90.00	110.	200.	950.	20,000.	—
1875 S	4,487,000	55.00	65.00	75.00	90.00	170.	675.	10,000.	—
1875 S/CC	Inc. Above	220.	270.	350.	500.	725.	1600.	—	—
1876	456,150	65.00	75.00	90.00	110.	200.	675.	10,000.	20,000.
1876 CC	509,000	80.00	90.00	110.	160.	240.	1000.	15,000.	—
1876 S	5,227,000	55.00	65.00	75.00	90.00	170.	675.	10,000.	—
1877	3,039,710	65.00	70.00	80.00	100.	185.	675.	10,000.	20,000.
1877 CC	534,000	90.00	105.	125.	180.	280.	1250.	15,000.	—
1877 S	9,519,000	55.00	65.00	75.00	90.00	170.	675.	10,000.	—
1878	900			PROOF ONLY					24,000.
1878 CC	97,000	200.	250.	340.	475.	800.	2650.	—	—
1878 S	4,162,000	55.00	65.00	75.00	90.00	170.	675.	10,000.	—
1879	1,541			PROOF ONLY					24,000.
1880	1,987			PROOF ONLY					22,000.
1881	960			PROOF ONLY					22,000.
1882	1,097			PROOF ONLY					22,000.
1883	979			PROOF ONLY					22,000.
1884	10		May 1985 Hanks & Associates Sale—PROOF						50,000.
1885	5		August 1980 Auction '80 Sale—PROOF						110,000.

MORGAN TYPE
1878-1921

DIAMETER—38.1mm
WEIGHT—26.73 Grams
COMPOSITION—.900 Silver,
.100 Copper
DESIGNER—George T. Morgan
EDGE—Reeded
PURE SILVER CONTENT—.77344 Tr. Oz.

DATE	MINTAGE	VG-8	F-12	VF-20	EF-40	AU-50	MS-60	MS-65	Prf-65
1878 8 Tail Feathers	750,000	11.00	13.00	15.00	22.50	30.00	45.00	1275.	7000.
1878 7/8 Tail Feathers	9,759,550	13.50	16.00	20.00	29.00	44.00	65.00	2400.	—
1878 7 Tail Feathers, 2nd Reverse	Inc. Above	—	—	12.00	13.50	20.00	26.00	1250.	8500.
1878 7 Tail Feathers, 3rd Reverse	Inc. Above	12.00	13.50	16.00	18.50	24.00	30.00	2700.	—
1878 S	9,744,000	—	—	—	12.00	16.00	25.00	295.	—
1878 CC	2,212,000	20.00	24.00	28.00	34.00	48.00	72.50	1200.	—
1879	14,807,100	—	—	—	11.50	15.00	25.00	1100.	4500.
1879 O	2,887,000	—	—	—	11.50	23.00	36.00	4250.	—
1879 S 2nd Reverse	9,110,000	12.00	13.00	16.00	20.00	31.00	77.00	5000.	—
1879 S 3rd Reverse	Inc. Above	—	—	11.50	12.50	15.00	22.00	135.	—
1879 CC	756,000	32.00	36.00	67.00	200.	520.	1250.	17,500.	—
1880	12,601,335	—	—	—	11.50	13.50	26.00	2000.	4500.
1880 8/7	Inc. Above	95.00	120.	185.	265.	425.	—	—	—
1880 O	5,305,000	—	—	—	11.50	23.00	39.00	20,000.	—
1880 O 8/7	Inc. Above	42.50	52.50	65.00	80.00	100.	200.	21,000.	—
1880 S	8,900,000	—	—	—	11.50	15.00	21.00	135.	—
1880 S 8/7	Inc. Above	—	—	—	—	—	80.00	—	—
1880/79 CC 2nd Rev.	591,000	46.00	55.00	70.00	87.50	125.	235.	2000.	—
1880 CC 2nd Rev.	Inc. Above	32.00	42.00	62.00	94.00	125.	150.	1250.	—
1880 CC 3rd Rev.	Inc. Above	32.00	42.00	62.00	90.00	115.	130.	625.	—
1880 CC 8/7 3rd Rev. High 7	Inc. Above	—	—	—	—	—	235.	2000.	—
1880 CC 8/7 3rd Rev. Low 7	Inc. Above	—	—	—	—	—	375.	2000.	—
1881	9,163,975	—	—	—	11.50	15.00	25.00	1200.	4500.
1881 O	5,708,000	—	—	—	11.50	13.50	21.00	2200.	—
1881 S	12,760,000	—	—	—	12.50	14.00	21.00	135.	—
1881 CC	296,000	72.00	85.00	105.	125.	135.	150.	475.	—
1882	11,101,100	—	—	—	11.50	13.50	25.00	775.	4800.
1882 O	6,090,000	—	—	—	12.00	13.50	23.00	1450.	—
1882 O/S	Inc. Above	—	—	—	13.00	15.00	30.00	1800.	—
1882 S	9,250,000	—	—	—	12.50	16.00	22.00	135.	—
1882 CC	1,133,000	23.00	30.00	37.50	45.00	54.00	70.00	320.	—
1883	12,291,039	—	—	—	11.50	13.00	24.00	165.	4500.

DATE	MINTAGE	VG-8	F-12	VF-20	EF-40	AU-50	MS-60	MS-65	Prf-65
1883 O	8,725,000	—	—	—	11.00	12.00	16.00	135.	—
1883 S	6,250,000	—	12.00	15.00	20.00	97.00	325.	22,500.	—
1883 CC	1,204,000	23.00	30.00	38.00	45.00	52.00	67.00	250.	—
1884	14,070,875	—	—	—	11.50	15.00	21.00	320.	4500.
1884 O	9,730,000	—	—	—	11.50	13.00	21.00	135.	—
1884 S	3,200,000	—	12.00	15.00	29.00	195.	3500.	115,000.	—
1884 CC	1,136,000	50.00	54.00	55.00	56.00	58.00	70.00	270.	—
1885	17,787,767	—	—	—	11.50	13.00	16.00	160.	4500.
1885 O	9,185,000	—	—	—	11.00	12.00	21.00	140.	—
1885 S	1,497,000	11.00	15.00	17.50	21.00	45.00	72.00	2500.	—
1885 CC	228,000	165.	175.	185.	195.	205.	220.	575.	—
1886	19,963,886	—	—	—	11.00	12.00	16.00	140.	4800.
1886 O	10,710,000	—	12.00	15.00	18.50	45.00	200.	27,500.	—
1886 S	750,000	13.00	16.00	21.00	32.00	52.00	100.	2500.	—
1887	20,290,710	—	—	—	11.00	12.00	16.00	140.	4500.
1887 O	11,550,000	—	—	—	13.00	21.00	35.00	3900.	—
1887 S	1,771,000	—	13.50	15.00	18.50	32.00	60.00	3900.	—
1888	19,183,833	—	—	—	11.50	12.50	18.00	230.	5000.
1888 O	12,150,000	—	—	—	12.00	15.00	22.00	1300.	—
1888 S	657,000	15.00	20.00	25.00	32.00	67.00	125.	3000.	—
1889	21,726,811	—	—	—	11.00	12.00	18.00	525.	5000.
1889 O	11,875,000	—	—	11.50	16.00	32.00	72.00	4000.	—
1889 S	700,000	13.00	18.50	23.00	26.00	46.00	77.00	1300.	—
1889 CC	350,000	140.	170.	255.	625.	2500.	6700.	125,000.	—
1890	16,802,590	—	—	—	12.00	13.50	22.00	3800.	4500.
1890 O	10,710,000	—	—	—	13.00	21.00	32.00	4250.	—
1890 S	8,230,373	—	—	11.50	14.00	23.00	40.00	850.	—
1890 CC	2,309,041	20.00	24.00	28.00	40.00	80.00	210.	4600.	—
1890 CC Tail Bar	Inc. Above	20.00	24.00	28.00	40.00	80.00	210.	4600.	—
1891	8,694,206	—	—	12.50	15.00	23.00	40.00	4600.	4500.
1891 O	7,954,529	—	—	13.50	18.50	32.00	65.00	6750.	—
1891 S	5,296,000	—	—	11.50	13.50	22.00	40.00	1250.	—
1891 CC	1,618,000	21.00	26.00	30.00	40.00	77.00	115.	2500.	—
1892	1,037,245	13.50	14.50	15.00	18.50	47.50	87.00	2100.	4500.
1892 O	2,744,000	12.00	13.00	16.00	17.50	45.00	90.00	5600.	—
1892 S	1,200,000	14.00	17.00	42.00	110.	1750.	10,000.	68,000.	—
1892 CC	1,352,000	27.50	33.00	45.00	85.00	175.	290.	4200.	—
1893	378,792	42.00	52.50	65.00	75.00	145.	230.	5100.	4500.
1893 O	300,000	52.00	60.00	70.00	150.	350.	1400.	85,000.	—
1893 S	100,000	600.	900.	1150.	2700.	12,500.	20,000.	145,000.	—
1893 CC	677,000	44.00	60.00	105.	385.	700.	1100.	35,000.	—
1894	110,972	180.	215.	250.	300.	500.	800.	13,500.	4800.
1894 O	1,723,000	12.00	20.00	23.00	28.00	120.	600.	32,000.	—
1894 S	1,260,000	13.00	23.00	34.00	78.00	160.	300.	5000.	—
1895	12,880			STRUCK IN PROOF ONLY					30,000.
1895 O	450,000	52.00	65.00	85.00	170.	850.	6100.	35,000.	—
1895 S	400,000	95.00	120.	165.	370.	575.	975.	18,000.	—
1896	9,967,762	—	—	—	11.00	12.50	21.00	210.	4500.
1896 O	4,900,000	—	11.50	13.00	16.00	100.	700.	36,500.	—
1896 S	5,000,000	11.00	16.00	36.00	105.	290.	650.	7600.	—
1897	2,822,731	—	—	—	11.00	12.50	15.00	420.	6000.

DATE	MINTAGE	VG-8	F-12	VF-20	EF-40	AU-50	MS-60	MS-65	Prf-65
1897 O	4,004,000	—	—	12.50	16.00	65.00	575.	24,000.	—
1897 S	5,825,000	—	—	11.50	15.00	21.00	42.50	420.	—
1898	5,884,735	—	—	—	11.50	13.00	16.00	315.	4800.
1898 O	4,440,000	—	12.00	13.00	14.00	15.00	16.00	140.	—
1898 S	4,102,000	12.50	13.50	17.50	25.00	50.00	115.	2000.	—
1899	330,846	20.00	27.50	32.00	42.50	58.00	80.00	1000.	5000.
1899 O	12,290,000	—	—	—	11.50	13.00	18.00	140.	—
1899 S	2,562,000	12.50	13.50	18.50	26.00	57.50	110.	1250.	—
1900	8,880,938	—	—	—	11.00	12.50	21.00	210.	4800.
1900 O	12,590,000	—	—	—	13.00	14.00	21.00	150.	—
1900 O/CC	Inc. Above	17.50	20.00	23.00	28.00	78.00	175.	1550.	—
1900 S	3,540,000	11.00	13.50	17.50	26.00	45.00	90.00	2400.	—
1901	6,962,813	15.00	17.50	26.00	40.00	160.	1200.	85,000.	6500.
1901 O	13,320,000	—	—	—	11.50	13.50	22.00	210.	—
1901 S	2,284,000	13.50	16.00	22.00	40.00	90.00	220.	3500.	—
1902	7,994,777	—	—	12.00	13.00	23.00	37.50	900.	6300.
1902 O	8,636,000	—	—	—	11.00	12.50	16.00	200.	—
1902 S	1,530,000	17.50	29.00	40.00	58.00	90.00	150.	3100.	—
1903	4,652,755	13.50	15.00	16.00	17.50	20.00	30.00	260.	4800.
1903 O	4,450,000	115.	130.	135.	140.	145.	150.	420.	—
1903 S	1,241,000	14.00	20.00	58.00	165.	700.	1800.	5400.	—
1904	2,788,650	—	—	12.00	16.00	31.00	58.00	3250.	4800.
1904 O	3,720,000	—	—	12.00	13.00	14.00	16.00	140.	—
1904 S	2,304,000	13.50	17.50	33.00	115.	440.	800.	7700.	—
1921	44,690,000	—	—	—	—	10.00	12.00	160.	—
1921 D	20,345,000	—	—	—	—	12.00	26.00	420.	—
1921 S	21,695,000	—	—	—	—	12.00	26.00	1500.	—

PEACE TYPE
1921-1935

DIAMETER—38.1mm
WEIGHT—26.73 Grams
COMPOSITION—
.900 Silver, .100 Copper
DESIGNER—
Anthony De Francisci
EDGE—Reeded
PURE SILVER CONTENT—
.77344 Tr. Oz.

DATE	MINTAGE	VG-8	F-12	VF-20	EF-40	AU-50	MS-60	MS-65
1921	1,006,473	20.00	26.00	35.00	45.00	80.00	125.	1600.
1922	51,737,000	—	—	—	—	8.00	11.00	210.
1922 D	15,063,000	—	—	—	—	11.00	22.00	575.
1922 S	17,475,000	—	—	—	—	11.00	22.00	2450.
1923	30,800,000	—	—	—	—	9.00	11.00	210.
1923 D	6,811,000	—	—	—	—	15.00	26.00	2100.
1923 S	19,020,000	—	—	—	—	11.00	22.00	5700.
1924	11,811,000	—	—	—	—	10.00	12.00	525.
1924 S	1,728,000	—	11.00	13.50	16.00	48.00	130.	8200.
1925	10,198,000	—	—	—	—	10.00	12.00	210.

DATE	MINTAGE	VG-8	F-12	VF-20	EF-40	AU-50	MS-60	MS-65
1925 S	1,610,000	—	10.00	12.00	15.00	27.00	52.00	6000.
1926	1,939,000	—	—	10.00	12.00	16.00	23.00	525.
1926 D	2,348,700	—	—	10.00	13.50	28.00	47.00	850.
1926 S	6,980,000	—	—	10.00	12.50	17.00	29.00	2500.
1927	848,000	13.50	16.00	17.50	22.00	31.00	52.00	6500.
1927 D	1,268,900	12.00	13.00	16.00	23.00	70.00	160.	4200.
1927 S	866,000	13.00	14.00	15.00	20.00	57.00	87.00	6700.
1928	360,649	95.00	100.	105.	115.	145.	180.	3250.
1928 S	1,632,000	11.00	12.50	13.50	16.00	40.00	80.00	17,000.
1934	954,057	13.50	15.00	16.00	21.00	33.00	75.00	1300.
1934 D	1,569,500	12.50	13.50	15.00	18.50	33.00	100.	3400.
1934 S	1,011,000	12.50	16.00	40.00	155.	450.	1000.	5600.
1935	1,576,000	11.00	12.50	13.50	17.50	23.00	42.50	950.
1935 S	1,964,000	—	11.00	13.50	17.50	62.50	100.	1350.

EISENHOWER TYPE
1971-1978

DIAMETER—38.1mm
WEIGHT—Silver Clad—24.50 Grams,
  Copper-Nickel Clad—22.68 Grams
COMPOSITION—Silver Issue, .800 Silver,
  .200 Copper Outer Layers
  .210 Silver, .790 Copper Inner Core
  .400 Silver Overall
  Copper Clad Issue—.750 Copper, .
  250 Nickel Outer Layers, Pure Copper Inner Core
DESIGNER—Frank Gasparro
EDGE—Reeded
PURE SILVER CONTENT FOR SILVER ISSUE—.31625 Tr. Oz.

NOTE: This type has been divided into two separate listings
because different metallic compositions were used concurrently
from 1971 to 1974. The Eisenhower dollars of 1976 are listed
on page 138 with the other bicentennial coinage.

.400 SILVER CLAD COMPOSITION 1971-1974

DATE	MINTAGE	MS-65	Prf-65
1971 S	6,868,530	4.00	—
1971 S Proof	4,265,234	—	4.00
1972 S	2,193,056	4.50	—
1972 S Proof	1,811,631	—	5.00
1973 S	1,883,140	5.00	—
1973 S Proof	1,013,646	—	30.00
1974 S	1,900,000	4.50	—
1974 S Proof	1,306,579	—	11.00

COPPER-NICKEL CLAD COMPOSITION 1971-1978

DATE	MINTAGE	MS-65	Prf-65
1971	47,799,000	3.00	—
1971 D	68,587,424	2.50	—
1972	75,890,000	3.00	—
1972 D	92,548,511	2.25	—
1973	2,000,056	6.00	—
1973 D	2,000,000	6.00	—
1973 S	2,769,624	PROOF ONLY	5.00
1974	27,366,000	2.25	—
1974 D	35,466,000	2.25	—
1974 S	2,617,350	PROOF ONLY	5.00
1977	12,596,000	1.75	—
1977 D	32,938,006	1.75	—
1977 S	3,251,152	PROOF ONLY	4.25
1978	25,702,000	1.75	—
1978 D	33,012,890	1.75	—
1978 S	3,127,788	PROOF ONLY	4.25

SUSAN B. ANTHONY TYPE
1979-1981

DIAMETER—26.5mm
WEIGHT—8.1 Grams
COMPOSITION—Copper-Nickel Clad Copper
DESIGNER—Frank Gasparro
EDGE—Reeded

DATE	MINTAGE	MS-65	Prf-65
1979 P	360,222,000	1.50	—
1979 D	288,015,744	1.50	—
1979 S	109,576,000	2.00	8.00
1980 P	27,610,000	1.75	—
1980 D	41,628,708	1.75	—
1980 S	20,422,000	3.00	8.00
1981 P	3,000,000	4.50	—
1981 D	3,250,000	4.50	—
1981 S	3,492,000	4.50	8.00

BICENTENNIAL COINAGE DATED 1776-1976

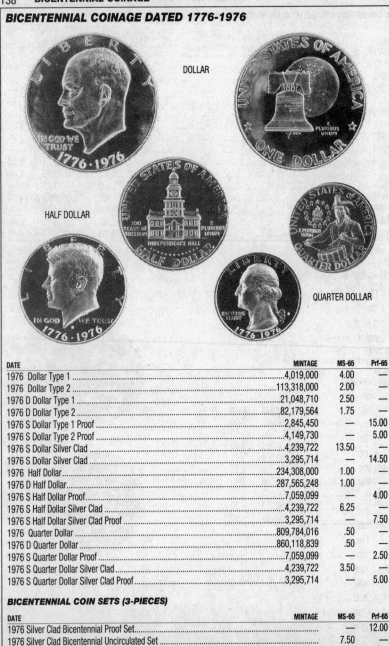

DOLLAR

HALF DOLLAR

QUARTER DOLLAR

DATE	MINTAGE	MS-65	Prf-65
1976 Dollar Type 1	4,019,000	4.00	—
1976 Dollar Type 2	113,318,000	2.00	—
1976 D Dollar Type 1	21,048,710	2.50	—
1976 D Dollar Type 2	82,179,564	1.75	—
1976 S Dollar Type 1 Proof	2,845,450	—	15.00
1976 S Dollar Type 2 Proof	4,149,730	—	5.00
1976 S Dollar Silver Clad	4,239,722	13.50	—
1976 S Dollar Silver Clad	3,295,714	—	14.50
1976 Half Dollar	234,308,000	1.00	—
1976 D Half Dollar	287,565,248	1.00	—
1976 S Half Dollar Proof	7,059,099	—	4.00
1976 S Half Dollar Silver Clad	4,239,722	6.25	—
1976 S Half Dollar Silver Clad Proof	3,295,714	—	7.50
1976 Quarter Dollar	809,784,016	.50	—
1976 D Quarter Dollar	860,118,839	.50	—
1976 S Quarter Dollar Proof	7,059,099	—	2.50
1976 S Quarter Dollar Silver Clad	4,239,722	3.50	—
1976 S Quarter Dollar Silver Clad Proof	3,295,714	—	5.00

BICENTENNIAL COIN SETS (3-PIECES)

DATE	MINTAGE	MS-65	Prf-65
1976 Silver Clad Bicentennial Proof Set		—	12.00
1976 Silver Clad Bicentennial Uncirculated Set		7.50	—

United States Gold Coins

Almost since the beginning of recorded time, gold has been the world's most sought after, prized metal. Historically speaking, gold coins have traditionally carried the highest face value of any nation's coinage system, and the United States is no exception. In this section, there is a brief chronology of American gold coinage, followed by some general comments concerning gold coins as investment devices.

The first United States gold coins were issued for circulation in 1795. They were the $5 and $10 coins, as specified by the law of April 2, 1792. Eventually, a total of six gold denominations saw service in America's channels of commerce. These denominations were $1, $2½, $3, $5, and $10, and $20. The government toyed with the notion of striking $4 and $50 denominations for regular circulation also, but those visions never got off the ground. Before these plans were finally scrubbed, however, several hundred $4 gold patterns were struck, as well as a few $50 gold specimens. These prizes are each valued at tens of thousands of dollars on today's market.

Numismatists still make use of the names originally given to the gold issues. The basic gold coin unit was the $10 piece, called the "eagle." Thus the $2½ coins were called the "quarter eagles," the $5 coins were the "half eagles," and the $20 pieces became known as "double eagles." There were no special names given to the $1 and $3 gold issues.

Despite the troubles gold coins had in circulating during the early 19th century (because of the face value to metal value imbalances), the production of gold coins was necessary and so it continued. In the absence of a stable paper currency system, gold coins were the primary medium used to conduct very large business transactions, particularly with foreign governments. The need for gold coins decrease after 1861, with the advent of a standardized paper money system backed by the United States government. However, in response to a growing nation, production of gold coins actually increased following the implementation of the paper money network.

Coinage of the gold denominations went on until 1933. That year President Franklin Roosevelt, in an attempt to lift the nation out of the Great Depression, made it illegal to own gold bullion. Collectors were allowed to keep their gold coins, however. Nevertheless, all gold coins stored in Treasury and bank vaults were rounded up and melted down, which represented the vast majority of all existing American gold coins. Once the gold had been secured, Uncle Sam pushed the price of gold bullion from $20.67 an ounce to $35 an ounce, realizing a tidy profit in the process. The price of gold was then controlled by the government to varying degrees until January 1, 1975, when all gold ownership and price regulations were terminated.

The Gold Order of 1933, coupled with the heavy meltings of the early 1800's, leaves collectors and investors of today with but a very small fraction of the original number of gold coins to scramble for. Indeed, between 1795 and 1933, the United States struck a face value of 4.25 billion dollars in gold coinage, with only less than an estimated 300 million dollars surviving today.

As an investor of American gold coins, you have two factors working in your favor: bullion value and numismatic value. The bullion factor acts as a shield against the erosion of the United States dollar and simultaneously will benefit from any price increases in gold bullion. The price movements of well-worn, common date gold coins rely mainly upon the direction of the metals market.

Gold coins have numismatic value because of their inclusions in date set or type set collections. Naturally, demand and rarity go hand-in-hand in determining specific values. It is the numismatic value that provides a price floor for gold coins when bullion prices collapse. The numismatic factor is also responsible for price jumps of gold coins during periods of sluggish activity on the metals market. In fact, it is clear that the best performances over the years are caused by collector interest, and not so much the bullion factor, although both methods of appreciation have done extremely well in the past.

The gold coin market has bounced back nicely since the bullion shake-out in early 1980, despite the fact that gold prices have been languishing in the doldrums, and may have an even greater future in store for them than anything seen in the past. Indeed, the best for American gold coins is yet to come.

The smallest gold coin, the $1 piece, was one of the last gold denominations to be introduced. Immediately, the gold dollar became an important coin, as large quantities released by the mints remained in circulation, even more so than the silver dollar of the time. The reason for this was that the relative value of gold had declined due to the large influx of the metal discovered during the California Gold Rush.

By the mid-1860's, the price of gold began to rise, resulting in the disappearance of many of the gold dollars. Smaller numbers were minted thereafter. When legislation required the massive production of silver dollars starting in 1878, the gold dollar series toiled in virtual anonymity until Congress ordered its cancellation following the release of the 1889 issues.

There were three types of gold dollars produced. Type I, or the Liberty Head dollars, were minted from 1849 to 1854. In 1854 the gold dollar was redesigned larger in diameter (but thinner), and the woman on the obverse side donned a feathered headdress. Her head was also reduced in size, compared to the Type I head. The Small Indian Head dollars, or Type II dollars, ran only until 1856. The Type III dollar, also known as the large Indian Head dollar, was distinguished from Type II dollars by a slight enlargement of the figure's head size. These dollars were struck every year until 1889.

Nearly all the upper grade gold dollars, Almost Uncirculated or better, advanced sharply in the late 1980's and first part of the 1990's, but have leveled off for now. With this in mind, these high grade dollars still represent solid investments, especially if considered as long term holdings. For most dates and mint marks in lower circulated grades, gold dollars are priced at levels well below those of the past. Right now is a tremendous time to obtain the most significant numismatic gold dollars. These are unbelievably rare coins being offered at affordable prices.

The 1861-D is probably the most famous of all $1 gold pieces. No one knows know many were made, but the number is assuredly very small. The 1861-D dollars were struck by the Confederacy following the takeover of the Dahlonega Mint by southern forces in April 1861. It is believed that a small quantity of gold on hand at the time of the seizure was used to produce the coins. For the well-to-do investors of the modern world, this historical rarity must be purchased at prices considerably higher than a few years ago, but this is nothing compared to the dizzying height we will see in the future. The 1861-D will continue to go higher in response to demands placed upon it by both collectors and investors. If you have thousands of dollars to spend on a $1 gold, give this beauty some serious thought...if you can find one for sale, that is.

Quarter eagles were authorized by the law of April 2,1792, although quarter eagles did not appear until 1796. The first type was the Liberty Cap design, minted for eight years between 1796 and 1807. Strangely, the face value designation was not a part of the coin's features.

The track record for the premier quarter eagle type is a good one. Liberty Cap quarter eagles are among the most consistent advancers of all United States coins, and there is no reason to expect this to change. Even in their lowest conditions, unfortunately, Liberty Cap quarter eagles are limited primarily to wealthy buyers.

The Turban Head type made its debut in 1808, and was minted sporadically until 1834. These coins were minted only in very small numbers because the increasing value of gold prevented them from staying in circulation. Because the 1808 issue had a slightly larger diameter than the other Turban Head quarter eagles, it is considered a type all by itself. Because of a very low mintage and unrelenting pressure from type set collectors, the 1808 is an excellent investment, for either short term or long term growth. if you want to consider other Turban Head quarter eagles, you'll be happy to know they also have excellent potential. Be advised, for here too, you'll need a bundle of money to get started.

The Classic Head type was released in 1834. These quarter eagles were reduced in size and weight to take the profit out of exportation and meltdowns. They were minted in much larger quantities than their predecessors. With the exception of the 1838-C, the Classic Head quarter eagles have been rather quiet over the last few years, indicating that we're bound to see some upward price movement. As far as the aforementioned 1838-C is concerned, here is a piece destined to continue its impressive climb, just as it has done for most of the better part of four decades.

In 1840, the quarter eagle was redesigned slightly to match the style of the half eagle and eagle. The new type was called the Coronet quarter eagle. The Coronet quarter eagle was minted every year up to and including 1907, making it one of the longest series of United States coins, along with the Coronet half eagle and eagle.

One of the most valuable Coronet quarter eagles is the 1848 CAL. specimen. These coins were minted from a special shipment of gold sent from California to the east coast following the fabulous gold strike. The letters "CAL." were counterstamped on the reverse above the eagle by mint officials to show that they were coined out of gold originating from the California gold fields. Only 1,389 of these quarter eagles were produced, and it is a real sleeper with an interesting historical aspect, yet it hasn't appreciated much in over ten years. This artifact of the Old West cannot be ignored much longer by collectors and investors. Be careful when you buy the 1848 CAL. quarter eagle, as there are many forgeries of this rarity.

For those with fewer funds to part with, the Coronet quarter eagles present numerous opportunities as well. You'll discover a surprising number of dates priced barely above bullion levels despite mintages of under 10,000. Those prices are in the same ballpark as the common date quarter eagles. The injustice becomes more acute when you consider specific examples. For instance, the 1869 issue, with an original mintage of 4,345, is valued in Fine condition only a little above the 1853 quarter eagle, having an original mintage of 1,404,668. Even though these mintage figures can be misleading because of the huge meltdowns, it is inconceivable that the 1853 is almost as rare as the 1869, as their values would suggest. Take advantage of the low prices for these very rare coins. If nothing else, you'll benefit from bullion increases, but you'll probably also reap extra profits as these coins attract more numismatic attention in the upcoming years.

The final quarter eagle, the Indian Head type, was minted from 1908 to 1929, with a ten year lapse between the 1915 and 1925. The values of all the Indian Head quarter eagles are remarkably similar with the one notable exception being the 1911-D. The 1911-D has had a checkered history, as some of the appreciation in the past has been very slow. This is surprising for a "key" coin in a series. Having experienced plunging prices in the 1990's in all grades from Fine to MS-65. In light of this fact, you ought to do well with this quarter eagle as a long term investment.

Take special notice of what has happened with the common date quarter eagles of the Coronet and Indian Head series. Since the middle of 1990, many MS-60 coins of this vintage have doubled in price. How much longer we'll see upward price movements here is anyone's guess, but it's safe to say that most of the appreciation for now has probably already occurred. MS-63's also saw sharp increases during this time, though not as much, and not for most Coronet quarter eagles minted in Philadelphia. If you're interested in obtaining MS-63 quarter eagles, these Philadelphia products could be your most cost effective purchase. Once again, however, if you're looking at the long term situation, you should do very well by owning quarter eagles in clean MS-60 or MS-63 condition.

The $3 gold piece, introduced in 1854, was one of the most unpopular coins of all time. Scholars today guess that the $3 denomination was minted because a sheet of 100 postage stamps, a frequently purchased item, cost three dollars to buy. The three cent charge for a single stamp was the primary reason for the origination of the 3 cent trime, as you'll recall.

Because of its unacceptability to the public, $3 gold coins were produced in tiny quantities only. During its 36 year lifespan from 1854 to 1889, only about half a million pieces were struck in all the mints combined. Subtract from this total all the ones that were lost or destroyed, and you'll come up with a very small number of $3 gold coins remaining today.

For much of the early 1980's, led by the MS-65 coins, the $3 gold series experienced strong advances. As has so much of the high quality material, prices have plummeted since then. Their negative behavior has poised them for an active market in a few years, or less; after all, coins this rare will not go un-noticed forever. Spend your investment dollars on the highest grade possible, being certain it has been professionally graded.

The $5 gold piece, or half eagle, was the first gold coin actually struck for the United States, in 1795. It is the only denomination of United States coinage to be produced in as many as seven mints. The history of type changes for the half eagles closely parallels that of the quarter eagles, with weight specifications always being double those of the smaller coin.

Low grade half eagles are relatively common and advance or decline in unison with the gold bullion market. This fact indicates these particular eagles to be a strong hedge against inflation, not to mention a slight numismatic premium attachment.

Gold half eagles in uncirculated grades, even common date examples, have shown consistent appreciation over time, with a few slips here and there. Fortunantly for 1993 buyers, the most recent reversal has taken place over the last three years, indicating a clear "buy" signal. This downward trend will eventually correct itself as investors and speculators rediscover the allure of high grade gold half eagles.

For investors bitten by the numismatic bug, pre-1839 half eagles,and rare dates issued in 1839 and beyond, are proven winners, although expensive. Half eagles meeting these criteria, in problem-free condition, should always be in demand by collectors from now until the end of the world, regardless if they are uncirculated or not. Many experts argue that there is far greater potential here than with gem quality common date material.

The general advice mentioned about the half eagle can be extended to any discussion involving eagles and double eagles, with the exception that there are no pre-1839 double eagles (regular production did not commence until 1850).

The $10 gold piece, or eagle, was the largest denomination authorized by the original coinage act. Many of the early specimens have file marks, created by mint employees to adjust the weight to meet legal specifications.

There are not as many types of $10 gold coins as seen with some of the smaller gold coins. The basic types (with slight variations within each type) are the Liberty Cap, the Coronet, and the Indian Head types. The Indian Head eagle type bears a different depiction from the Indian Head quarter eagle and the Indian Head half eagle. Designed by perhaps America's finest sculptor of the time, Augustus Saint Gaudens, the Indian Head eagle is one of the most highly acclaimed artistic coins in the world.

The largest ever regular issue United States coin was the $20 gold piece. The coin came into being as a result of the discovery of massive new gold reserves in California. The first double eagles released for circulation came in 1850. A single double eagle specimen was struck in 1849 and today resides in the Smithsonian Institute in Washington, D.C.

The double eagles quickly became the preferred denomination for international transactions and bank deposit holdings. Thus, larger quantities of double eagles were minted than any other gold denominations.

The Coronet double eagles, often called the Liberty Head double eagles, were produced continuously from 1850 to 1907. The same year the Coronet double eagle series came to an end, the Saint-Gaudens type was released. Although designed by the same sculptor, these coins were completely different in appearance than the Indian Head eagles. The Saint-Gaudens double eagle was praised as a marvelous work of art just as much if not more than the Indian Head eagle.

The double eagle denomination ceased in 1933. There were over 400,000 double eagles struck in the final year, but none were ever placed in circulation. It is assumed that the Gold Order sent all of the 1933 examples to the melting pot. Should anyone ever offer up for sale a 1933 double eagle, he/she might get in trouble with Uncle Sam, for ownership of such a piece is declared illegal.

Traditionally, the double eagles are the most sought after gold coins by speculators. Double eagles are favored because there is a relatively large supply of them, and they each contain nearly one ounce of gold. In addition, even the common dates carry some numismatic value.

Double eagles appear to be terrific investments on today's market. For the most part, MS-60 to MS-65 prices are attractive for buyers in comparison to a few years ago. Currently, the cost of acquiring an uncirculated double eagle is about as low as it can get. You can bet that when the market heats up, millions of speculators will push for choice eagles, driving prices higher and higher. Buy now before the herd comes thundering along!

To reiterate, the purchase of gold coins in any denomination should consist of high grade issues, or coins of great interest to collectors. By remembering these simple facts, there is very little chance of picking a loser. In addition to owning a historically important artifact, you'll have a lot of fun in the pursuit!

There is so much to be said about American gold that these pages cannot detail it all. As with any other facet of life, the more you learn about a particular subject, the better qualified you are to make wise decisions. Investing in gold coinage is no exception. A good learning tool for any prospective buyer is a book entitled *United States Gold Coins: An Illustrated History*, by Q. David Bowers. Several chapters of the book are devoted to each gold denomination. Information is given concerning availability of individual issues and other pertinent details. You can check out this book from the American Numismatic Association Library in Colorado, or perhaps your local library may have it. At any rate, whether you are a collector, an investor, or the intellectual sort, American gold coinage is a topic worthy of extensive study.

GOLD DOLLARS
1849-1889

TYPE 1 - LIBERTY HEAD 1849-1854

DIAMETER—13mm
WEIGHT—1.672 Grams
COMPOSITION—.900 Gold, .100 Copper
DESIGNER—James B. Longacre
EDGE—Reeded
PURE GOLD CONTENT—.04837 Tr. Oz.

DATE	MINTAGE	F-12	VF-20	EF-40	MS-60
1849 Open Wreath	688,567	140.	160.	200.	550.
1849 Closed Wreath	Inc. Above	140.	160.	200.	550.
1849 C Open Wreath	11,634	Auction '79 Sale EF $90,000.			
1849 C Closed Wreath	Inc. Above	275.	450.	675.	4250.
1849 D	21,588	325.	750.	1000.	2950.
1849 O	215,000	135.	210.	250.	925.
1850	481,953	125.	150.	180.	425.
1850 C	6,966	250.	575.	775.	6250.
1850 D	8,382	350.	750.	1000.	6000.
1850 O	14,000	135.	225.	275.	2750.
1851	3,317,671	125.	150.	180.	425.
1851 C	41,267	250.	450.	575.	2250.
1851 D	9,882	275.	800.	1000.	3750.
1851 O	290,000	125.	150.	180.	700.
1852	2,045,351	125.	150.	180.	425.
1852 C	9,434	275.	575.	775.	3250.
1852 D	6,360	275.	800.	1000.	5800.
1852 O	140,000	170.	200.	240.	1000.
1853	4,076,051	125.	150.	180.	425.
1853 C	11,515	250.	440.	675.	4250.
1853 D	6,583	250.	800.	1000.	6500.
1853 O	290,000	125.	150.	240.	600.
1854	736,709	125.	150.	180.	425.
1854 D	2,935	375.	1000.	1600.	14,000.
1854 S	14,632	250.	350.	450.	1850.

TYPE 2 - INDIAN HEAD SMALL HEAD 1854-1856

DIAMETER—15mm
WEIGHT—1.672 Grams
COMPOSITION—.900 Gold, .100 Copper
DESIGNER—James B. Longacre
EDGE—Reeded
PURE GOLD CONTENT—.04837 Tr. Oz.

DATE	MINTAGE	F-12	VF-20	EF-40	MS-60
1854	902,736	220.	280.	525.	3000.
		Nov. 1979 Garrett Sale Proof $90,000.			
1855	758,269	220.	280.	525.	3000.
1855 C	9,803	700.	1000.	2400.	11,000.
1855 D	1,811	1500.	2500.	5000.	20,000.
1855 O	55,000	365.	600.	850.	7000.
1856 S	24,600	365.	675.	1200.	8000.

TYPE 3 - INDIAN HEAD, LARGE HEAD 1856-1889

DIAMETER—15mm
WEIGHT—1.672 Grams
COMPOSITION—.900 Gold, .100 Copper
DESIGNER—James B. Longacre
EDGE—Reeded
PURE GOLD CONTENT—.04837 Tr. Oz.

DATE	MINTAGE	F-12	VF-20	EF-40	MS-60	Prf-65
1856 Upright 5	1,762,936	125.	150.	175.	600.	—
1856 Slant 5	Inc. Above	125.	150.	175.	400.	—
1856 D	1,460	2350.	3850.	6750.	22,000.	—
1857	774,789	125.	150.	175.	400.	—
1857 C	13,280	225.	500.	1200.	10,000.	—
1857 D	3,533	375.	825.	1850.	11,500.	—
1857 S	10,000	300.	500.	800.	8700.	—
1858	117,995	125.	150.	175.	400.	18,500.
1858 D	3,477	475.	800.	1350.	7800.	—
1858 S	10,000	325.	425.	650.	6750.	
1859	168,244	125.	150.	175.	400.	12,500.
1859 C	5,235	225.	500.	800.	11,000.	—
1859 D	4,952	250.	800.	1400.	7800.	—
1859 S	15,000	225.	325.	450.	7100.	—
1860	36,668	125.	150.	175.	400.	12,500.
1860 D	1,566	2100.	3650.	6000.	26,000.	—
1860 S	13,000	225.	340.	390.	2300.	—
1861	527,499	125.	150.	175.	400.	18,500.
1861 D	Unknown	3650.	8250.	14,000.	40,000.	—
1862	1,361,390	125.	150.	175.	400.	12,500.
1863	6,250	225.	475.	800.	4500.	12,500.
1864	5,950	225.	450.	625.	1550.	12,500.
1865	3,725	225.	450.	750.	1650.	12,500.
1866	7,130	225.	340.	450.	1150.	12,500.
1867	5,250	225.	340.	425.	1250.	12,500.
1868	10,525	225.	340.	375.	1150.	12,500.
1869	5,925	225.	350.	400.	1400.	12,500.
1870	6,335	225.	340.	400.	1100.	12,500.
1870 S	3,000	375.	525.	1200.	3100.	—
1871	3,930	225.	362.	525.	775.	18,500.
1872	3,530	225.	365.	525.	925.	18,500.
1873 Closed 3	125,125	225.	315.	575.	3400.	18,500.
1873 Open 3	Inc. Above	125.	150.	175.	400.	—
1874	198,820	125.	150.	175.	400.	19,000.
1875	420	1850.	2650.	3750.	9250.	40,000.
1876	3,245	225.	345.	400.	925.	12,500.
1877	3,920	225.	365.	575.	785.	25,000.
1878	3,020	225.	365.	575.	800.	12,500.
1879	3,030	225.	365.	600.	575.	12,500.
1880	1,636	225.	365.	600.	950.	12,500.
1881	7,707	225.	340.	365.	500.	12,500.
1882	5,125	225.	340.	390.	500.	12,500.
1883	11,007	150.	200.	240.	500.	12,500.

DATE	MINTAGE	F-12	VF-20	EF-40	MS-60	Prf-65
1884	6,236	225.	315.	365.	500.	12,500.
1885	12,261	150.	200.	240.	500.	12,500.
1886	6,016	225.	340.	400.	500.	12,500.
1887	8,543	165.	225.	250.	500.	12,500.
1888	16,580	150.	200.	240.	500.	12,500.
1889	30,729	150.	200.	240.	400.	12,500.

QUARTER EAGLES
1796-1929

($2.50 GOLD PIECES)

**VARIETY ONE
NO STARS ON
OBVERSE 1796**

LIBERTY CAP TYPE
1796-1807

DIAMETER—20mm
WEIGHT—4.37 Grams
COMPOSITION—.9167 Gold,
  .0833 Copper
DESIGNER—Robert Scot
EDGE—Reeded

**VARIETY TWO
STARS ON OBVERSE
1796-1807**

DATE	MINTAGE	F-12	VF-20	EF-40	MS-60
1796 No Stars	963	10,000.	20,000.	32,500.	90,000.
1976 Stars	432	7000.	9500.	15,000.	75,000.
1797	427	7000.	9500.	15,000.	45,000.
1798	1,094	2500.	4000.	6500.	25,000.
1802/1	3,035	2500.	3800.	5800.	16,500.
1804 13 Star Reverse	3,327	13,000.	18,000.	30,000.	—
1804 14 Star Reverse	Inc. Above	2500.	3800.	5800.	16,500.
1805	1,781	2500.	3800.	5800.	16,500.
1807/4	1,616	2500.	3800.	5800.	16,500.
1806/5	Inc. Above	4200.	6750.	12,000.	20,000.
1807	6,812	2500.	3800.	5800.	16,500.

CAPPED BUST TO LEFT 1808

DIAMETER—20mm
WEIGHT—4.37 Grams
COMPOSITION—.9167 Gold, .0833 Copper
DESIGNER—John Reich
EDGE—Reeded

DATE	MINTAGE	F-12	VF-20	EF-40	MS-60
1808	2,710	12,500.	18,000.	30,000.	55,000.

CAPPED HEAD TO LEFT
1821-1834

DIAMETER—1821-1827 18.5mm
1829-1834 18.2mm
WEIGHT—4.37 Grams
COMPOSITION— .9167 Gold, .0833 Copper
DESIGNER—John Reich
EDGE—Reeded

VARIETY ONE - LARGE DIAMETER 1821-1827

DATE	MINTAGE	F-12	VF-20	EF-40	MS-60
1821	6,448	3200.	4250.	6000.	16,000.
1824/21	2,600	3200.	4250.	6000.	15,000.
1825	4,434	3200.	4250.	6000.	15,000.
1826/25	760	3650.	5750.	10,500.	19,000.
1827	2,800	3200.	4250.	6000.	14,500.

VARIETY TWO - SMALL DIAMETER 1829-1834

DATE	MINTAGE	F-12	VF-20	EF-40	MS-60
1829	3,403	3200.	3750.	5000.	10,000.
1830	4,540	3200.	3750.	5000.	9,000.
1831	4,520	3200.	3750.	5000.	9,000.
1832	4,400	3200.	3750.	5000.	9,000.
1833	4,160	3200.	3750.	5000.	9,000.
1834	4,000	6500.	9500.	16,000.	32,000.

CLASSIC HEAD TYPE
1834-1839

DIAMETER—18.2mm
WEIGHT—4.18 Grams
COMPOSITION—.8992 Gold, .1008 Copper
DESIGNER—William Kneass
EDGE—Reeded

DATE	MINTAGE	F-12	VF-20	EF-40	MS-60
1834	112,234	275.	325.	525.	3200.
1835	131,402	275.	280.	525.	2900.
1836	547,986	275.	280.	525.	2900.
1837	45,080	275.	280.	525.	2900.
1838	47,030	275.	280.	525.	2900.
1838 C	7,880	600.	1000.	2400.	20,000.
1839	27,021	275.	280.	525.	6200.
1839 C	18,140	325.	575.	1850.	14,000.
1839 D	13,674	600.	1000.	2800.	18,500.
1839 O	17,781	325.	500.	1200.	6700.

CORONET OR LIBERTY HEAD TYPE
1840-1907

DIAMETER—18mm
WEIGHT—4.18 Grams
COMPOSITION—.900 Gold, .100 Copper
DESIGNER— Christian Gobrecht
EDGE—Reeded
PURE GOLD CONTENT—.12094 Tr. Oz.

DATE	MINTAGE	F-12	VF-20	EF-40	MS-60	Prf-65
1840	18,859	200.	350.	575.	2250.	—
1840 C	12,822	275.	500.	1300.	12,500.	—
1840 D	3,532	1250.	2200.	3500.	—	—
1840 O	33,580	200.	250.	350.	6500.	—
1841	Unknown	U.S. Gold Coll. Oct. '82 Prf-63 $82,500.				
1841 C	10,281	200.	365.	550.	13,500.	—
1841 D	4,164	750.	1500.	2600.	15,000.	—
1842	2,823	275.	525.	850.	13,500.	—
1842 C	6,729	325.	600.	900.	13,000.	—
1842 D	4,643	750.	1400.	2400.	15,500.	—
1842 O	19,800	200.	275.	450.	12,500.	—
1843	100,546	200.	240.	250.	750.	—
1843 C Sm. Date	26,064	775.	1600.	2600.	17,500.	—
1843 C Lg. Date	Inc. Above	200.	400.	625.	6500.	—
1843 D	36,209	200.	525.	850.	6600.	—
1843 O Sm. Date	368,002	200.	240.	250.	1100.	—
1843 O Lg. Date	Inc. Above	200.	250.	325.	2000.	—
1844	6,784	200.	365.	625.	4000.	—
1844 C	11,622	200.	365.	550.	15,500.	—
1844 D	17,332	200.	525.	850.	6500.	—
1845	91,051	200.	280.	330.	1000.	—
1845 D	19,460	200.	500.	750.	5400.	—
1845 O	4,000	425.	900.	1350.	9200.	—
1846	21,598	200.	250.	325.	5000.	—
1846 C	4,808	250.	625.	900.	13,500.	—
1846 D	19,303	325.	550.	850.	7000.	—
1846 O	66,000	200.	250.	325.	3200.	—
1847	29,814	200.	250.	325.	3000.	—
1847 C	23,226	250.	365.	550.	7600.	—
1847 D	15,784	325.	500.	850.	7600.	—
1847 O	124,000	200.	250.	325.	2800.	—
1848	7,497	325.	525.	850.	6500.	—
1848 CAL	1,389	3650.	4700.	8250.	32,000.	—
1848 C	16,788	200.	365.	575.	8200.	—
1848 D	13,771	325.	525.	850.	7000.	—
1849	23,294	200.	250.	325.	2650.	—
1849 C	10,220	250.	365.	575.	20,000.	—
1849 D	10,945	250.	575.	950.	6600.	—
1850	252,923	180.	200.	225.	875.	—
1850 C	9,148	250.	365.	575.	13,500.	—
1850 D	12,148	250.	525.	850.	13,500.	—

DATE	MINTAGE	F-12	VF-20	EF 40	MS-65	Prf-65
1850 O	84,000	200.	250.	325.	2350.	—
1851	1,372,748	180.	200.	225.	750.	—
1851 C	14,923	250.	365.	525.	12,000.	—
1851 D	11,264	250.	525.	900.	11,000.	—
1851 O	148,000	200.	250.	325.	5600.	—
1852	1,159,681	180.	200.	225.	500.	—
1852 C	9,772	275.	450.	850.	17,500.	—
1852 D	4,078	250.	650.	1500.	18,000.	—
1852 O	140,000	200.	250.	325.	1750.	—
1853	1,404,668	180.	200.	225.	500.	—
1853 D	3,178	250.	625.	1200.	16,500.	—
1854	596,258	180.	200.	225.	500.	—
1854 C	7,295	200.	365.	650.	14,500.	—
1854 D	1,760	2200.	3600.	5400.	18,000.	—
1854 O	153,000	200.	250.	325.	1500.	—
1854 S	246	11,500.	22,500.	34,000.	—	—
1855	235,480	180.	200.	225.	800.	—
1855 C	3,677	525.	850.	1350.	15,000.	—
1855 D	1,123	2200.	3750.	5400.	24,000.	—
1856	384,240	200.	250.	325.	450.	35,000.
1856 C	7,913	225.	425.	575.	14,000.	—
1856 D	874	2100.	4200.	6250.	35,000.	—
1856 O	21,100	200.	250.	325.	6300.	—
1856 S	71,120	200.	250.	325.	5200.	—
1857	214,130	180.	200.	225.	425.	—
1857 D	2,364	250.	800.	1200.	10,000.	—
1857 O	34,000	200.	250.	325.	6000.	—
1857 S	69,200	200.	250.	325.	4100.	—
1858	47,377	200.	250.	325.	1400.	22,000.
1858 C	9,056	250.	375.	525.	9200.	—
1859	39,444	200.	250.	325.	1400.	22,000.
1859 D	2,244	250.	750.	1100.	24,000.	—
1859 S	14,200	200.	250.	325.	6300.	—
1860	22,675	200.	250.	325.	1300.	22,000.
1860 C	7,469	250.	375.	600.	20,000.	—
1860 S	35,600	200.	250.	325.	4250.	—
1861	1,283,878	170.	185.	210.	375.	22,000.
1861 S	24,000	200.	250.	325.	5600.	—
1862	98,543	200.	250.	325.	1500.	22,000.
1862/1	Inc. Above	—	1100.	1600.	14,000.	—
1962 S	8,000	200.	250.	400.	16,000.	—
1863	30		PROOF ONLY			80,000.
1863 S	10,800	200.	250.	325.	6700.	—
1864	2,874	1300.	5500.	11,000.	45,000.	22,000.
1865	1,545	1000.	4400.	9800.	34,000.	22,000.
1865 S	23,376	200.	250.	325.	3750.	—
1866	3,110	225.	315.	525.	17,000.	22,000.
1866 S	38,960	200.	250.	325.	8500.	—
1867	3,250	225.	275.	475.	5000.	22,000.
1867 S	28,000	200.	250.	325.	5000.	—
1868	3,625	250.	315.	425.	2650.	22,000.

DATE	MINTAGE	F-12	VF-20	EF-40	MS-60	Prf-65
1868 S	34,000	200.	250.	350.	4500.	—
1869	4,345	200.	250.	350.	4900.	22,000.
1869 S	29,500	200.	250.	325.	4250.	—
1870	4,555	215.	270.	375.	3900.	22,000.
1870 S	16,000	200.	250.	325.	4850.	—
1871	5,350	215.	275.	350.	2450.	22,000.
1871 S	22,000	200.	250.	325.	2450.	—
1872	3,030	225.	275.	425.	4600.	22,000.
1872 S	18,000	200.	250.	325.	4400.	—
1873 Closed 3	178,025	175.	225.	250.	1150.	22,000.
1873 Open 3	Inc. Above	200.	250.	325.	375.	
1873 S	27,000	200.	250.	325.	3750.	—
1874	3,940	225.	315.	400.	3750.	22,000.
1875	420	1600.	3150.	5750.	10,500.	40,000.
1875 S	11,600	200.	250.	325.	4600.	—
1876	4,221	215.	250.	325.	5200.	22,000.
1876 S	5,000	215.	250.	350.	5200.	—
1877	1,652	340.	475.	750.	3500.	50,000.
1877 S	35,400	160.	190.	225.	875.	—
1878	286,260	130.	160.	180.	260.	19,000.
1878 S	178,000	130.	160.	180.	400.	—
1879	88,990	130.	160.	180.	275.	19,000.
1879 S	43,500	130.	160.	180.	1500.	—
1880	2,996	215.	250.	350.	1500.	22,000.
1881	691	625.	1000.	1850.	15,000.	22,000.
1882	4,067	165.	250.	350.	1250.	19,000.
1883	2,002	165.	250.	425.	2250.	22,000.
1884	2,023	165.	250.	425.	1500.	34,000.
1885	887	525.	900.	1600.	6000.	34,000.
1886	4,088	215.	250.	325.	1350.	19,000.
1887	6,282	200.	250.	325.	1300.	19,000.
1888	16,098	160.	190.	225.	525.	19,000.
1889	17,648	160.	190.	225.	475.	19,000.
1890	8,813	160.	190.	225.	500.	19,000.
1891	11,040	160.	190.	225.	475.	19,000.
1892	2,545	190.	250.	375.	875.	19,000.
1893	30,106	135.	175.	200.	300.	19,000.
1894	4,122	200.	250.	350.	875.	19,000.
1895	6,199	160.	180.	210.	450.	19,000.
1896	19,202	125.	155.	175.	260.	19,000.
1897	29,904	125.	155.	175.	260.	19,000.
1898	24,165	125.	155.	175.	260.	19,000.
1899	27,350	125.	155.	175.	260.	19,000.
1900	67,205	125.	155.	175.	260.	19,000.
1901	91,322	125.	155.	175.	260.	19,000.
1902	133,733	125.	155.	175.	260.	17,000.
1903	201,257	125.	155.	175.	260.	17,000.
1904	160,960	125.	155.	175.	260.	17,000.
1905	217,944	125.	155.	175.	260.	17,000.
1906	176,490	125.	155.	175.	260.	17,000.
1907	336,448	125.	155.	175.	260.	17,000.

INDIAN HEAD TYPE
1908-1929

DIAMETER—18mm
WEIGHT—4.18 Grams
COMPOSITION—.900 Gold, .100 Copper
DESIGNER— Bela Lyon Pratt
EDGE—Reeded
PURE GOLD CONTENT—.12094 Tr. Oz.

DATE	MINTAGE	F-12	VF-20	EF-40	MS-60	Prf-65
1908	565,057	120.	135.	160.	300.	18,000.
1909	441,899	120.	135.	160.	300.	18,000.
1910	492,682	120.	135.	160.	300.	18,000.
1911	704,191	120.	135.	160.	300.	18,000.
1911 D	55,680	600.	750.	1000.	3300.	—
1912	616,197	120.	135.	160.	300.	18,000.
1913	722,165	120.	135.	160.	300.	18,000.
1914	240,117	120.	135.	160.	300.	19,000.
1914 D	448,000	120.	135.	160.	300.	—
1915	606,100	120.	135.	160.	300.	22,000.
1925 D	578,000	120.	135.	160.	300.	—
1926	446,000	120.	135.	160.	300.	—
1927	388,000	120.	135.	160.	300.	—
1928	416,000	120.	135.	160.	300.	—
1929	532,000	120.	135.	160.	300.	—

THREE DOLLAR GOLD PIECES
1854-1889

DIAMETER—20.5mm
WEIGHT—5.015 Grams
COMPOSITION—.900 Gold, .100 Copper
DESIGNER—James B. Longacre
EDGE—Reeded
PURE GOLD CONTENT—.14512 Tr. Oz.

DATE	MINTAGE	F-12	VF-20	EF-40	MS-60	Prf-65
1854	138,618	375.	550.	675.	2400.	38,000.
1854 D	1,120	4000.	7000.	11,000.	30,000.	—
1854 O	24,000	375.	625.	800.	4250.	—
1855	50,555	375.	550.	675.	2400.	—
1855 S	6,600	565.	775.	1000.	8750.	—
1856	26,010	375.	600.	725.	2500.	—
1856 S	34,500	550.	750.	850.	5600.	—
1857	20,891	375.	550.	725.	2500.	38,000.
1857 S	14,000	550.	775.	950.	5300.	—
1858	2,133	600.	825.	1000.	4800.	38,000.
1859	15,638	375.	550.	750.	2500.	38,000.
1860	7,155	575.	775.	875.	2500.	38,000.

DATE	MINTAGE	F-12	VF-20	EF-40	MS-60	Prf-65
1860 S	7,000	550.	775.	1100.	5800.	—
1861	6,072	575.	775.	900.	3800.	38,000.
1862	5,785	550.	775.	900.	3800.	38,000.
1863	5,039	625.	775.	900.	4600.	38,000.
1864	2,680	625.	775.	975.	4300.	38,000.
1865	1,165	750.	850.	1250.	7500.	38,000.
1866	4,030	550.	775.	1250.	5000.	38,000.
1867	2,650	625.	850.	1000.	4400.	38,000.
1868	4,875	550.	775.	900.	4400.	38,000.
1869	2,525	600.	775.	925.	5000.	38,000.
1870	3,535	550.	775.	925.	4600.	38,000.
1870 S	2	UNIQUE U.S.Gold Coll. Oct.'82 EF-40 $687,500.				
1871	1,330	575.	900.	1000.	4600.	38,000.
1872	2,030	550.	825.	975.	4400.	38,000.
1873 Open 3	25			PROOF ONLY		75,000.
1873 Closed 3 Restrike	Inc. Above	—	—	—	11,000.	65,000.
1874	41,820	375.	525.	675.	3500.	38,000.
1875	20	U.S. Gold Coll. Oct. '82 Prf-65 $110,000.				
1876	45			PROOF ONLY		80,000.
1877	1,488	650.	950.	1500.	5400.	38,000.
1878	82,324	375.	525.	675.	2400.	35,000.
1879	3,030	575.	825.	1000.	3600.	35,000.
1880	1,036	575.	925.	1000.	3600.	35,000.
1881	554	950.	1300.	1800.	4600.	35,000.
1882	1,576	575.	825.	1000.	3800.	35,000.
1883	989	575.	950.	1200.	3800.	35,000.
1884	1,106	575.	850.	1000.	3900.	35,000.
1885	910	575.	850.	1100.	4500.	35,000.
1886	1,142	575.	950.	1000.	4000.	35,000.
1887	6,160	550.	775.	750.	2400.	35,000.
1888	5,291	550.	775.	750.	2400.	35,000.
1889	2,429	550.	775.	750.	2400.	35,000.

FOUR DOLLAR GOLD (STELLA)

*THE STELLAS ARE ACTUALLY PATTERN
COINS THAT, BECAUSE OF THEIR UNIQUE
DENOMINATION, HAVE BEEN COLLECTED
ALONG WITH THE REGULAR SERIES.*

DATE	MINTAGE		Prf-65
1879 Flowing Hair	415		50,000.
1879 Coiled Hair	10	Aug. 1980 Auction '80 Sale	$175,000.
1880 Flowing Hair	15	Aug. 1980 Auction '80 Sale	$105,000.
1880 Coiled Hair	10		145,000.

HALF EAGLES
1795-1929

($5.00 GOLD PIECES)

LIBERTY CAP TYPE
SMALL EAGLE REVERSE
1795-1798

DIAMETER—25mm
WEIGHT—8.75 Grams
COMPOSITION—.9167 Gold,
   .0833 Copper
DESIGNER—Robert Scot
EDGE—Reeded

DATE	MINTAGE	F-12	VF-20	EF-40	MS-60
1795 Sm. Eagle	8,707	5000.	7500.	9500.	35,000.
1796/5	6,196	5000.	7750.	9750.	24,000.
1797 15 Stars	3,609	5250.	8000.	10,000.	26,000.
1797 16 Stars	Inc. Above	5250.	8000.	10,000.	26,000.
1798 Sm. Eagle	6 Known	U.S. Gold Coll. Oct. '82 VF 77,000.			

LIBERTY CAP TYPE
HERALDIC EAGLE REVERSE
1795-1807

DIAMETER—25mm
WEIGHT—8.75 Grams
COMPOSITION—.9167 Gold,
   .0833 Copper
DESIGNER—Robert Scot
EDGE—Reeded

DATE	MINTAGE	F-12	VF-20	EF-40	MS-60
1795 Heraldic Eagle	Inc. w/1798	7000.	10,000.	15,000.	45,000.
1797/5	Inc. w/1798	4500.	5500.	9500.	24,000.
1797 16 Stars	Inc. w/1798	UNIQUE - Smithsonian Collection			
1798 Small 8	24,867	1250.	2000.	3800.	10,000.
1798 Lg. 8, 13 Star Rev.	Inc. Above	1250.	2000.	3800.	10,000.
1798 Lg. 8, 14 Star Rev.	Inc. Above	1600.	2750.	4800.	13,000.
1799	7,451	1200.	1900.	3800.	10,000.
1800	37,628	1200.	1600.	2400.	6500.
1802/1	53,176	1200.	1600.	2200.	6500.
1803/2	33,508	1200.	1600.	2200.	6500.
1804 Small 8	30,475	1200.	1600.	2200.	6500.
1804 Large 8	Inc. Above	1200.	1600.	2200.	6500.
1805	33,183	1200.	1600.	2200.	6500.
1806 Pointed 6	64,093	1200.	1600.	2400.	10,000.
1806 Round 6	Inc. Above	1200.	1600.	2200.	6500.
1807	32,488	1200.	1600.	2200.	6500.

CAPPED BUST TO LEFT
1807-1812

DIAMETER—25mm
WEIGHT—8.75 Grams
COMPOSITION—.9167 Gold, .0833 Copper
DESIGNER—John Reich
EDGE—Reeded

DATE	MINTAGE	F-12	VF-20	EF-20	MS-60
1807	51,605	1300.	1700.	2300.	6500.
1808/7	55,578	1500.	1800.	2500.	9500.
1808	Inc. Above	1300.	1700.	2300.	6500.
1809/8	33,875	1300.	1700.	2300.	6500.
1810 Sm. Date, Sm. 5	100,287	EXTREMELY RARE			
1810 Sm. Date, Lg. 5	Inc. Above	1300.	1700.	2500.	6500.
1810 Lg. Date, Sm. 5	Inc. Above	3500.	4500.	7500.	20,000.
1810 Lg. Date, Lg. 5	Inc. Above	1300.	1500.	2200.	6200.
1811 Small 5	99,581	1300.	1500.	2200.	6200.
1811 Large 5	Inc. Above	1300.	1500.	2200.	6200.
1812	58,087	1300.	1500.	2200.	6200.

CAPPED HEAD TO LEFT
1813-1834

DIAMETER—1813-1829 25mm,
   1829-1834 22.5mm
WEIGHT—8.75 Grams
COMPOSITION—.9167 Gold;
   .0833 Copper
DESIGNER—John Reich
EDGE—Reeded

VARIETY ONE - LARGE DIAMETER 1813-1829

DATE	MINTAGE	F-12	VF-20	EF-40	MS-60
1813	95,428	1400.	1600.	2400.	6800.
1814/13	15,454	1700.	2100.	3250.	10,000.
1815	635	EXTREMELY RARE			
1818	48,588	1600.	2000.	2900.	9000.
1819	51,723	EXTREMELY RARE			
1820 Curved Base 2, Sm. Letters	263,806	1600.	2000.	4500.	15,000.
1820 Curved Base 2, Lg. Letters	Inc. Above	1600.	2000.	4500.	15,500.
1820 Square Base 2	Inc. Above	1600.	2000.	3250.	9,000.
1821	34,641	2300.	3800.	7500.	22,000.

DATE	MINTAGE	F-12	VF-20	EF-40	MS-60
1822	17,796	U.S.Gold Coll. Oct.'82 VF $687,500.			
1823	14,485	3400.	5000.	8500.	15,000.
1824	17,340	EXREMELY RARE			
1825/21	29,060	3400.	5250.	8000.	16,000.
1825/24	Inc. Above	U.S.Gold Coll. Oct.'82 Prf $220,000.			
1826	18,069	2850.	6000.	8000.	20,000.
1827	24,913	EXTREMELY RARE			
1828/7	28,029	EXTREMELY RARE			
1828	Inc. Above	Auction '79 Sale MS-65 $110,000.			
1829 Large Date	57,442	Superior Sale July'85 MS-65 $104,500.			

VARIETY TWO - SMALL DIAMETER 1829-1834

DATE	MINTAGE	F-12	VF-20	EF-40	MS-60
1829 Small Date	Inc. Above	EXTREMELY RARE			
1830 Small 5D	126,351	3600.	4400.	5500.	16,000.
1830 Large 5D	Inc. Above	3600.	4400.	5500.	16,000.
1831	140,594	3600.	4400.	5500.	16,000.
1832 Curved Base 2, 12 Stars	157,487	EXTREMELY RARE			
1832 Square Base 2, 13 Stars	Inc. Above	4000.	6700.	9000.	22,000.
1833	193,630	3600.	4400.	5500.	16,000.
1834 Plain 4	50,141	3600.	4400.	5500.	16,000.
1834 Crosslet 4	Inc. Above	3600.	4400.	5500.	16,000.

CLASSIC HEAD TYPE
1834-1838

DIAMETER—22.5mm
WEIGHT—8.36 Grams
COMPOSITION—.8992 Gold, .1008 Copper
DESIGNER—William Kneass
EDGE—Reeded

DATE	MINTAGE	F-12	VF-20	EF-40	MS-60
1834 Plain 4	658,028	250.	300.	520.	3000.
1834 Crosslet 4	Inc. Above	550.	1200.	2400.	10,500.
1835	371,534	250.	300.	520.	3000.
1836	553,147	250.	300.	520.	3000.
1837	207,121	275.	340.	550.	3600.
1838	286,588	250.	300.	520.	3300.
1838 C	17,719	600.	1600.	4200.	20,000.
1838 D	20,583	550.	1500.	3600.	12,000.

CORONET OR LIBERTY HEAD TYPE
1839-1908
VARIETY ONE - NO MOTTO
ABOVE EAGLE 1839-1866

DIAMETER—21.6mm
WEIGHT—8.359 Grams
COMPOSITION—.900 Gold, .100 Copper
DESIGNER—Christian Gobrecht
EDGE—Reeded
PURE GOLD CONTENT—.24187 Tr. Oz.

DATE	MINTAGE	F-12	VF-20	EF-40	MS-60
1839	118,143	200.	225.	425.	3400.
1939 C	17,205	450.	900.	2000.	20,000.
1839 D	18,939	400.	775.	1600.	10,000.
1840	137,382	200.	225.	350.	4000.
1840 C	18,992	400.	700.	1600.	15,000.
1840 D	22,896	400.	700.	1450.	10,000.
1840 O	40,120	200.	340.	700.	7500.
1841	15,833	200.	350.	1100.	7500.
1841 C	21,467	325.	650.	1400.	11,000.
1841 D	30,495	325.	575.	1200.	11,000.
1841 O	50	2 KNOWN—EXCEEDINGLY RARE			
1842 Sm. Letters	27,578	200.	300.	1250.	9500.
1842 Lg. Letters	Inc. Above	200.	675.	2000.	10,000.
1842 C Sm. Date	28,184	1700.	3500.	11,000.	—
1842 C Lg. Date	Inc. Above	350.	725.	1450.	17,000.
1842 D Sm. Date	59,608	350.	625.	1200.	11,500.
1842 D Lg. Date	Inc. Above	1200.	2200.	6000.	17,500.
1842 O	16,400	350.	1000.	5000.	22,500.
1843	611,205	155.	185.	220.	2200.
1843 C	44,201	350.	575.	1350.	12,500.
1843 D	98,452	350.	550.	1000.	7800.
1843 O Sm. Letters	19,075	325.	525.	1350.	10,500.
1843 O Lg. Letters	82,000	200.	325.	875.	14,500.
1844	340,330	155.	190.	220.	2000.
1844 C	23,631	300.	700.	2600.	13,000.
1844 D	88,982	350.	525.	1000.	9500.
1844 O	364,600	165.	200.	575.	4800.
1845	417,099	155.	190.	220.	2700.
1845 D	90,629	350.	825.	1800.	10,500.
1845 O	41,000	200.	325.	1050.	9200.
1846	395,942	155.	190.	220.	2900.
1846 C	12,995	400.	875.	2400.	17,000.
1846 D	80,294	375.	525.	1300.	9000.
1846 O	58,000	200.	350.	1400.	12,500.
1847	915,981	155.	190.	220.	1800.
1847 C	84,151	350.	550.	1400.	16,000.
1847 D	64,405	400.	500.	1050.	9000.
1847 O	12,000	450.	2250.	11,000.	30,000
1848	260,775	155.	190.	220.	2450.
1848 C	64,472	400.	625.	1500.	15,000.
1848 D	47,465	400.	500.	1450.	12,500.
1849	133,070	155.	190.	300.	2650.

DATE	MINTAGE	F-12	VF-20	EF-40	MS-60	Prf-65
1849 C	64,823	325.	475.	1050.	11,000.	—
1849 D	39,036	325.	675.	1300.	11,000.	—
1850	64,491	200.	325.	850.	5600.	—
1850 C	63,591	300.	525.	1050.	12,500.	—
1850 D	43,984	325.	475.	1450.	17,500.	—
1851	377,505	155.	190.	220.	2750.	—
1851 C	49,176	300.	575.	1050.	10,500.	—
1851 D	62,710	325.	500.	1325.	11,000.	—
1851 O	41,000	300.	625.	1500.	3000.	—
1852	573,901	155.	190.	220.	1800.	—
1852 C	72,574	325.	525.	1050.	11,500.	—
1852 D	92,584	325.	475.	950.	8800.	—
1853	305,770	155.	190.	220.	2200.	—
1853 C	65,571	325.	500.	950.	11,500.	—
1853 D	89,678	325.	475.	875.	8800.	—
1854	160,675	175.	200.	475.	2900.	—
1854 C	39,283	400.	600.	1500.	14,000.	—
1854 D	56,413	325.	475.	975.	9200.	—
1854 O	46,000	240.	300.	500.	6750.	—
1854 S	268	U.S. Gold Coll. Oct. '82 AU-55 $187,000.				
1855	117,098	155.	190.	240.	2400.	—
1855 C	39,788	325.	600.	1700.	13,000.	—
1855 D	22,432	375.	575.	1450.	15,000.	—
1855 O	11,100	325.	675.	2800.	15,500.	—
1855 S	61,000	200.	400.	1050.	10,000.	—
1856	197,990	180.	320.	350.	3400.	—
1856 C	28,457	325.	575.	1250.	11,500.	—
1856 D	19,786	375.	575.	1250.	7700.	—
1856 O	10,000	375.	775.	2750.	—	—
1856 S	105,100	200.	300.	775.	—	—
1857	98,188	170.	210.	260.	2900.	65,000.
1857 C	31,360	290.	575.	1250.	7900.	—
1857 D	17,046	290.	575.	1200.	7900.	—
1857 O	13,000	300.	700.	2000.	—	—
1857 S	87,000	200.	300.	700.	7000.	—
1858	15,136	200.	275.	775.	5200.	65,000.
1858 C	38,856	350.	775.	1200.	10,500.	—
1858 D	15,362	290.	575.	1150.	11,500.	—
1858 S	18,600	325.	625.	2500.	—	—
1859	16,814	200.	270.	575.	6400.	65,000.
1859 C	31,847	290.	500.	1350.	12,500.	—
1859 D	10,366	375.	700.	2000.	11,000.	—
1859 S	13,220	450.	1200.	4800.	—	—
1860	19,825	200.	300.	575.	6400.	65,000.
1860 C	14,813	325.	775.	2000.	11,000.	—
1860 D	14,635	300.	775.	1750.	13,000.	—
1860 S	21,200	425.	1150.	2750.	18,000.	—
1861	688,150	155.	190.	220.	1850.	65,000.
1861 C	6,879	700.	1450.	3300.	25,000.	—
1861 D	1,597	2600.	4700.	7200.	—.	—
1861 S	18,000	450.	1050.	4500.	—	—

DATE	MINTAGE	F-12	VF-20	EF-40	MS-60	Prf-65
1862	4,465	450.	750.	2500.	—	65,000.
1862 S	9,500	1500.	4500.	10,000.	—	—
1863	2,472	500.	1100.	3500.	—	65,000.
1863 S	17,000	400.	1150.	4600.	—	—
1864	4,220	375.	575.	2000.	11,000.	65,000.
1864 S	3,888	2000.	6600.	15,000.	—	—
1865	1,295	575.	1150.	3100.	—	65,000.
1865 S	27,612	400.	1150.	3500.	—	—
1866 S	9,000	575.	1500.	6000.	—	—

VARIETY TWO - MOTTO ABOVE EAGLE 1866-1908

DIAMETER—21.6mm
WEIGHT—3.359 Grams
COMPOSITION—.900 Gold, .100 Copper
DESIGNER—Christian Gobrecht
EDGE—Reeded
PURE GOLD CONTENT—.24187 Tr. Oz.

DATE	MINTAGE	F-12	VF-20	EF-40	MS-60	Prf-65
1866	6,730	400.	750.	1750.	12,000.	36,000.
1866 S	34,920	700.	1300.	4500.	18,000.	—
1867	6,920	250.	600.	2400.	8000.	36,000.
1867 S	29,000	600.	1500.	5000.	—	—
1868	5,725	250.	650.	1750.	10,000.	36,000.
1868 S	52,000	200.	500.	2350.	—	—
1869	1,785	500.	850.	2250.	—	36,000.
1869 S	31,000	200.	375.	2350.	—	—
1870	4,035	250.	700.	2750.	—	36,000.
1870 CC	7,675	2500.	4250.	9000.	—	—
1870 S	17,000	700.	1150.	4000.	—	—
1871	3,230	250.	850.	2100.	—	36,000.
1871 CC	20,770	425.	950.	3000.	—	—
1871 S	25,000	200.	550.	2000.	17,000.	—
1872	1,690	525.	725.	2000.	15,000.	36,000.
1872 CC	16,980	525.	825.	3400.	—	—
1872 S	36,400	200.	500.	1800.	—	—
1873 Closed 3	49,305	200.	225.	245.	2750.	36,000.
1873 Open 3	63,200	200.	225.	245.	2750.	—
1873 CC	7,416	900.	2100.	6500.	—	—
1873 S	31,000	200.	850.	2700.	—	—
1874	3,508	250.	600.	2100.	—	36,000.
1874 CC	21,198	250.	650.	1700.	11,500.	—
1874 S	16,000	200.	700.	3700.	—	—
1875	220		VERY RARE			
1875 CC	11,828	600.	1450.	5200.	—	—
1875 S	9,000	250.	925.	3250.	—	—
1876	1,477	425.	1000.	2000.	15,000.	36,000.
1876 CC	6,887	425.	1400.	5600.	—	—
1876 S	4,000	1000.	1600.	5000.	—	—
1877	1,152	525.	775.	2400.	11,500.	36,000.
1877 CC	8,680	425.	1000.	3200.	—	—
1877 S	26,700	250.	300.	875.	—	—
1878	131,740	130.	150.	225.	1000.	36,000.

DATE	MINTAGE	F-12	VF-20	EF-40	MS-60	Prf-65
1878 CC	9,054	1500.	3400.	9000.	—	—
1878 S	144,700	130.	145.	170.	225.	—
1879	301,950	130.	145.	170.	225.	22,000.
1879 CC	17,281	225.	375.	1250.	—	—
1879 S	426,200	130.	145.	170.	225.	—
1880	3,166,436	130.	145.	170.	225.	22,000.
1880 CC	51,017	225.	350.	850.	7500.	—
1880 S	1,348,900	130.	145.	170.	225.	—
1881	5,708,802	130.	145.	170.	225.	22,000.
1881/80	Inc. Above	2 KNOWN—EXCEEDINGLY RARE				
1881 CC	13,886	250.	525.	1450.	8800.	—
1881 S	969,000	130.	145.	170.	225.	—
1882	2,514,568	130.	145.	170.	225.	22,000.
1882 CC	82,817	200.	350.	700.	5000.	—
1882 S	969,000	130.	145.	170.	225.	—
1883	233,461	130.	145.	170.	225.	22,000.
1883 CC	12,958	200.	350.	800.	11,500.	—
1883 S	83,200	130.	145.	170.	225.	—
1884	191,078	130.	145.	170.	225.	22,000.
1884 CC	16,402	325.	450.	800.	—	—
1884 S	177,000	130.	145.	170.	225.	—
1885	601,506	130.	145.	170.	225.	22,000.
1885 S	1,211,500	130.	145.	170.	225.	—
1886	388,432	130.	145.	170.	225.	22,000.
1886 S	3,268,000	130.	145.	170.	225.	—
1887	87	PROOF ONLY				100,000.
1887 S	1,912,000	130.	145.	170.	225.	—
1888	18,296	130.	145.	170.	225.	22,000.
1888 S	293,900	130.	145.	170.	225.	—
1889	7,565	250.	315.	425.	—	22,000.
1890	4,328	200.	250.	425.	3400.	22,000.
1890 CC	53,800	200.	225.	550.	1200.	—
1891	61,413	150.	175.	250.	750.	22,000.
1891 CC	208,000	200.	250.	375.	825.	—
1892	753,572	130.	145.	170.	225.	22,000.
1892 CC	82,968	250.	300.	575.	1500.	—
1892 O	10,000	400.	600.	1200.	4500.	—
1892 S	298,400	130.	145.	170.	225.	—
1893	1,528,197	130.	145.	170.	225.	22,000.
1893 CC	60,000	230.	280.	400.	2000.	—
1893 O	110,000	175.	200.	280.	2000.	—
1893 S	224,000	130.	145.	170.	225.	—
1894	957,955	130.	145.	170.	225.	22,000.
1894 O	16,600	175.	200.	350.	2000.	—
1894 S	55,900	225.	275.	350.	3600.	—
1895	1,345,936	130.	145.	175.	225.	22,000.
1895 S	112,000	200.	250.	350.	4800.	—
1896	59,063	130.	145.	170.	225.	22,000.
1896 S	155,400	130.	145.	170.	225.	—
1897	867,883	130.	145.	170.	225.	22,000.

DATE	MINTAGE	F-12	VF-20	EF-40	MS-60	Prf-65
1897 S	354,000	130.	145.	170.	225.	—
1898	633,495	130.	145.	170.	225.	22,000.
1898 S	1,397,400	130.	145.	170.	225.	—
1899	1,710,729	130.	145.	170.	225.	22,000.
1899 S	1,545,000	130.	145.	170.	225.	—
1900	1,405,730	130.	145.	170.	225.	22,000.
1900 S	329,000	130.	145.	170.	225.	—
1901	616,040	130.	145.	170.	225.	14,000.
1901 S 1/0	3,648,000	130.	145.	170.	225.	—
1901 S	Inc. Above	130.	145.	170.	225.	—
1902	172,562	130.	145.	170.	225.	14,000.
1902 S	939,000	130.	145.	170.	225.	—
1903	227,024	130.	145.	170.	225.	17,000.
1903 S	1,855,000	130.	145.	170.	225.	—
1904	392,136	130.	145.	170.	225.	14,000.
1904 S	97,000	130.	145.	170.	225.	—
1905	302,308	130.	145.	170.	225.	14,000.
1905 S	880,700	130.	145.	170.	225.	—
1906	348,820	130.	145.	170.	225.	14,000.
1906 D	320,000	130.	145.	170.	225.	—
1906 S	598,000	130.	145.	170.	225.	—
1907	626,192	130.	145.	170.	225.	22,000.
1907 D	888,000	130.	145.	170.	225.	—
1908	421,874	130.	145.	170.	225.	—

INDIAN HEAD TYPE
1908-1929

DIAMETER—21.6mm
WEIGHT—8.359 Grams
COMPOSITION—.900 Gold, .100 Copper
DESIGNER—Bela Lyon Pratt
EDGE—Reeded
PURE GOLD CONTENT—.24187 Tr. Oz.

DATE	MINTAGE	F-12	VF-20	EF-40	MS-60	Prf-65
1908	578,012	180.	200.	230.	375.	24,000.
1908 D	148,000	180.	200.	230.	375.	—
1908 S	82,000	250.	275.	425.	1800.	—
1909	627,138	180.	200.	230.	375.	28,000.
1909 D	3,423,560	180.	200.	230.	375.	—
1909 O	34,200	400.	625.	950.	7000.	—
1909 S	297,200	225.	250.	300.	1300.	—
1910	604,250	225.	250.	275.	460.	26,000.
1910 D	193,600	225.	250.	275.	530.	—
1910 S	770,200	225.	250.	375.	1900.	—
1911	915,139	180.	200.	230.	375.	27,000.
1911 D	72,500	250.	365.	525.	5500.	—
1911 S	1,416,000	225.	250.	275.	875.	—
1912	790,144	180.	200.	230.	375.	26,000.
1912 S	392,000	225.	250.	275.	1600.	—
1913	916,099	180.	200.	230.	375.	27,000.

DATE	MINTAGE	F-12	VF-20	EF-40	MS-60	Prf-65
1913 S	408,000	225.	350.	450.	3000.	—
1914	247,125	180.	200.	230.	375.	27,000.
1914 D	247,000	180.	200.	230.	375.	—
1914 S	263,000	180.	200.	230.	1050.	—
1915	588,075	180.	200.	230.	375.	34,000.
1915 S	164,000	250.	300.	350.	2750.	—
1916 S	240,000	180.	200.	230.	900.	—
1929	662,000	1600.	2100.	3400.	7000.	—

EAGLES 1795-1933
($10.00 GOLD PIECES)

LIBERTY CAP TYPE
SMALL EAGLE
REVERSE
1795-1797

DIAMETER—33mm
WEIGHT—17.50 Grams
COMPOSITION—.9167 Gold,
 .0833 Copper
DESIGNER—Robert Scot
EDGE—Reeded

DATE	MINTAGE	F-12	VF-20	EF-40	MS-60
1795	5,583	6500.	9000.	12,000.	35,000.
1796	4,146	6500.	9000.	12,000.	35,000.
1797 (Sm. Eagle)	3,615	6500.	9000.	12,000.	35,000.

LIBERTY CAP TYPE
HERALDIC EAGLE
REVERSE
1797-1804

DIAMETER—33mm
WEIGHT—17.50 Grams
COMPOSITION—.9167 Gold,
 .0833 Copper
DESIGNER—Robert Scot
EDGE—Reeded

DATE	MINTAGE	F-12	VF-20	EF-40	MS-60
1797 (Lg. Eagle)	10,940	2500.	3750.	5500.	17,000.
1798/97 9 Stars Left, 4 Right	900	Oct.'80 Garrett Sale MS-65 $52,500.			
1798/97 7 Stars Left, 6 Right	842	Oct.'80 Garrett Sale AU-55 $120,000.			
1799	37,449	2500.	3250.	4500.	15,000.
1800	5,999	2500.	3500.	4750.	15,000.
1801	44,344	2500.	3250.	4500.	15,000.
1803	15,017	2500.	3500.	4500.	15,000.
1804	3,757	2800.	4200.	7500.	35,000.

CORONET OR LIBERTY HEAD TYPE
1838-1907

**VARIETY ONE - NO MOTTO
ABOVE EAGLE 1838-1866**

DIAMETER—27mm
WEIGHT—16.718 Grams
COMPOSITION—.900 Gold, .100 Copper
DESIGNER—Christian Gobrecht
EDGE—Reeded
PURE GOLD CONTENT—.48375 Tr. Oz.

DATE	MINTAGE	F-12	VF-20	EF-40	MS-60	Prf-65
1838	7,200	625.	1350.	2800.	22,000.	—
1839 Lg. Letters	38,248	425.	750.	2400.	15,000.	—
		U.S. Gold Coll. Oct '82 Prf-65 $121,000.				
1839 Sm. Letters	Inc. Above	675.	1500.	3700.	—	—
1840	47,338	365.	400.	725.	12,000.	—
1841	63,131	365.	400.	650.	13,000.	—
1841 O	2,500	875.	2000.	5500.	—	—
1842 Sm. Date	81,507	365.	400.	700.	—	—
1842 Lg. Date	Inc. Above	365.	400.	750.	13,000.	—
1842 O	27,400	365.	400.	700.	12,000.	—
1843	75,462	365.	400.	700.	7700.	—
1843 O	175,162	365.	400.	600.	7800.	—
1844	6,361	450.	1000.	3000.	—	—
1844 O	118,700	365.	400.	600.	10,000.	—
1845	26,153	365.	725.	2000.	—	—
1845 O	47,500	365.	400.	675.	12,000.	—
1846	20,095	500.	850.	2800.	—	—
1846 O	81,780	365.	440.	900.	—	—
1847	862,258	230.	250.	325.	5200.	—
1847 O	571,500	250.	280.	400.	4600.	—
1848	145,484	320.	375.	400.	5400.	—
1848 O	38,850	380.	600.	1300.	—	—
1849	653,618	230.	250.	280.	3800.	—
1849 O	23,900	425.	700.	2300.	—	—
1850	291,451	230.	250.	280.	3800.	—
1850 O	57,500	365.	400.	600.	—	—
1851	176,328	300.	340.	550.	9000.	—
1851 O	263,000	270.	320.	550.	—	—
1852	263,106	300.	400.	500.	—	—
1852 O	18,000	400.	525.	1800.	—	—
1853	201,253	230.	250.	280.	3800.	—
1853 O	51,000	365.	400.	550.	—	—
1854	54,250	365.	400.	675.	—	—
1854 O	52,500	365.	400.	550.	11,000.	—
1854 S	123,826	260.	300.	550.	10,000.	—
1855	121,701	230.	250.	280.	3800.	—
1855 O	18,000	365.	575.	1800.	—	—
1855 S	9,000	825.	1600.	3700.	—	—
1856	60,490	290.	320.	380.	4600.	—
1856 O	14,500	400.	575.	2000.	—	—
1856 S	68,000	320.	375.	600.	9500.	—

DATE	MINTAGE	F-12	VF-20	EF-40	MS-60	Prf-65
1857	16,606	320.	375.	900.	—	—
1857 O	5,500	675.	1000.	2200.	—	—
1857 S	26,000	365.	500.	775.	—	—
1858	2,521	2600.	5000.	10,000.	—	90,000.
1858 O	20,000	320.	375.	800.	11,000.	—
1858 S	11,800	725.	2100.	5000.	4500.	—
1859	16,093	320.	375.	950.	4200.	90,000.
1859 O	2,300	1250.	3500.	8800.	—	—
1859 S	7,000	875.	2400.	7200.	4200.	—
1860	15,105	320.	375.	950.	12,000.	90,000.
1860 O	11,100	365.	550.	1150.	13,000.	—
1860 S	5,000	725.	2600.	6800.	6250.	—
1861	113,233	260.	300.	350.	5000.	90,000.
1861 S	15,500	650.	1800.	4700.	—	—
1862	10,995	340.	490.	1300.	—	90,000.
1862 S	12,500	700.	1900.	4700.	—	—
1863	1,248	2100.	3650.	8800.	—	90,000.
1863 S	10,000	700.	1650.	4000.	—	—
1864	3,580	775.	1850.	4800.	—	90,000.
1864 S	2,500	2700.	5600.	11,000.	—	—
1865	4,005	725.	2100.	5200.	—	90,000.
1865 S	16,700	1400.	4500.	9000.	—	—
1865 Over Inverted 186	Inc. Above	1000.	2500.	7400.	—	—
1866 S	8,500	1250.	3000.	6400.	—	—

VARIETY TWO -
MOTTO ABOVE EAGLE
1866-1907

DIAMETER—27mm
WEIGHT—16.718 Grams
COMPOSITION—.900 Gold, .100 Copper
DESIGNER—Christian Gobrecht
EDGE—Reeded
PURE GOLD CONTENT—.48375 Tr. Oz.

DATE	MINTAGE	F-12	VF-20	EF-40	MS-60	Prf-65
1866	3,780	365.	725.	1500.	—	65,000.
1866 S	11,500	365.	1700.	3800.	—	—
1867	3,140	365.	1750.	4400.	—	65,000.
1867 S	9,000	400.	2300.	7800.	—	—
1868	10,655	365.	600.	1350.	14,000.	65,000.
1868 S	13,500	1500.	4200.	950.	—	—
1869	1,855	1700.	4200.	3000.	—	65,000.
1869 S	6,430	1500.	4200.	1000.	—	—
1870	4,025	400.	725.	1400.	—	65,000.
1870 CC	5,908	2500.	5600.	10,500.	—	—
1870 S	8,000	400.	1500.	5800.	—	—
1871	1,820	1000.	1500.	4000.	3600.	65,000.
1871 CC	8,085	475.	1900.	4700.	—	—
1871 S	16,500	365.	1700.	4600.	—	—
1872	1,650	1200.	3000.	7800.	—	65,000.
1872 CC	4,600	475.	1700.	7600.	—	—

DATE	MINTAGE	F-12	VF-20	EF-40	MS-60	Prf-65
1872 S	17,300	365.	625.	950.	—	—
1873	825	2500.	3500.	5500.	—	80,000.
1873 CC	4,543	1000.	1500.	1850.	—	—
1873 C	12,000	350.	400.	575.	2100.	—
1874	53,160	350.	400.	420.	—	65,000.
1874 CC	16,767	365.	425.	950.	—	—
1874 S	10,000	365.	425.	675.	—	—
1875	120	U.S. Gold Coll. Oct.'82 Prf-65 $104,500.				
1875 CC	7,715	525.	800.	1400.	—	—
1876	732	1600.	2350.	4200.	—	55,000.
1876 CC	4,696	1100.	1300.	1850.	—	—
1876 S	5,000	450.	725.	1100.	—	—
1877	817	1600.	2600.	4750.	—	45,000.
1877 CC	3,332	1300.	1800.	2350.	—	—
1877 S	17,000	350.	375.	425.	—	—
1878	73,800	280.	290.	320.	1400.	45,000.
1878 CC	3,244	1250.	1800.	2350.	—	—
1878 S	26,100	350.	375.	400.	—	—
1879	384,770	270.	290.	315.	900.	45,000.
1879 CC	1,762	3650.	5500.	7800.	—	—
1879 O	1,500	1300.	2600.	3650.	—	—
1879 S	224,000	290.	300.	325.	1800.	—
1880	1,644,876	270.	290.	305.	450.	45,000.
1880 CC	11,190	350.	375.	725.	3600.	—
1880 O	9,200	350.	425.	625.	3300.	—
1880 S	506,250	250.	275.	290.	650.	—
1881	3,877,260	240.	260.	280.	350.	45,000.
1881 CC	24,015	350.	375.	475.	4000.	—
1881 O	8,350	350.	375.	525.	3600.	—
1881 S	970,000	240.	260.	280.	475.	—
1882	2,324,480	240.	260.	280.	350.	45,000.
1882 CC	6,764	350.	375.	575.	4900.	—
1882 O	10,820	350.	375.	400.	3300.	—
1882 S	132,000	240.	260.	280.	1150.	—
1883	208,740	240.	260.	280.	475.	45,000.
1883 CC	12,000	350.	375.	725.	4500.	—
1883 O	800	2600.	3650.	5250.	19,000.	—
1883 S	38,000	240.	260.	280.	1400.	—
1884	76,905	240.	260.	280.	1900.	55,500.
1884 CC	9,925	350.	375.	575.	6700.	—
1884 S	124,250	240.	260.	280.	1200.	—
1885	253,527	240.	260.	280.	800.	45,000.
1885 S	228,000	240.	260.	280.	625.	—
1886	236,160	240.	260.	280.	1150.	45,000.
1886 S	826,000	240.	260.	280.	350.	—
1887	53,680	250.	280.	300.	1450.	45,000.
1887 S	817,000	240.	260.	280.	500.	—
1888	132,996	240.	260.	280.	1550.	45,000.
1888 O	21,335	350.	375.	400.	775.	—
1888 S	648,700	240.	260.	280.	525.	—
1889	4,485	350.	425.	675.	1950.	45,000.

DATE	MINTAGE	F-12	VF-20	EF-40	MS-60	Prf-65
1889 S	425,400	240.	260.	280.	400.	—
1890	58,043	250.	280.	300.	1850.	45,000.
1890 CC	17,500	350.	375.	475.	1500.	—
1891	91,868	240.	260.	280.	375.	45,000.
1891 CC	103,732	350.	375.	475.	900.	—
1892	797,552	240.	260.	280.	350.	45,000.
1892 CC	40,000	350.	375.	625.	1850.	—
1892 O	28,688	350.	375.	400.	750.	—
1892 S	115,500	240.	260.	280.	750.	—
1893	1,840,895	240.	260.	280.	350.	45,000.
1893 CC	14,000	350.	375.	475.	2500.	—
1893 O	17,000	350.	375.	400.	900.	—
1893 S	141,350	250.	280.	300.	775.	—
1894	2,470,778	240.	260.	280.	350.	45,000.
1894 O	107,500	250.	280.	300.	1350.	—
1894 S	25,000	325.	475.	650.	3800.	—
1895	567,826	240.	260.	280.	350.	45,000.
1895 O	98,000	290.	300.	325.	675.	—
1895 S	49,000	350.	525.	750.	3600.	—
1896	76,348	290.	300.	325.	375.	45,000.
1896 S	123,750	275.	290.	375.	3800.	—
1897	1,000,159	240.	260.	280.	350.	45,000.
1897 O	42,500	290.	300.	325.	875.	—
1897 S	234,750	240.	260.	280.	1700.	—
1898	812,197	240.	260.	280.	350.	45,000.
1898 S	473,600	240.	260.	280.	550.	—
1899	1,262,305	240.	260.	280.	350.	45,000.
1899 O	37,047	290.	300.	325.	1000.	—
1899 S	841,000	240.	260.	280.	500.	—
1900	293,960	240.	260.	280.	350.	45,000.
1900 S	81,000	290.	300.	325.	1350.	—
1901	1,718,825	240.	260.	280.	350.	45,000.
1901 O	72,041	290.	300.	325.	700.	—
1901 S	2,812,750	240.	260.	280.	350.	—
1902	82,513	250.	275.	300.	350.	45,000.
1902 S	469,500	240.	260.	280.	350.	—
1903	125,926	240.	260.	280.	350.	45,000.
1903 O	112,771	240.	260.	280.	580.	—
1903 S	538,000	240.	260.	280.	395.	—
1904	162,038	240.	260.	280.	350.	45,000.
1904 O	108,950	240.	260.	280.	600.	—
1905	201,078	240.	260.	280.	350.	45,000.
1905 S	369,250	240.	260.	280.	2500.	—
1906	165,497	240.	260.	280.	350.	45,000.
1906 D	981,000	240.	260.	280.	350.	—
1906 O	86,895	290.	300.	325.	675.	—
1906 S	457,000	240.	260.	280.	700.	—
1907	1,203,973	240.	260.	280.	350.	45,000.
1907 D	1,030,000	240.	260.	280.	350.	—
1907 S	210,500	240.	260.	280.	1000.	—

INDIAN HEAD TYPE
1907-1933

VARIETY ONE -
NO MOTTO ON REVERSE 1907-1908

DIAMETER—27mm
WEIGHT—16.718 Grams
COMPOSITION—.900 Gold, .100 Copper
DESIGNER—Augustus Saint-Gaudens
EDGE—46 Raised Stars
PURE GOLD CONTENT—.48375 Tr. Oz.

DATE	MINTAGE	F-12	VF-20	EF-40	MS-60
1907 Rolled Edge, Periods Before and After E PLURIBUS UNUM 42					50,000.
1907 Same, Plain Edge	Unique			UNIQUE	
1907 Wire Edge, Periods	500	—	—	3200.	10,000.
1907 No Periods	239,406	450.	525.	575.	1050.
1908 No Motto	33,500	450.	525.	625.	1200.
1908 D No Motto	210,000	450.	525.	575.	1000.

VARIETY TWO -
MOTTO ON REVERSE 1908-1933

DIAMETER—27mm
WEIGHT—16.718 Grams
COMPOSITION—.900 Gold, .100 Copper
DESIGNER—Augustus Saint-Gaudens
EDGE—1908-1911-46 Raised Stars
   1912-1933-48 Raised Stars
PURE GOLD CONTENT—.48375 Tr. Oz.

DATE	MINTAGE	F-12	VF-20	EF-40	MS-60	Prf-65
1908	341,486	360.	400.	425.	450.	38,000.
1908 D	836,500	430.	475.	560.	725.	—
1908 S	59,850	500.	560.	725.	2600.	—
1909	184,863	360.	400.	425.	500.	38,000.
1909 D	121,540	360.	400.	425.	950.	—
1909 S	292,350	430.	475.	560.	875.	—
1910	318,704	360.	400.	425.	450.	38,000.
1910 D	2,356,640	360.	400.	425.	450.	—
1910 S	811,000	430.	475.	560.	1100.	—
1911	505,595	360.	400.	425.	450.	38,000.
1911 D	30,100	575.	750.	1000.	5000.	—
1911 S	51,000	430.	475.	650.	1600.	—
1912	405,083	360.	400.	425.	450.	38,000.
1912 S	300,000	430.	475.	560.	950.	—
1913	442,071	360.	400.	425.	450.	38,000.
1913 S	66,000	475.	625.	950.	5300.	—
1914	151,050	360.	420.	440.	450.	38,000.
1914 D	343,500	360.	400.	425.	450.	—
1914 S	208,000	425.	475.	525.	670.	—
1915	351,075	360.	400.	425.	500.	40,000.
1915 S	59,000	475.	525.	600.	2800.	—
1916 S	138,500	430.	475.	500.	775.	—

DATE	MINTAGE	F-12	VF-20	EF-40	MS-60	Prf-65
1920 S	126,500	6000.	7000.	8500.	15,000.	—
1926	1,014,000	360.	400.	425.	470.	—
1930 S	96,000	2500.	3650.	5250.	8700.	—
1932	4,463,000	360.	400.	425.	470.	—
1933	312,500	Oct. 1980 Stack's Sale MS-63 $97,500.				

DOUBLE EAGLES
1849-1933

($20.00 GOLD PIECES)

CORONET OR LIBERTY HEAD TYPE
1849-1907

VARIETY ONE - NO MOTTO, TWENTY D. 1849-1866

DIAMETER—34mm
WEIGHT—33.436 Grams
COMPOSITION—.900 Gold, .100 Copper
DESIGNER—James B. Longacre
EDGE—Reeded
PURE GOLD CONTENT—.96750 Tr. Oz.

DATE	MINTAGE	VF-20	EF-40	AU-50	MS-60	Prf-65
1849	1	UNIQUE-U.S. MINT COLLECTION				
1850	1,170,261	525.	650.	1000.	4200.	—
1850 O	141,000	625.	950.	2700.	7600.	—
1851	2,087,155	500.	550.	650.	2600.	—
1851 O	315,000	625.	800.	1750.	7600.	—
1852	2,053,026	500.	550.	700.	2500.	—
1852 O	190,000	625.	800.	1950.	7200.	—
1853	1,261,326	500.	625.	825.	5600.	—
1853 O	71,000	650.	1000.	3400.	7600.	—
1854	757,899	500.	650.	1000.	5600.	—
1854 O	3,250	Auction '79 Sale XF $45,000.				
1854 S	141,468	575.	850.	1100.	4850.	—
1855	364,666	500.	550.	1000.	6200.	—
1855 O	8,000	3200.	6500.	12,500.	—	—
1855 S	879,675	500.	600.	1250.	6000.	—
1856	329,878	500.	550.	1000.	6000.	—
1856 O	2,250	Stack's Sale 1979 XF $70,000.				
1856 S	1,189,750	500.	550.	875.	5900.	—
1857	439,375	500.	550.	850.	4600.	—
1857 O	30,000	800.	1750.	4000.	—	—
1857 S	970,500	500.	550.	875.	6000.	—
1858	211,714	500.	550.	975.	5400.	—
1858 D	35,250	875.	1500.	6000.	8000.	—
1858 S	846,710	500.	550.	950.	6100.	—
1859	43,597	950.	1600.	7500.	17,500.	95,000.
1859 O	9,100	2700.	4600.	10,000.	—	—
1859 S	636,445	500.	625.	1000.	6300.	—

DATE	MINTAGE	VF-20	EF-40	AU-50	MS-60	Prf-65
1860	577,670	500.	750.	3250.	5500.	90,000.
1860 O	6,600	4200.	7500.	15,000.	—	—
1860 S	544,950	500.	625.	1500.	7400.	—
1861	2,976,453	500.	525.	650.	2900.	90,000.
1861 A.C. Paquet Reverse	Inc. Above	Bower's & Merena Sale 1988 MS-67 $660,000.				
1861 O	17,741	1800.	3800.	7200.	—	—
1861 S	768,000	550.	625.	1850.	7600.	—
1861 S A.C. Paquet Reverse	Inc. Above	Auction '79 Sale AU $20,000.				
1862	92,133	575.	1400.	3800.	10,000.	90,000.
1862 S	854,173	550.	800.	1750.	8100.	—
1863	142,790	525.	925.	2000.	9000.	90,000.
1863 S	966,570	500.	550.	1450.	6300.	—
1864	204,285	525.	725.	4600.	8600.	90,000.
1864 S	793,660	525.	850.	2900.	5300.	—
1865	351,200	550.	950.	1450.	5000.	90,000.
1865 S	1,042,500	500.	550.	1450.	8000.	—
1866 S	842,250	1400.	3200.	6700.	—	—

VARIETY TWO - MOTTO ABOVE EAGLE, TWENTY D. 1866-1876

DIAMETER—34mm
WEIGHT—33.436 Grams
COMPOSITION—.900 Gold,
.100 Copper
DESIGNER—James B. Longacre
EDGE—Reeded
PURE GOLD CONTENT—.96750 Tr. Oz

DATE	MINTAGE	VF-20	EF-40	AU-50	MS-60	Prf-65
1866	698,775	490.	550.	1250.	6000.	80,000.
1866 S	Inc. Above	525.	850.	2500.	—	—
1867	251,065	490.	500.	775.	1550.	80,000.
1867 S	920,750	490.	725.	1500.	—	—
1868	98,600	550.	875.	2400.	7500.	80,000.
1868 S	837,500	490.	700.	1800.	6000.	—
1869	175,155	490.	725.	2100.	6000.	80,000.
1869 S	686,750	490.	575.	1050.	4600.	—
1870	155,185	525.	1000.	2750.	—	80,000.
1870 CC	3,789	Stack's Sale 1979 AU $28,500.				
1870 S	982,000	490.	575.	800.	4350.	—
1871	80,150	650.	1300.	3200.	6600.	80,000.
1871 CC	17,387	1950.	4500.	9500.	—	—
1871 S	928,000	490.	525.	1000.	4000.	—
1872	251,880	490.	520.	700.	4000.	80,000.
1872 CC	26,900	775.	1500.	6000.	13,000.	—
1872 S	780,000	490.	520.	675.	2600.	—
1873 Closed 3	1,709,825	750.	800.	1800.	15,000.	80,000.
1873 Open 3	Inc. Above	490.	520.	550.	700.	—
1873 CC	22,410	800.	1750.	4000.	—	—
1873 S	1,040,600	490.	520.	550.	2000.	—

DATE	MINTAGE	VF-20	EF-40	AU-50	MS-60	Prf-65
1874	366,800	490.	525.	850.	1950.	80,000.
1874 CC	115,085	675.	675.	1750.	7500.	—
1874 S	1,214,000	490.	520.	675.	1650.	—
1875	295,740	490.	520.	575.	1000.	80,000.
1875 CC	111,151	725.	625.	1250.	2000.	—
1875 S	1,230,000	490.	520.	575.	1150.	—
1876	583,905	490.	520.	575.	925.	80,000.
1876 CC	138,441	700.	850.	1650.	5500.	—
1876 S	1,597,000	490.	520.	575.	1150.	—

VARIETY THREE - TWENTY DOLLARS SPELLED OUT 1877-1907

DIAMETER—34mm
WEIGHT—33.436 Grams
COMPOSITION—.900 Gold,
 .100 Copper
DESIGNER—James B. Longacre
EDGE—Reeded
PURE GOLD CONTENT—.96750 Tr. Oz.

DATE	MINTAGE	VF-20	EF-40	AU-50	MS-60	Prf-65
1877	397,670	490.	525.	575.	900.	75,000.
1877 CC	42,565	650.	875.	1350.	5800.	—
1877 S	1,735,000	490.	525.	550.	1000.	—
1878	543,645	490.	525.	575.	800.	75,000.
1878 CC	13,180	800.	1250.	3750.	—	—
1878 S	1,739,000	490.	525.	550.	1500.	—
1879	207,630	490.	550.	600.	1600.	75,000.
1879 CC	10,708	900.	1600.	4500.	—	—
1879 O	2,325	2400.	3600.	11,000.	25,000.	—
1879 S	1,223,800	490.	525.	575.	1600.	—
1880	51,456	590.	610.	1200.	3500.	75,000.
1880 S	836,000	490.	525.	725.	2250.	—
1881	2,260	2600.	6000.	7800.	15,000.	75,000.
1881 S	727,000	490.	525.	675.	1750.	—
1882	630	8500.	15,000.	25,000.	37,000.	75,000.
1882 CC	39,140	750.	850.	1100.	3800.	—
1882 S	1,125,000	490.	525.	550.	1000.	—
1883	92	U.S. Gold Coll. Oct. '82 Prf-67 $88,000.				
1883 CC	59,962	750.	775.	925.	3000.	—
1883 S	1,189,000	490.	525.	550.	750.	—
1884	71	U.S. Gold Coll. Oct. '82 Prf-65 $82,500.				
1884 CC	81,139	750.	775.	1100.	3000.	—
1884 S	916,000	490.	525.	550.	650.	—
1885	828	6000.	10,000.	14,000.	28,000.	75,000.
1885 CC	9,450	1000.	1600.	3500.	9000.	—
1885 S	683,500	490.	525.	550.	650.	—

DATE	MINTAGE	VF-20	EF-40	AU-50	MS-60	Prf-65
1886	1,106	5250.	10,500.	14,500.	24,000.	75,000.
1887	121	U.S. Gold Coll. Oct. '82 Prf-65 $46,750.				
1887 S	283,000	490.	525.	550.	750.	—
1888	226,266	490.	525.	575.	1000.	75,000.
1888 S	859,600	490.	525.	550.	650.	—
1889	44,111	700.	750.	825.	1000.	75,000.
1889 CC	30,945	850.	950.	1200.	3100.	—
1889 S	774,700	490.	525.	550.	700.	—
1890	75,995	700.	730.	725.	1000.	75,000.
1890 CC	91,209	850.	925.	1000.	3800.	—
1890 S	802,750	490.	525.	550.	1500.	—
1891	1,442	2500.	3600.	5000.	8250.	75,000.
1891 CC	5,000	1800.	2400.	3000.	5400.	—
1891 S	1,228,125	490.	500.	510.	600.	—
1892	4,523	1250.	1800.	2400.	7000.	75,000.
1892 CC	27,265	850.	1000.	1300.	3800.	—
1892 S	930,150	490.	500.	510.	600.	—
1893	344,339	490.	500.	510.	600.	75,000.
1893 CC	18,402	700.	950.	1200.	2900.	—
1893 S	996,175	490.	500.	510.	600.	—
1894	1,368,990	490.	500.	510.	600.	75,000.
1894 S	1,048,550	490.	500.	510.	600.	—
1895	1,114,656	490.	500.	510.	600.	75,000.
1895 S	1,143,500	490.	500.	510.	600.	—
1896	792,663	490.	500.	510.	600.	75,000.
1896 S	1,403,925	490.	500.	510.	600.	—
1897	1,383,261	490.	500.	510.	600.	75,000.
1897 S	1,470,250	490.	500.	510.	600.	—
1898	170,470	490.	500.	510.	600.	75,000.
1898 S	2,575,175	490.	500.	510.	600.	—
1899	1,669,384	490.	500.	510.	600.	75,000.
1899 S	2,010,300	490.	500.	510.	600.	—
1900	1,874,584	490.	500.	510.	600.	75,000.
1900 S	2,459,500	490.	500.	510.	600.	—
1901	111,526	490.	500.	510.	600.	75,000.
1901 S	1,596,000	490.	500.	510.	600.	—
1902	31,254	575.	600.	625.	1050.	75,000.
1902 S	1,753,625	490.	500.	510.	600.	—
1903	287,428	490.	500.	510.	600.	75,000.
1903 S	954,000	490.	500.	510.	600.	—
1904	6,256,797	490.	500.	510.	600.	75,000.
1904 S	5,134,175	490.	500.	510.	600.	—
1905	59,011	550.	600.	650.	1500.	75,000.
1905 S	1,813,000	490.	500.	510.	600.	—
1906	69,690	625.	675.	825.	1050.	75,000.
1906 D	620,250	490.	500.	510.	600.	—
1906 S	2,065,750	490.	500.	510.	600.	—
1907	1,451,864	490.	500.	510.	600.	75,000.
1907 D	842,250	490.	500.	510.	600.	—
1907 S	2,165,800	490.	500.	510.	600.	—

SAINT-GAUDENS TYPE
1907-1933

VARIETY ONE - HIGH RELIEF, ROMAN NUMERAL DATE 1907

DIAMETER—34mm
WEIGHT—33.436 Grams
COMPOSITION—.900 Gold, .100 copper
DESIGNER—Augustus Saint-Gaudens
EDGE—E PLURIBUS UNUM
  with stars dividing the words
PURE GOLD CONTENT—.96750 Tr. Oz.

DATE	MINTAGE	VF-20	EF-40	AU-50	MS-60	Prf-65
1907 Extremely High Relief, Plain Edge	Unique		UNIQUE			
1907 Extremely High Relief, Lettered Edge	Unknown	U.S. Gold Coll. Oct. '82 Prf-67			$242,000.	
1907 High Relief, Wire Rim	11,250	2500.	5000.	6500.	9500.	—
1907 High Relief, Flat Rim	Inc. Above	2500.	5000.	6500.	9500.	—

VARIETY TWO - ARABIC NUMERALS, NO MOTTO 1907-1908

DIAMETER—34mm
WEIGHT—33.436 Grams
COMPOSITION—.900 Gold,
  .100 Copper
DESIGNER—Augustus Saint-Gaudens
EDGE—E PLURIBUS UNUM
  With Stars Dividing The Words
PURE GOLD CONTENT-.96750 Tr. Oz.

DATE	MINTAGE	VF-20	EF-40	AU-50	MS-60	Prf-65
1907 Lg. Letters on Edge	Unique	UNIQUE—PROOF ONLY				
1907 Sm. Letters on Edge	361,667	500.	520.	550.	625.	—
1908	4,271,551	500.	520.	550.	625.	—
1908 D	663,750	500.	520.	550.	625.	—

VARIETY THREE - MOTTO ADDED BELOW EAGLE 1908-1933

DIAMETER—34mm
WEIGHT—33.436 Grams
COMPOSITION—.900 Gold,
  .100 Copper
DESIGNER—Augustus Saint-Gaudens
EDGE—E PLURIBUS UNUM
  With Stars Dividing the Words
PURE GOLD CONTENT-.96750 Tr. Oz.

DATE	MINTAGE	VF-20	EF-40	AU-50	MS-60	Prf-65
1908	156,359	495.	510.	525.	625.	65,000.
1908 D	349,500	495.	510.	525.	625.	—
1908 S	22,000	850.	1000.	1350.	2800.	—
1909/8	161,282	540.	560.	590.	1900.	—
1909	Inc. Above	540.	560.	590.	900.	65,000.
1909 D	52,500	600.	625.	700.	1600.	—
1909 S	2,774,925	495.	510.	525.	625.	—
1910	482,167	495.	510.	525.	625.	65,000.
1910 D	429,000	495.	510.	525.	625.	—
1910 S	2,128,250	495.	510.	525.	625.	—
1911	197,350	495.	510.	525.	625.	—
1911 D	846,500	495.	510.	525.	625.	—
1911 S	775,750	495.	510.	525.	625.	—
1912	149,824	495.	510.	525.	625.	65,000.
1913	168,838	495.	510.	525.	625.	65,000.
1913 D	393,500	495.	510.	525.	625.	—
1913 S	34,000	600.	700.	800.	1200.	—
1914	95,320	540.	560.	590.	750.	65,000.
1914 D	453,000	495.	510.	525.	625.	—
1914 S	1,498,000	495.	510.	525.	625.	—
1915	152,050	495.	510.	525.	625.	65,000.
1915 S	567,500	495.	510.	525.	625.	—
1916 S	796,000	495.	510.	525.	625.	—
1920	228,250	495.	510.	525.	625.	—
1920 S	558,000	5250.	9500.	12,500.	20,000.	—
1921	528,500	8500.	12,500.	16,500.	28,000.	—
1922	1,375,500	495.	510.	525.	625.	—
1922 S	2,658,000	575.	650.	850.	1200.	—
1923	566,000	495.	510.	525.	625.	—
1923 D	1,702,250	540.	560.	590.	675.	—
1924	4,323,500	495.	510.	525.	625.	—
1924 D	3,049,500	700.	950.	1200.	2300.	—
1924 S	2,927,500	700.	950.	1200.	2000.	—
1925	2,831,750	495.	510.	525.	625.	—
1925 D	2,938,500	900.	1200.	1500.	2400.	—
1925 S	3,776,500	900.	1200.	1500.	3000.	—
1926	816,750	495.	510.	525.	625.	—
1926 D	481,000	1000.	1150.	1550.	2850.	—
1926 S	2,041,500	900.	1200.	1400.	1650.	—
1927	2,946,750	495.	510.	525.	625.	—
1927 D	180,000	July 1983 Private Sale MS-65 $290,000.				
1927 S	3,107,000	2600.	4500.	5500.	10,000.	—
1928	8,816,000	495.	510.	525.	625.	—
1929	1,779,750	1850.	3650.	4750.	9000.	—
1930 S	74,000	6250.	11,000.	13,500.	20,000.	—
1931	2,938,250	4500.	7750.	11,500.	15,500.	—
1931 D	106,500	3900.	7500.	10,500.	20,000.	—
1932	1,101,750	5250.	9500.	12,500.	22,500.	—
1933	445,500	None Placed in Circulation				

Mint Sets 1947 To Date

Mint sets consist of one uncirculated business strike coin from each mint of every denomination minted during a given year. Official mint sets are assembled and packaged by the Treasury's Bureau of the Mint, and are sold directly from the government to collectors and dealers.

The United States first began offering mint sets in 1947. Mint assembled sets through 1958 contained two examples of each coin from the various mints. Beginning in 1959, only one specimen of each coin struck for the year was included in the sets.

No official government mint sets were produced in 1950, 1982, and 1983, although many sets were assembled by private means. During the years 1965-1967, the government issued what were called "Special Mint Sets." At a time when silver coins were rapidly disappearing from circulation, Treasury officials decided to adopt measures that would discourage collecting to alleviate the coin shortage. The Special Mint Sets contained only five coins (as compared to at least ten in all the previous years), but were sold at almost double the cost of a 1964 Mint set. The 1965 sets were sealed in pliofilm packets and had low quality specimens. In 1966 and 1967 the coins were encased in plastic holders and possessed a proof-like appearance. The Mint renewed the nominal Mint set program in 1968.

Mint sets are good long term investments, primarily because of the potential for the Uncirculated coins contained within the sets. In the years ahead, Uncirculated examples existing today will be worth many times more than their present values. Of course, Mint sets containing choice examples will be worth more than those that don't.

Some dealers believe the Special Mint Sets are severely underpriced because they are such oddities. If you're looking at inexpensive mint sets with a "wild card" factor, then these sets may fit the bill.

By virtue of being a "set," Mint sets have some promise by themselves. No set older than 1959 was produced in quantities greater than 55,000, and many of those were broken up. Compare that with the two million or more sold each year recently, and the promise becomes more evident. Moreover, because Mint sets are sealed at the Mint, grading concerns are not paramount, because buyers feel assured they're getting what they paid for...uncirculated coins. This factor could provide some upward impetus for Mint sets. When buying Mint sets, don't totally abandon caution, however, for it is possible that someone could have cleverly substituted lesser specimens for some of the coins.

The figures listed in the "mintage" column below do not actually indicate a separate actual mintage for these coins, but actually the number of sets packaged by the Treasury Department for the specified year.

MINT SETS 1947 TO DATE LISTING

This listing applies to United States Government packaged mint sets. These sets consist of two coins of each denomination for each mint from 1947 to 1958 and one coin of each denomination and mint from 1959 to date. Mint sets were not produced in 1950, and from 1965 to 1967, and 1982 to 1983. The "mintage" listed does not actually indicate a separate actual mintage for these coins, and is actually the number of sets packaged by the Treasury Department for the specified year.

DATE	MINTAGE	VALUE	DATE	MINTAGE	VALUE
1947	Est. 5,000	900.	1972	2,750,000	3.25
1948	Est. 6,000	240.	1973	1,767,691	15.00
1949	Est. 5,200	780.	1974	1,975,981	5.25
1951	8,654	400.	1975	1,921,488	7.50
1952	11,499	260.	1976	1,892,513	5.50
1953	15,538	230.	1977	2,006,869	7.00
1954	25,599	140.	1978	2,162,609	8.00
1955	49,656	85.00	1979	2,526,000	6.50
1956	45,475	75.00	1980	2,813,118	9.00
1957	32,324	100.	1981	2,908,145	11.00
1958	50,315	95.00	1984	1,832,857	17.00
1959	187,000	24.00	1985	1,710,571	18.00
1960	260,485	18.00	1986	1,153,536	42.00
1961	223,704	18.00	1987	2,890,758	7.00
1962	385,285	18.00	1988	1,646,204	15.00
1963	606,622	18.00	1989	1,987,915	9.00
1964	978,157	15.00	1990		9.00
1968	2,105,128	4.00	1991		9.00
1969	1,306,723	4.25	1992		9.00
1970	2,150,000	24.00	1993		9.00
1971	2,193,396	3.25			

NOTE: The Eisenhower Dollars were not included in the 1971 and 1972 Mint Sets. The 1979 S Susan B. Anthony Dollar is not included in the 1979 Mint Set.

SPECIAL MINT SETS 1965-1967

These sets were sold to collectors during the suspension of proof coinage from 1965 to 1967. These coins possess a proof-like surface and are of better quality than regular circulation strikes. However, the 1965 special mint sets are of lower quality than the 1966 and 1967 sets.

DATE	MINTAGE	VALUE
1965	2,360,000	5.00
1966	2,261,583	6.50
1967	1,863,344	8.00

Proof Sets 1936 To Date

Proof sets are composed of examples of each Proof coin produced during a single year. They are sealed together and shipped directly from the Mint to private citizens. The values for Proof sets are listed here beginning with the 1936 edition, although the United States Mint began striking Proof coins in the 1820's and has annually offered Proof sets and individual Proofs to the public since 1858 with several lapses, including the periods between 1916 to 1936, and 1942 to 1950. There were no Proof sets per se offered from 1965-1967, but the Special Mint Sets of those years were proclaimed by the government to be adequate substitutes for the Proof sets. Prior to 1968, all regular Proof coins were struck at the Philadelphia Mint, but since then they have been produced at the San Francisco facility. The most notable exception to this was the striking of 20 proof 1938 O half dollars to commemorate the opening of the New Orleans Branch Mint. There are a few other branch mint proof coins of various types and all are very rare.

The Proof sets of the 1930's, 1940's and 1950's have increased profoundly during intervals in the past. Presently, their movement has stagnated or even retreated. For those who have been holding out for more bargain prices, 1993 is an opportune time to acquire such a set.

Many of the Proof sets of the 1960's, 1970's and 1980's can now be purchased at prices below their original costs. The price movement from here cannot be any direction but upward, although this probably will not occur immediately. Thus, as long term investments, these sets are attractive. Another contributor to the potential of the more recent Proof sets is the fact that many of them have been dismantled to furnish collectors with singles so they can include the Proof-only San Francisco coins in their collections.

Proof sets do not increase in value solely on the basis of the Proof coins themselves. Proof sets have been a highly visible segment of the coin market to collectors and investors, being advertised every year by the Mint. The sets are housed in attractive, compact display holders, and are popular even with the casual coin collector. 1993 is no exception, as the Mint reports strong sales at the years midpoint. As millions of new collectors enter the hobby in the future, Proof sets are certainly destined for even greater things to come.

PROOF SETS 1936 TO DATE LISTING

The U.S. Mint began striking proof coins in the 1820's and started offering proof sets to collectors in 1858 and continued selling them through 1915. All U.S. proof coins throughout this period, and during the period between 1936 and 1964, were struck at the Philadelphia Mint. Perhaps the most notable exception to this was the striking of 20 proof 1938 O half dollars to commemorate the opening of the New Orleans Branch Mint. There are a few other branch mint proof coins of various types and all are very rare. Starting in 1968, proof coinage was transferred from Philadelphia to the San Francisco Mint. All U.S. proof coins are presently produced at this facility.

The listing below contains the popular modern era proof coinage from 1936 to date. Proof coinage was suspended by the Mint between 1943-1949 and 1965-1967. Proof sets from 1936 to 1972 contain the cent through half dollar. Starting in 1973, the dollar coin was included.

DATE	MINTAGE	VALUE	DATE	MINTAGE	VALUE
1936	3,837	3300.	1970 S Sm. Date 1¢	Inc. Above	90.00
1937	5,542	2000.	1970 S No Mintmark 10¢	Est. 2,200	650.
1938	8,045	1100.	1971 S	3,224,138	8.00
1939	8,795	975.	1971 S No Mintmark 5¢	Est. 1,655	850.
1940	11,246	825.	1972 S	3,267,667	7.50
1941	15,287	750.	1973 S	2,769,624	13.00
1942 Both Nickels	21,120	900.	1974 S	2,617,350	10.00
1942 One Nickel	Inc. Above	750.	1975 S	2,909,369	12.50
1950	51,386	550.	1975 S No Mintmark 10¢	Inc. Above	—
1951	57,500	350.	1976 S	4,149,730	10.00
1952	81,980	240.	1977 S	3,251,152	12.00
1953	128,800	150.	1978 S	3,127,788	13.00
1954	233,300	75.00	1979 S	3,677,175	20.00
1955 Box Pack	378,200	70.00	1979 1979 S Type II	Inc. Above	100.
1955 Flat Pack	Inc. Above	85.00	1980 S	3,554,806	10.00
1956	669,384	32.50	1981 S	4,063,083	13.00
1957	1,247,952	22.00	1982 S	3,857,479	12.50
1958	875,652	27.00	1983 S	3,138,765	12.00
1959	1,149,291	22.00	1984 S	2,748,430	22.50
1960 Lg. Date 1¢	1,691,602	17.50	1985 S	3,362,821	18.00
1960 Sm. Date 1¢	Inc. Above	27.00	1986 S	2,411,180	23.00
1961	3,028,244	15.00	1987 S	3,792,233	11.00
1962	3,218,019	15.00	1988 S	3,031,287	14.00
1963	3,075,645	15.00	1989 S	3,009,107	12.00
1964	3,950,752	15.00	1990 S		20.00
1968 S	3,041,509	12.00	1991 S		15.00
1968 S No Mintmark 10¢	Inc. Above	8500.	1992 S		15.00
1969 S	2,934,631	10.00	1992 S		15.00
1970 S Lg. Date 1¢	2,632,810	14.00	1993 S		15.00

United States Commemorative Coins

Commemorative coins are issued by the United States government to remember past events and things or to honor certain historical persons. They are sold to the general public at prices well above the face values of the coins themselves. Sometimes the money raised from these sales is used to fund a monument or to support some cause. Commemoratives offer variety, beauty, and history, qualities which have endeared them to collectors.

The first American commemorative coin made its debut in 1892. It was the Columbian half dollar, issued to mark the 400th anniversary of Columbus' discovery of the New World. Up to 1954 many commemoratives were released, observing a wide variety of subjects. No commemoratives were produced after 1954 until 1982, when the George Washington half dollar ushered in an era of modern commemoratives.

In considering the older commemorative coins, few of them were struck in great numbers. In fact, many of them have mintages under 30,000. Since they were never intended as spending money, commemoratives have survived in Uncirculated condition in far higher proportions than regular issues. Occasionally, a collector will encounter slightly worn commemoratives, especially for those types struck before the Great Depression. During those tough economic times, some people did not have the luxury of keeping souvenir coins. Adding to the supply of circulated commemoratives was the federal government itself, which sometimes released unsold examples into circulation at face value.

Of the remaining stock of older Uncirculated commemoratives, not too many have survived to this day in MS-65 condition or better. Mishandling and the passage of time have certainly taken their toll on these coins. Some of the lower grade Uncirculated coins have been cleaned or dipped to resemble nicer specimens, so be alert for this sort of thing.

While it is true that the older commemoratives have been consistently popular with collectors, based solely on their intrinsic merits, their wild price fluctuations could make you think otherwise. The reason for these pricing irregularities is because of the heavy influence promoters exert from time to time. These commemoratives are ideal targets for promoters. They have attractive designs, interesting topics, a large collector base to support the market, a high percentage of Uncirculated examples, and are affordable to most buyers. Because many of the older commemorative types have low mintages, a large dealer or group of dealers can corner a fair share of the available supply of a particular commemorative type (which acts to push prices higher by itself), effectively promote the coin and sell out later at much higher prices. This has happened in the past and undoubtedly will take place again. Don't let this sort of activity prevent you from purchasing commemoratives for the sake of investing. If you play your cards right, you can actually use the promoter influence to your advantage. The age-old adage "buy low, sell high" should be your guiding principle.

At the present time, the cost of obtaining an older commemorative is generally down from what it was in 1989 by a considerable margin. This holds true for all grades. Inevitably, the spotlight will shine brightly upon them again, and when this happens, watch for the older commemoratives to post impressive gains. If you've been putting off buying that commemorative you've always dreamed about, check into it soon. The chances are good that you'll never see a better opportunity than now.

As far as long range planners are concerned, every older commemorative issue in collectible grades will be a winner. Excellent long term growth is part of their nature. Thus, today's investors are virtually assured of future profits if only they have patience.

The reinstatement of commemorative coinage in 1982 was met with applause, but 11 years later, many individuals involved with the coin industry are unhappy with the program. One complaint is that too many commemoratives are being issued, with no expectation that the situation will improve. For example, several dozen varieties of Olympic coins observing the 1996 Atlanta games are being planned! Another distasteful characteristic for many is the political pressure by special interests to have their topic immortalized (not to mention extra revenue brought in by the coin sales). This is the sort of thing that doomed the first commemorative era. And lastly, there has been appreciation on only a very few of the modern commemoratives, a fact quite possibly linked to the occurrence above. In fact, most of them can be had for far less than their original costs. Understandably, not many people are excited about this set of circumstances.

On the positive side, some of the newer commemoratives are truly beautiful coins that can be yours today at true bargains. That may not be the case in another ten years or so. Either way, you have very little to lose at the present moment.

Buying commemoratives can be downright fun. Take a look at all the different subject matters commemoratives depict. Consult some of the books listed in the Suggested Reading List to gain a historical perspective for commemorative coin collecting. Persons having a general appreciation for American history especially could spend many enjoyable years putting together a collection of commemoratives, and no doubt would be justly pleased with the final project.

The entire United States commemorative coin set consists of many beautiful designs, laced with patriotic overtones. It's easy to understand why collectors are so fond of commemorative coinage.

UNITED STATES COMMEMORATIVE COINS

QUARTER DOLLAR

DATE	MINTAGE	EF-40	AU-50	MS-60	MS-65
1893 Isabella, Columbian Exposition	24,214	140.	195.	400.	3000.

SILVER DOLLAR

1900 Lafayette	36,026	280.	425.	675.	10,000.

HALF DOLLARS

1921 Alabama 2X2	6,000	100.	125.	280.	3900.
1921 Alabama	53,038	67.50	80.00	200.	4200.

DATE	MINTAGE	EF-40	AU-50	MS-60	MS-65
1935 Albany	17,671	180.	195.	225.	725.

DATE	MINTAGE	EF-40	AU-50	MS-60	MS-65
1937 Antietam	18,028	350.	400.	460.	775.

DATE	MINTAGE	EF-40	AU-50	MS-60	MS-65
1935 Arkansas PDS Set	5,505	—	—	265.	1400.
1936 Arkansas PDS Set	9,660	—	—	265.	1400.
1937 Arkansas PDS Set	5,505	—	—	280.	1600.
1938 Arkansas PDS Set	3,155	—	—	350.	3100.
1939 Arkansas PDS Set	2,104	—	—	700.	3500.
Arkansas-Type Coin	—	35.00	45.00	90.00	480.

DATE	MINTAGE	EF-40	AU-50	MS-60	MS-65
1936 S.F. - Oakland Bay Bridge	71,424	45.00	65.00	120.	500.

DATE	MINTAGE	EF-40	AU-50	MS-60	MS-65
1934 Daniel Boone	10,007	60.00	85.00	100.	210.
1935 Boone PDS Set	5,005	—	—	300.	525.
1935 Boone PDS Set W/1934 on Rev.	2,003	—	—	550.	1800.
1936 Boone PDS Set	5,005	—	—	300.	525.
1937 Boone PDS Set	2,506	—	—	575.	1500.
1938 Boone PDS Set	2,100	—	—	750.	2500.
Boone, Type Coin	—	60.00	85.00	100.	200.

1936 Bridgeport	25,015	80.00	95.00	120.	535.

1925 S California Jubilee	86,594	70.00	85.00	125.	900.

DATE	MINTAGE	EF-40	AU-50	MS-60	MS-65
1936 Cincinnati, PDS Set	5,005	—	—	800.	2700.
1936 Cincinnati, Type Coin	—	210.	230.	275.	900.

1936 Cleveland-Great Lakes	50,030	35.00	45.00	75.00	385.

1936 Columbia, PDS Set	9,007	—	—	580.	1000.
1936 Columbia, Type Coin	—	95.00	150.	210.	350.

1892 Columbian Exposition	950,000	16.00	24.00	75.00	1400.
1893 Columbian Exposition	1,550,405	15.00	22.00	68.00	1700.

DATE	MINTAGE	EF-40	AU-50	MS-60	MS-65
1935 Connecticut	25,018	140.	200.	225.	1000.
1936 Delaware	20,993	140.	180.	225.	700.
1936 Elgin, Illinois	20,015	120.	175.	225.	450.
1936 Gettysburg	26,928	150.	210.	240.	850.

DATE	MINTAGE	EF-40	AU-50	MS-60	MS-65
1922 Grant, With Star	4,256	300.	350.	900.	10,500.
1922 Grant	67,405	60.00	75.00	90.	1300.

| 1928 Hawaiian | 10,008 | 575. | 600. | 1100. | 5500. |

| 1935 Hudson | 10,008 | 350. | 375. | 475. | 2250. |

| 1924 Huguenot-Walloon | 142,080 | 47.50 | 65.00 | 90.00 | 825. |

DATE	MINTAGE	EF-40	AU-50	MS-60	MS-65
1918 Illinois - Lincoln	100,058	50.00	75.00	100.	900.

1946 Iowa	100,057	60.00	65.00	75.00	135.

1925 Lexington - Concord	162,013	30.00	40.00	70.00	1200.

1936 Long Island	81,826	55.00	65.00	75.00	600.

DATE	MINTAGE	EF-40	AU-50	MS-60	MS-65
1936 Lynchburg	20,013	130.	155.	175.	625.
1920 Maine	50,028	50.00	60.00	85.00	1000.
1934 Maryland	25,015	90.00	100.	160.	550.
1921 Missouri-2x4	5,000	220.	250.	375.	8000.
1921 Missouri	15,428	160.	175.	320.	7500.

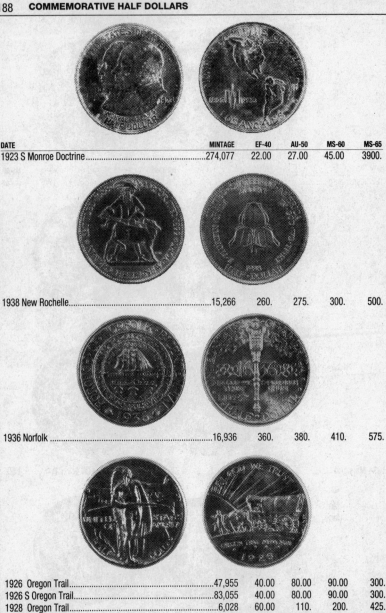

DATE	MINTAGE	EF-40	AU-50	MS-60	MS-65
1923 S Monroe Doctrine	274,077	22.00	27.00	45.00	3900.
1938 New Rochelle	15,266	260.	275.	300.	500.
1936 Norfolk	16,936	360.	380.	410.	575.
1926 Oregon Trail	47,955	40.00	80.00	90.00	300.
1926 S Oregon Trail	83,055	40.00	80.00	90.00	300.
1928 Oregon Trail	6,028	60.00	110.	200.	425.
1933 D Oregon Trail	5,008	90.00	140.	275.	525.
1934 D Oregon Trail	7,006	50.00	100.	200.	500.
1936 Oregon Trail	10,006	40.00	95.00	150.	325.

DATE	MINTAGE	EF-40	AU-50	MS-60	MS-65
1936 S Oregon Trail	5,006	60.00	110.	220.	375.
1937 D Oregon Trail	12,008	40.00	95.00	125.	325.
1938 Oregon Trail, PDS Set	6,005	—	—	530.	1250.
1939 Oregon Trail, PDS Set	3,004	—	—	1200.	2400.
Oregon Trail, Type Coin	—	40.00	80.00	90.00	300.

DATE	MINTAGE	EF-40	AU-50	MS-60	MS-65
1915 S Panama-Pacific Exposition	27,134	150.	200.	300.	3200.

DATE	MINTAGE	EF-40	AU-50	MS-60	MS-65
1920 Pilgrim	152,112	30.00	45.00	65.00	875.
1921 Pilgrim	20,053	55.00	75.00	95.00	1200.

DATE	MINTAGE	EF-40	AU-50	MS-60	MS-65
1936 Rhode Island, PDS Set	15,010	—	—	275.	1350.
1936 Rhode Island, Type Coin	—	60.00	75.00	90.00	460.

DATE	MINTAGE	EF-40	AU-50	MS-60	MS-65
1937 Roanoke	29,030	100.	180.	200.	325.
1936 Robinson - Arkansas	25,265	65.00	80.00	90.00	540.
1935 S San Diego	70,132	60.00	65.00	75.00	140.
1936 D San Diego	30,092	60.00	65.00	75.00	150.
1926 Sesquicentennial	141,120	30.00	45.00	75.00	6200.
1935 Spanish Trail	10,008	575.	625.	800.	1100.

DATE	MINTAGE	EF-40	AU-50	MS-60	MS-65
1925 Stone Mountain	1,314,709	20.00	27.50	42.00	240.

1934 Texas	61,463	70.00	80.00	120.	180.
1935 Texas-PDS Set	9,994	—	—	350.	550.
1936 Texas-PDS Set	8,911	—	—	350.	550.
1937 Texas-PDS Set	6,571	—	—	350.	550.
1938 Texas-PDS Set	3,775	—	—	625.	1400.
Texas, Type Coin	—	70.00	80.00	120.	180.

1925 Fort Vancouver	14,994	200.	220.	300.	1300.

1927 Vermont	28,142	100.	125.	175.	1450.

DATE	MINTAGE	EF-40	AU-50	MS-60	MS-65
1946 B.T. Washington - PDS Set	200,113	—	—	36.00	150.
1947 B.T. Washington - PDS Set	100,017	—	—	50.00	290.
1948 B.T. Washington - PDS Set	8,005	—	—	90.00	190.
1949 B.T. Washington - PDS Set	6,004	—	—	100.	325.
1950 B.T. Washington - PDS Set	6,004	—	—	100.	225.
1951 B.T. Washington - PDS Set	7,004	—	—	80.00	235.
B.T. Washington, Type Coin	(3,091,205 Total for Type)	10.00	12.00	12.50	50.00

DATE	MINTAGE	EF-40	AU-50	MS-60	MS-65
1951 Washington - Carver PDS Set	10,004	—	—	75.00	640.
1952 Washington - Carver PDS Set	8,006	—	—	75.00	375.
1953 Washington - Carver PDS Set	8,003	—	—	100.	500.
1954 Washington - Carver PDS Set	12,006	—	—	75.00	600.
Washington - Carver, Type Coin	(2,422,392 Total for Type)	10.00	12.00	15.00	90.00

DATE	MINTAGE	MS-65	Prf-65
1982 D Geo. Washington-250th Anniversary	2,210,502	8.00	—
1982 S Geo. Washington-250th Anniversary	4,894,044	—	8.00

DATE	MINTAGE	EF-40	AU-50	MS-60	MS-65
1936 Wisconsin	25,015	160.	180.	220.	310.

1936 York County	25,015	150.	170.	200.	315.

GOLD DOLLARS

1903 Louisiana Purchase-Jefferson	17,500	—	350.	450.	2900.
1903 Louisiana Purchase-McKinley	17,500	—	350.	450.	2900.

1904 Lewis and Clark Exposition	10,025	—	475.	750.	6500.
1905 Lewis and Clark Exposition	10,041	—	475.	1000.	15,000.

1915 S Panama-Pacific Exposition	15,000	—	350.	425.	2900.
1916 McKinley Memorial	9,977	—	365.	450.	3000.
1917 McKinley Memorial	10,000	—	375.	475.	3400.

DATE	MINTAGE	AU-50	MS-60	MS-65
1922 Grant Memorial with Star	5,016	900.	1450.	3200.
1922 Grant Memorial	5,000	925.	1500.	3400.

QUARTER EAGLES ($2.50 Gold Pieces)

1915 S Panama - Pacific Exposition	6,749	1000.	1400.	5500.

1926 Philadelphia Sesquicentennial	46,019	280.	375.	10,000.

FIFTY DOLLARS GOLD

1915 S Panama - Pacific Exposition - Round	483	21,500.	25,000.	90,000.
1915 S Panama - Pacific Exposition - Octagonal	645	19,000.	22,000.	80,000.

1984
OLYMPIC GAMES, LOS ANGELES
SILVER DOLLARS

DATE	MINTAGE	MS-65	Prf-65
1983 P	294,543	15.00	—
1983 D	174,014	28.00	—
1983 S	174,014	21.00	—
1983 S PROOF	1,577,025	—	13.00

1984 P	217,954	18.00	—
1984 D	116,675	42.00	—
1984 S	116,675	45.00	—
1984 S PROOF	1,801,210	—	15.00

EAGLE

1984 W	75,886	260.	—
1984 W PROOF	381,085	—	260.
1984 P	33,309	—	300.
1984 D	34,533	—	275.
1984 S	48,551	—	260.

1986
STATUE OF LIBERTY CENTENNIAL
HALF DOLLAR

DATE	MINTAGE	MS-65	Prf-65
1986 D	928,008	4.25	—
1986 S	6,925,627	—	4.25

SILVER DOLLAR

1986 P	723,635	18.00	—
1986 S	6,414,638	—	14.00

HALF EAGLE

1986 W	95,248	120.	—
1986 W PROOF	404,013	—	125.

1987
CONSTITUTION BICENTENNIAL

SILVER DOLLAR

DATE	MINTAGE	MS-65	Prf-65
1987 P 451,629		12.00	—
1987 S...2,747,116		—	12.00

HALF EAGLE

1987 W 214,225		125.	—
1987 W PROOF 651,659		—	125.

1988
OLYMPIAD

SILVER DOLLAR

DATE	MINTAGE	MS-65	Prf-65
1988 D	191,368	27.00	—
1988 S	1,359,366	—	12.00

HALF EAGLE

	MINTAGE	MS-65	Prf-65
1988 W	62,913	125.	—
1988 W PROOF	281,465	—	130.

1989
BICENTENNIAL OF CONGRESS

HALF DOLLAR

DATE	MINTAGE	MS-65	Prf-65
1989 D	163,753	12.50	—
1989 S	767,897	—	11.00

SILVER DOLLAR

1989 D	135,203	36.00	—
1989 S	762,198	—	27.50

HALF EAGLE

1989 W	46,899	125.	—
1989 W PROOF	164,690	—	120.

1990
EISENHOWER CENTENNIAL

SILVER DOLLAR

DATE	MINTAGE	MS-65	Prf-65
1990 W	—	30.00	—
1990 P	—	—	20.00

1991
MOUNT RUSHMORE

HALF DOLLAR

DATE	MINTAGE	MS-65	Prf-65
1991 D	—	16.00	—
1991 S	—	—	18.00

SILVER DOLLAR

| 1991 P | — | 45.00 | — |
| 1991 S | — | — | 32.00 |

HALF EAGLE

| 1991 W | — | 180. | 200. |

1991
KOREAN WAR

SILVER DOLLAR

DATE	MINTAGE	MS-65	Prf-65
1991 D	—	22.50	—
1991 P	—	—	25.00

1991
U.S.O. FIFTIETH ANNIVERSARY

SILVER DOLLAR

DATE	MINTAGE	MS-65	Prf-65
1991 D	—	85.00	—
1991 S	—	—	50.00

1992
OLYMPIC GAMES

HALF DOLLAR

DATE	MINTAGE	MS-65	Prf-65
1992 P..—		7.25	—
1992 S..—		—	11.00

SILVER DOLLAR

| 1992 D..— | | 26.00 | — |
| 1992 S..— | | — | 30.00 |

HALF EAGLE

| 1992 W..— | | 230. | 210. |

1992
COLUMBUS QUINTENCENTURY

HALF DOLLAR

DATE	MINTAGE	MS-65	Prf-65
1992 D	—	11.00	—
1992 S	—	—	13.00

SILVER DOLLAR

1992 D	—	36.00	—
1992 S	—	—	38.00

HALF EAGLE

1992 W	—	225.	210.

1992
WHITE HOUSE
200TH ANNIVERSARY

SILVER DOLLAR

DATE	MINTAGE	MS-65	Prf-65
1992 D	—	80.00	—
1992 W	—	—	90.00

UNITED STATES BULLION COINS

AMERICAN EAGLES
FIFTY DOLLARS—1 OUNCE

DIAMETER—32.7mm
WEIGHT—33.931 Grams
COMPOSITION—.9167 Gold,
  .03 Silver, .0533 Copper
DESIGNER—Augustus Saint-Gaudens
  (Obverse), Miley Busiek (Reverse)
EDGE—Reeded
PURE GOLD CONTENT—1.000 Tr. Oz.

DATE	MINTAGE	MS-65	Prf-65
1986	1,362,650	420.	—
1986 W	446,290	—	500.
1987	1,045,500	420.	—
1987 W	147,498	—	500.
1988	465,500	420.	—
1988 W	87,133	—	500.
1989	415,790	420.	—
1989 W	54,570	—	500.
1990	373,210	420.	—
1990 W	—	—	510.
1991	—	420.	—
1991 W	—	—	620.
1992	—	420.	—
1992 W	—	—	650.

TWENTY-FIVE DOLLARS— 1/2 OUNCE

DIAMETER—27mm
WEIGHT—16.966 Grams
COMPOSITION—.9167 Gold,
  .03 Silver, .0533 Copper
DESIGNER—Augustus Saint-Gaudens
  (Obverse), Miley Busiek (Reverse)
EDGE—Reeded
PURE GOLD CONTENT—.50 Tr. Oz.

DATE	MINTAGE	MS-65	Prf-65
1986	599,566	225.	—
1987	131,255	225.	—
1987 P	143,398	—	250.
1988	45,000	225.	—
1988 P	76,528	—	250.
1989	44,829	225.	—
1989 P	44,798	—	250.
1990	31,000	225.	—
1990 P	—	—	340.

DATE	MINTAGE	MS-65	Prf-65
1991	—	280.	—
1991 P	—	—	280.
1992	—	225.	—
1992 P	—	—	270

TEN DOLLARS— 1/4 OUNCE

DIAMETER—22mm
WEIGHT—8.483 Grams
COMPOSITION—.9167 Gold,
  .03 Silver, .0533 Copper
DESIGNER—Augustus Saint-Gaudens
  (Obverse), Miley Busiek (Reverse)
EDGE—Reeded
PURE GOLD CONTENT—.25 Tr. Oz.

DATE	MINTAGE	MS-65	Prf-65
1986	726,031	105.	—
1987	269,255	105.	—
1988	49,000	105.	—
1988 P	98,028	—	125.
1989	81,789	105.	—
1989 P	54,170	—	125.
1990	41,000	105.	—
1990 P	—	—	125.
1991	—	125.	—
1991 P	—	—	150.
1992	—	110.	—
1992 P	—	—	—

FIVE DOLLARS—1/10 OUNCE

DIAMETER—16.5mm
WEIGHT—3.393 Grams
COMPOSITION—.9167 Gold,
  .03 Silver, .0533 Copper
DESIGNER—Augustus Saint-Gaudens
  (Obverse), Miley Busiek (Reverse)
EDGE—Reeded
PURE GOLD CONTENT—.10 Tr. Oz.

DATE	MINTAGE	MS-65	Prf-65
1986	912,609	50.00	—
1987	580,266	50.00	—
1988	159,500	50.00	—
1988 P	143,881	—	65.00
1989	264,790	50.00	—
1989 P	84,647	—	65.00
1990	210,210	50.00	—
1990 P	—	—	70.00
1991	—	50.00	—
1991 P	—	—	75.00
1992	—	50.00	—
1992 P	—	—	—

SILVER EAGLES
ONE DOLLAR—1 OUNCE

DIAMETER—40.6mm
WEIGHT—31.101 Grams
COMPOSITION—.9993 Silver,
   .0007 Copper
DESIGNER—Adolph A. Weinman
   (Obverse), John Mercanti (Reverse)
EDGE—Reeded
PURE SILVER CONTENT—1.000 Tr. Oz.

DATE	MINTAGE	MS-65	Prf-65
1986	5,393,005	14.00	—
1986 S	1,446,778	—	22.00
1987	11,442,335	7.50	—
1987 S	904,732	—	20.00
1988	5,004,646	7.50	—
1988 S	557,370	—	90.00
1989	5,203,327	7.50	—
1989 S	617,694	—	20.00
1990	5,750,000	7.50	—
1990 S	700,000	—	28.00
1991	—	7.50	—
1991 S	—	—	25.00
1992	—	7.50	—
1992 S	—	—	—

BULLION VALUES OF UNITED STATES COINS

SILVER COINS

Price of Silver Per Troy Ounce	$3.50	$4.00	$4.50	$5.00	$6.00	$7.00	$8.00	$9.00	$10.00
Wartime Nickels									
1942-45 (.350 Fine)	.20	.23	.25	.28	.34	.39	.45	.51	.56
Dimes (.900 Fine)									
1964 and Earlier	.25	.29	.33	.36	.43	.51	.58	.65	.72
Quarters (.900)									
1964 and Earlier	.63	.72	.81	.90	1.09	1.27	1.45	1.63	1.81
Half Dollars (.900 Fine)									
1964 and Earlier	1.27	1.45	1.63	1.81	2.17	2.53	2.89	3.26	3.62
Silver Dollars (.900 Fine)									
1935 and Earlier	2.71	3.09	3.48	3.87	4.64	5.41	6.19	6.96	7.73
Half Dollars (.400 Fine)									
1965-1970	.52	.59	.67	.74	.89	1.04	1.18	1.33	1.48
Ike Dollars (.400 Fine)									
(S-Mint)	1.11	1.27	1.42	1.58	1.90	2.21	2.53	2.85	3.16

GOLD COINS

Price of Gold Per Troy Ounce	$325.	$350.	$375.	$400.	$425.	$450.	$475.	$500.	$525.
Gold Dollars (.900 Fine)	15.72	16.93	18.14	19.35	20.56	21.77	22.98	24.19	25.39
Quarter Eagles ($2.50)									
(.900 Fine)	39.31	42.33	45.25	48.38	51.40	54.42	57.45	60.47	63.50
Three Dollars (.900 Fine)	47.16	50.79	54.42	58.05	61.68	65.30	68.93	72.56	76.19
Half Eagles ($5.00) (.900 Fine)	78.61	84.65	90.70	96.75	102.79	108.84	114.89	120.94	126.98
Eagles ($10.00) (.900 Fine)	157.22	169.31	181.41	193.50	205.59	217.69	229.78	241.88	253.97
Double Eagles ($20.00) (.900)	314.44	338.63	362.81	387.00	411.19	435.38	459.56	483.75	507.94

EXPLANATION OF BULLION VALUE CHARTS

Many newcomers to numismatics have the erroneous opinion that the prices of gold and silver are closely related to their bullion value. This assumption is quite far from the truth. Bullion value determines only the base value of coins. This value applies to the most common dates of the series and usually only coins that are not in choice condition. No U.S. silver coins minted before 1892 are affected significantly by this base value because they all have numismatic value in excess of their bullion value even in the lowest collectible grades.

For those who are interested in using the bullion value charts, the following information should be noted: Dealers will generally pay considerably less for silver coins than their full melt value (listed above). At the time that this book is being written, dealers were paying as much as 40% below melt value for silver.

The prices dealers are paying for bullion related (common date) United States gold coins are quite different. U.S. gold coins have already sold for a premium over actual melt value. This premium has changed considerably in the present volatile market, so we recommend that anyone wishing to sell common date gold coins should get several offers from dealers before selling to the highest bidder.

United States Mints and Mint Marks

The United States Mint at Philadelphia is the "parent" mint of the United States. Regular issue U.S. coinage was commenced at Philadelphia in 1793. From that time to date, all dies for U.S. coinage have been made at Philadelphia. It has been customary for coins of the Philadelphia mint to not carry a mint mark. The exceptions to this practice are the nickels of 1942-1945 and the Susan B. Anthony type dollar.

From time to time, branch mints have been established to increase coinage production to keep up with increasing commercial needs for coins. To distinguish coins struck at these branch mints, a letter (or letters) was punched into the dies sent from Philadelphia to the branch mints. The mint marks of these mints are as follows:

MINT MARK	MINT	DATES OF OPERATION
P	Philadelphia, Pennsylvania	1793 to date
O	New Orleans, Louisiana	1838-1861 and 1879-1909
D	Dahlonega, Georgia	1838-1861 (gold coins only)
C	Charlotte, North Carolina	1838-1861 (gold coins only)
S	San Francisco, California	1854-1955 & 1968 to date
CC	Carson City, Nevada	1870-1893
D	Denver, Colorado	1906 to date
W	West Point, New York	1984

Mint Mark Locations

DENOMINATION	TYPE	SIDE OF COIN	LOCATION OF MINT MARK
Cent	Indian Head	Reverse	Below Wreath
Cent	Lincoln	Obverse	Below Date
Three Cents (Silver)	—	Reverse	At Right of C
Five Cent Nickel	Liberty Head	Reverse	At Left of Cents Below Dot
Five Cent Nickel	Buffalo	Reverse	Below Five Cents
Five Cent Nickel	Jefferson 1938-64	Reverse	At Right of Building
Five Cent Nickel	Jefferson (Wartime)	Reverse	Large Mintmark Above Building
Five Cent Nickel	Jefferson 1968-Date	Obverse	Below Date
Half Dime	Liberty Seated	Reverse	Above or Below Bow of Wreath
Dime	Liberty Seated	Reverse	Above or Below Bow of Wreath
Dime	Barber	Reverse	Below Wreath
Dime	Mercury	Reverse	At Right of ONE
Dime	Roosevelt 1946-64	Reverse	At Left of Torch
Dime	Roosevelt 1968-Date	Obverse	Above Date
Twenty Cents	—	Reverse	Below Eagle
Quarter Dollar	Liberty Seated	Reverse	Below Eagle

DENOMINATION	TYPE	SIDE OF COIN	LOCATION OF MINT MARK
Quarter Dollar	Barber	Reverse	Below Eagle
Quarter Dollar	Standing Liberty	Obverse	At Left of Date
Quarter Dollar	Washington 1938-64	Reverse	Below Wreath
Quarter Dollar	" 1968-Date	Obverse	At Right of Ribbon
Half Dollar	Cap bust, Reed edge	Obverse	Above Date
Half Dollar	Liberty Seated	Reverse	Below Eagle
Half Dollar	Barber	Reverse	Below Eagle
Half Dollar	Liberty Walk 1916-17	Obverse	Below Motto
Half Dollar	Liberty Walk 1917-47	Reverse	Below Leaves at Left
Half Dollar	Franklin	Reverse	Above Yoke of Bell
Half Dollar	Kennedy 1964	Reverse	At Left of Branch
Half Dollar	Kennedy 1968-Date	Obverse	Above Date
Silver Dollar	Liberty Seated	Reverse	Below Eagle
Trade Dollar	—	Reverse	Below Eagle
Silver Dollar	Morgan	Reverse	Below Wreath
Silver Dollar	Peace	Reverse	Below ONE at Left of Wingtip
Dollar	Eisenhower	Obverse	Above Date
Dollar	S.B. Anthony	Obverse	At Left of Head
Gold Dollar	All Types	Reverse	Below Wreath
Quarter Eagle	Classic Head	Obverse	Above Date
Quarter Eagle	Coronet	Reverse	Below Eagle
Quarter Eagle	Indian Head	Reverse	At Left of Fasces
Three Dollars	—	Reverse	Below Wreath
Half Eagle	Classic Head	Obverse	Above Date
Half Eagle	Coronet 1939	Obverse	Above Date
Half Eagle	Coronet 1840-1908	Reverse	Below Eagle
Half Eagle	Indian Head	Reverse	At Left of Fasces
Eagle	Coronet	Reverse	Below Eagle
Eagle	Indian Head	Reverse	At Left of Fasces
Double Eagle	Coronet	Reverse	Below Eagle
Double Eagle	Saint-Gaudens	Obverse	Above Date

Recommended Reading

A fairly extensive listing of recommended books and periodicals concerning United States coins is being included because the editor believes that it is very important to read as much information as possible before spending large sums of money for coins. While *Edmund's United States Coin Prices* is intended to give you accurate price listings for all United States regular issue and commemorative coins, there is a wealth of detailed specific information in the publications on the following pages.

Periodicals

COIN WORLD (Weekly)	Post Office Box 150, Sidney, OH 45365
COINS MAGAZINE (Monthly)	Iola, WI 54945
COINage MAGAZINE (Monthly)	17337 Ventura Blvd., Encino, CA 91316
NUMISMATIC NEWS (Weekly)	Iola, WI 54945

General Reference

Yeoman, R.S., *A GUIDE BOOK OF UNITED STATES COINS*, 36th edition,
 1983 Racine, Wisconsin
Taxay, Don, *THE U.S. MINT AND COINAGE*, New York 1966 Reprinted 1969
Bressett, Ken and Kosoff, A., *OFFICIAL A.N.A. GRADING STANDARDS FOR
 UNITED STATES COINS*, Racine, Wisconsin 1977
Bowers, Q. David, *THE HISTORY OF UNITED STATES COINAGE, AS
 ILLUSTRATED BY THE GARRETT COLLECTION*, Los Angeles, California 1979
 IBID., *ADVENTURES WITH RARE COINS*, Los Angeles, California 1979
 IBID., *COINS AND COLLECTORS*, New York, New York 1971
Stack, Norman, *UNITED STATES TYPE COINS*, New York, New York 1977

Specialized Reference

NOTE: The following books are recommended to the collector who wishes to specialize in a particular series of United States coins. At the end of this listing, we have included a few books covering Colonial coins, Pattern coins and mint errors. These coins are somewhat related to the collecting of U.S. regular issue coins, but are not within the scope of this book.

Gilbert, Ebenezer, *UNITED STATES HALF CENTS*, New York 1916,
 Hewitt Reprint, Chicago
Sheldon, Wm. H., *PENNY WHIMSY (1793-1814)*, Lawrence, Mass. 1976
Newcomb, H.R., *UNITED STATES COPPER CENTS 1816-1857*, New York 1944
Valentine, D.W., *THE UNITED STATES HALF DIMES*, New York 1931
Kosoff, A., *UNITED STATES DIMES FROM 1796*, New York 1945
Ahwash, Kamal M., *ENCYCLOPEDIA OF UNITED STATES LIBERTY SEATED DIMES
 1837-1891*, Kamal Press 1977
Browning, A.W., *THE EARLY QUARTER DOLLARS OF THE UNITED STATES*

1796-1838, New York 1925

Haseltine, J.W., *TYPE TABLE OF UNITED STATES DOLLARS, HALF DOLLARS
AND QUARTER DOLLARS,* Phila, 1881 Reprinted 1968

Cline, *J.H. STANDING LIBERTY QUARTERS, 1976*

Kelman, Keith N., *STANDING LIBERTY QUARTERS, 1976*

Beistle, M.L., *REGISTER OF UNITED STATES HALF DOLLARS VARIETIES
AND SUBVARIETIES,* Shippensburg, Pa. 1929

Overton, Al C., *EARLY HALF DOLLAR DIE VARIETIES 1794-1836,*
Colorado Springs, 1967, Revised 1970

Bolender, M.H., *THE UNITED STATES EARLY SILVER DOLLARS FROM
1794-1803,* Freeport, Ill. 1950

Newman, Eric P. and Bressett, Kenneth E., *THE FANTASTIC 1804 DOLLAR,*
Racine, Wisconsin 1962

Willem, John M., *THE UNITED STATES TRADE DOLLAR,* Racine,
Wisconsin 1965

Van Allen, Leroy C. and Mallis, A. George, *COMPREHENSIVE CATALOGUE
AND ENCYCLOPEDIA OF U.S. MORGAN AND PEACE SILVER DOLLARS,*
New York 1976

Akers, David W., *UNITED STATES GOLD COINS, AN ANALYSIS OF
AUCTION RECORDS*

> *VOLUME I GOLD DOLLARS,* 1849-1889, Englewood, Ohio, 1975
> *VOLUME II QUARTER EAGLES, 1796-1929,* Englewood, Ohio, 1975
> V*OLUME III THREE DOLLAR GOLD PIECES 1854-*1889 AND FOUR
>   *DOLLAR GOLD PIECES 1879-1880,* Englewood, Ohio 1976
> *VOLUME IV HALF EAGLES 1795-1929,* Englewood, Ohio 1979
> *VOLUME V EAGLES 1795-1933,* Englewood, Ohio 1980
> *VOLUME VI DOUBLE EAGLES 1849-1933,* Englewood, Ohio 1982

Slabaugh, Arlie R., *UNITED STATES COMMEMORATIVE COINAGE,*
Racine, Wisconsin, 1975

Taxay, Don, *AN ILLUSTRATED HISTORY OF U.S. COMMEMORATIVE
COINAGE,* New York 1967

Breen, Walter, *WALTER BREEN'S ENCYCLOPEDIA OF UNITED STATES AND
COLONIAL PROOF COINS 1722-1977,* Albertson, New York, 1977

Judd, J. Hewitt, MD., *UNITED STATES PATTERN, EXPERIMENTAL AND
TRIAL PIECES,* Sixth edition, Racine, Wisconsin, 1977

Herbert, Alan, THE OFFICIAL PRICE GUIDE TO MINT ERRORS AND
VARIETIES, Orlando, Florida 1978

Durst, Sanford J., *COMPREHENSIVE GUIDE TO AMERICAN COLONIAL
COINAGE,* New York 1976

Crosby, S.S., *THE EARLY COINS OF AMERICA,* Boston 1875
(Reprints, 1945, 1965, 1975)

Kessler, Alan, *THE FUGIO CENTS,* Newtonville, Massachusetts 1976

Collector's Notes

Collector's Notes

Collector's Notes

To place an ad in the marketplace section...

Standard Rate: 30¢ per word. (30 word min.)
Classified Display: $35 per column inch
Hafl-Page Verticle: $215—1x (2¹⁄₁₆x6½)
Half-Page Horizontal: $215—1x (4¼x3¼)
Full Page: $400—1x (4¼x6½)

Ask about our discounts for consecutive insertions.

Classified/Display Advertising Requirements: Please print. Not responsible for errors due to longhand or poor copy. *Payment must be received with copy. Check, Money Order, Visa or MasterCard accepted.*

Call 407-767-0557 or fax 407-767-6583 or mail to: P.O. Box 1139, Longwood, FL 32752

Edmund's has recently introduced our new MarketPlace Section, allowing buyers and sellers of coins and related products the opportunity to relay their messages to their audience.

We consider all of our advertisers to be reliable in the products and services they offer.

If you ever have any questions or comments regarding our advertisers or advertising in the *MarketPlace* section, we welcome your calls at 407-767-0557.